# Praise for *Blurb Your Enthusiasm*

'A small masterpiece. There is something funny, notable or awe-inspiring on every single page. Some books simply slide into your life like good-humoured old friends. This is undoubtedly one of them.'

**Jenny Colgan, *Spectator***

'The bookiest book about books you'll ever read – I loved it.'

**Lucy Mangan**

'A charming guide not just to blurbs, but to first lines, hatchet jobs, puffs… I couldn't, as the cliché goes, put it down.'

***The Times*, Best Books of 2022**

'A little marvel… consummately brilliant.'

***Daily Mail***

'Truly delightful… charming and gracefully learned… I couldn't have had more fun.'

**Benjamin Dreyer, author of *Dreyer's English***

'Very funny, erudite and profound. A delight!'

**Nina Stibbe**

'Wise and witty… she is full of vim, blessed too with an unusual sense of enquiry, a comic turn of phrase and a talent for investigation into almost every nook and cranny of the business and pleasure of books.'

**Carmen Callil, *The Oldie***

'I love this book's sheer happiness and humanity. It is rich, wise and soul-awaking, exhilarating-like-the-snowman-flying-through-the-air-of-human-gloriousness.'

**Martin Latham, author of *The Bookseller's Tale***

'This book is ace! A must-read for any and every writer or book-obsessed person.'

**Sophie Hannah**

Also by Louise Willder

*Blurb Your Enthusiasm*

# THE BOOK WAS BETTER

## THE TRIUMPHS AND TRAVESTIES OF BOOK TO FILM ADAPTATION

LOUISE WILLDER

ONEWORLD

A Oneworld Book

First published by Oneworld Publications Ltd in 2026



A CIP record for this title is available from the British Library

ISBN 978-0-86154-772-2
eISBN 978-0-86154-773-9

Typeset by Oneworld Publications Ltd

Printed and bound in Great Britain by Clays Ltd, Elcograf S.p.A.



The authorised representative in the EEA is eucomply OÜ,
Pärnu mnt 139b–14, 11317 Tallinn, Estonia
(email: hello@eucompliancepartner.com / phone: +33757690241)

Oneworld Publications Ltd
10 Bloomsbury Street
London WC1B 3SR
England

For Tim,
it had to be you

'The tale is not beautiful if nothing is added to it'

Italo Calvino

'Adaptation is an act of creation in itself'

Hilary Mantel

'The summer movies are coming out. My advice:
just stay home and burn a good book'

Stephen Colbert

# Contents

# Introduction

## WHOSE BOOK IS IT ANYWAY?

'It's just a book.'

When the casting director of Emerald Fennell's scandalous *Wuthering Heights* adaptation, Kharmel Cochrane, uttered these words upon the film's announcement, it was like starting a fight in a pub with legions of drunken bibliophiles. It's never just a book! The irate Brontë fans became apoplectic when they saw the film's psychosexual smorgasbord of a trailer.* Then, after months of goading, when Fennell's movie/relentless marketing juggernaut finally reached cinemas, the bookworms really turned, decrying it as everything from 'florid, horny, juvenile fan fiction' to a 'bastardization' of the novel, 'insulting', 'disrespectful' and even 'degrading' to Brontë. The rage-baiting had worked. No doubt by the time this book is published, another hated adaptation will have taken "*Wuthering Heights*"'s place.

* When I saw Margot Robbie's wedding dress in the trailer, 'she looks like a big meringue' from *Four Weddings and a Funeral* popped into my head. When I saw the film, it was Alan Partridge crying, 'Lynn! These are sex people!' when he realises his new friend (brilliantly played by Stephen Mangan) is a wife-swapper.

There's always one waiting in the wings, ready to crush literary dreams everywhere.

Book lovers are jealous, possessive, territorial paramours. We get very twitchy without our beloveds – when my husband and I drove around Europe for three months, we stashed books into every available secret space of the car, even around the spare tyre, like drug smugglers. Books are a comfort and a joy. And when someone messes with a story we love, we become as fired up as people who generally like to sit alone in a quiet room can be.

Everyone has their own particular trauma. When I first started work on *The Book Was Better*, Disney+ had greenlit *Dissolution*, the first of mine and my sister's favourite historical mystery series by C. J. Sansom. We exchanged giddy messages, with that familiar feeling of excitement and fear. Would they really understand our beloved Tudor lawyer-turned-detective Shardlake in the way only we could? Or would they royally bugger it up and turn it into a panto with tights? Oh yes they did, dear reader. Then there was the dismal Netflix *Persuasion*, where Dakota Johnson Fleabagged to screen with lines like 'She's a total narcissist'; the painful prolongation of *The Hobbit* into an exhausting trilogy that felt like having a molar extracted; Tim Burton destroying my childhood by making Willy Wonka icky not impish; and Renée Zellweger being ordered to gain two stone to play Bridget Jones, when the whole point is that *she isn't overweight; it's all in her head, and who cares anyway?* (This still irks me today. At least in the fourth film, they finally stopped making weight an issue.)

But, just like the Martians in Jeff Wayne's *War of the Worlds*, still they come. Dozens of books have been adapted this year so far as I write, including *Carrie*, again, *Pride and Prejudice*, again, *The Thursday Murder Club*, oh dear, and *The Salt Path*, oh dear, oh dear. And there will be dozens more by the time you read this. There are two reasons for what many call a 'glut' of reworkings and retreads in our culture.

One, it makes ruthless commercial sense to adapt a pre-existing property.

Two, it makes ruthless commercial sense to adapt a pre-existing property.

Even in the 1970s, Stanley Kubrick knew that by basing a film on a novel, 'the more chances you can take with everything else'. And now, with a highly risk-averse film industry in post-Covid, post-streaming freefall, caught between the Marvel Universe and A24 arthouse with very little in between, an adaptation is more likely to get financial backing because there's already an idea people can wrap their heads around – perhaps, as Sophie Kaplan from Empire Studios says, slightly bleakly, 'a pre-existing fanbase' too.* When price-conscious audiences need a good reason to leave their sofas, it's a far safer bet to eke out every last drop from a known intellectual property or franchise, whether it's a movie adaptation, a spinoff, a video game or a continuation novel; part of an ongoing, interlocking universe of what film writer Peter Biskind calls 'megabudget narrative daisy chains' – especially as virality is usually the goal. Everything is up for grabs.

Before I get too depressed, though, it's worth noting that an adaptation also sells more copies of a book, sometimes those special 'tie-in' editions featuring a film's actors on the front cover (I remember Penguin once had the chutzpah to reissue

* There's also been a gold rush on literary estates, with media giants buying up the entire back catalogues of writers such as Winston Churchill, Frederick Forsyth and Roald Dahl.

Homer's *Odyssey* with one of these when the Coen brothers' *O Brother, Where Art Thou?*, *very* loosely inspired by the ancient epic, came out). It's a nicely reciprocal relationship, with backs scratched and bank accounts filled all round, at least in theory.

A book brings prestige to a project too. Some of the most lauded films this awards season just past are adaptations: Chloé Zhao's weep-fest/grief-porn movie (depending on your perspective) *Hamnet*, Guillermo del Toro's *Frankenstein*, Paul Thomas Anderson's *One Battle After Another*, the indie charmer *Pillion*, and *Nuremberg*, based on a book of reportage. In the recent madcap moviemaking satire *Official Competition*, a millionaire in search of a legacy decides he must bankroll a great film, 'the best' – and for that, his assistant tells him, he must acquire an award-winning novel to base it on (as well as a prestigious director, played with relish by Penélope Cruz in the most alarming wig ever placed on a human head). The billionaire, being a bit of a philistine, never reads it.

There's undeniably some kind of kudos to preferring the book, or maybe snobbery, or just braggery ('Oh you've only been to the sister restaurant? You must try the original').* I'm not saying all books are better than all films. They're just different, in fact almost antithetical – 'apples and giraffes', as novelist-screenwriter Dennis Lehane put it. Reading and watching use different parts of our brains, and because the verbal developed far later than the visual, deciphering particular words in a particular order makes us *work*: it's an act of creation in itself. This cognitive process of forming images in our minds when we read is common to most of humanity. The critic John Carey

* In Andy Miller's book *The Year of Reading Dangerously*, he suggests a useful response to the question 'Oh haven't you read...?' 'Not personally.'

calls it 'reader-creativity'. Here, he describes the sense of personal ownership we all feel, the sense that a book belongs to us:

> It seems absurd to claim, when you have read a piece of imaginative literature, that you have done the imagining. But this is what readers feel, and rightly. They know that imagining has happened inside their heads, and that it is special to them. Watching the grotesque liberties that a film or TV version takes with something you have read confirms that this view of the situation is correct. How can they have got this or that character so wrong? How can they have missed out this or that vital bit? The reader creates, and feels a creator's possessiveness.

This is why, in a sense, there's no such thing as a closed book. We all create meaning. Roland Barthes spoke gloomily of the death of the author, but I prefer Stephen King's cheery maxim that 'a good tale belongs to each reader in its own particular way'. Despite what the copyright page states, an author doesn't really own their book. It's 'a chrysalis, an inanimate object packed with the potential to burst into new life', as Susan Hill said, and we're bereft when we've finished (I believe the kids call this a book hangover). Even when we tell someone about a book, we're adapting the story. A film adaptation could be seen as a grand-scale – and ruinously expensive – way of getting over a book hangover by buttonholing a friend to say, 'you must read this!'*

We love retelling stories, and being retold them, whether it's a child wanting the same bedtime tale every night, clapping like Gertie in *E.T.* at the end of *Peter Pan* to keep the magic going;

* John Boorman once said that moviemaking was essentially a process of turning money into light and then back into money again (hopefully).

Shakespeare swiping ancient legends for the stage; or the act of passing on gossip, my personal favourite. As adaptation expert Linda Hutcheon puts it, 'The Victorians had a habit of adapting just about everything – poems, novels, plays, operas, paintings, songs, dances ... There are precious few stories around that have not been "lovingly ripped off" from others. In the workings of the human imagination, adaptation is the norm, not the exception.'* No story is 100 per cent original: it's the result of an author's life and times and the hundreds of stories that went before them.†

I wonder if this is why some of the best adaptations often acknowledge the fact that books belong to everybody and nobody, flirting with the source, taking frightful liberties and then abandoning it like a tabloid love rat: 'Steal the parts that you need, and then run as fast as you can,' advised Paul Thomas Anderson; Hitchcock claimed he read Daphne du Maurier's *The Birds* once before making his film, and never thought about it again. 'You've drunk the drink, and the taste that's left in your mouth is what you go with', as Anthony Minghella said of adapting *The Talented Mr Ripley*. And for every reader, that taste, or that memory, of a book is different. I loved discovering that Jodie Foster lobbied Jonathan Demme hard for the part of Clarice Starling in *The Silence of the Lambs*, adamant that the novel was about a woman saving the life of another woman, while 'all these f**king men' get in the way.‡

* From *A Theory of Adaptation*.

† 'The work of other writers is one of a writer's main sources,' said William Burroughs, and lots of other writers.

‡ Demme hired her and named his production company 'Strong Heart' in her honour.

Each of us, like Jodie, has our own little film running in our heads when we read. It's a book's greatest gift; it's also why we get so narked when they cast somebody with the wrong hair, or leave out the most important bit, or just, well, don't get it.* (It's also why many prefer reading the book before the film colonises our imaginations – like my niece, who was pleased to find a sticker saying 'Read *Wonder* Before You See the Film' on her edition of R. J. Palacio's bestselling novel.) An adaptation may just be a glimpse into another mind's eye, but their pictures rarely match the ones we'd imagined.

For this reason, I decided the anonymous, dream-destroying 'they', at whom we bookish types so often shake our weedy little fists upon leaving the cinema, should be at the heart of *The Book Was Better*. There are three parts. First of all, we look at 'what they get wrong', whether it's sexing up Jane Austen, ruining the ending of Tolkien, stomping over millions of childhoods with *The Dark is Rising*, perhaps not even reading the book at all, and a host of other crimes against fiction. Then, in a spirit of fairness and optimism, I look at 'what they get right'. Do the best thrillers come from twisty short stories? (As Billy Wilder put it, 'Let the audience add up two plus two. They'll love you forever.') How did the famously 'difficult' novelist Henry James write the perfect horror script? Are there certain tales and genres that resonate more than others, with something in their DNA that helps them jump medium?

Finally, we descend into the inferno of 'what the hell were they thinking?', where I brave the true horrors of some of the worst films and biggest flops ever made, do battle with the

* The omission of the Deathday Party from the *Harry Potter and the Chamber of Secrets* movie is my niece's particular bugbear.

unfilmables and watch the unwatchables. There is gossip. There is criticism. There is ham. There are hairpieces. (There is also, in the noble screen tradition, an added Christmas special, mostly so I could indulge my love of Dickens and *Die Hard*. Yippee ki yay!)*

So, join me, dear readers, as we screw our courage to the sticking place and set forth to discover whether 'they' can ever do justice to the films in our heads. Together, we will face the good, the bad, the mad and *Cats*. *The Book Was Better* is completely subjective and in no way comprehensive, but it does cover the most popular genres and tropes – from science fiction and fantasy to rom-coms, crime thrillers to fairy tales, classics to horror – and attempts to identify what makes an adaptation work (or not) in each case. I also bust a few myths along the way; for example, the idea that the best books always make the worst films and vice versa, or that some books don't translate to the screen, whereas the truth is, as every Nancy Meyers fan knows, it's complicated.

I hope you will find something to enjoy or disagree with here, whether it's an old favourite or a new discovery. Think of it as an adventure. Think of it as a therapy session. Think of it as a celebration of books and why they are capable of working magic. Especially that last one.

* Yes, it is based on a book! A little-known 1979 thriller called *Nothing Lasts Forever*. But, thanks to Bruce Willis, it did.

# PART I

## What They Get Wrong

# 1

# THEY MADE JANE AUSTEN FOR DUMMIES

'You're joking! Not another one? Oh for God's sake … I can't stand this.'

With these words, a woman known simply as 'Brenda from Bristol' briefly became world famous when a TV reporter door-stepped her with the news there was going to be a snap election in 2017 – after the UK had already gone to the polls twice in two years.

I felt a bit 'Je suis Brenda' when I was greeted with the prospect of the tenth English-language adaptation of *Pride and Prejudice*, this time written by Dolly Alderton for the two-hundred-and-fiftieth anniversary of Jane Austen's birth, as well as a new big-screen *Sense and Sensibility* in the works, starring Daisy Edgar-Jones. I adore and admire Austen's novels as much as the next hard-headed romantic, yet there is something about the thought of another empire line dress or bonnet that makes me want to fling myself into a lake like Colin Firth. And this was before I even forced myself to watch the dire Netflix *Persuasion* – more on that later.

Perhaps I should just keep my shirt on, though. If, in adaptation terms, Austen is the gift that keeps on giving (whether we want it or not), it's surely a sign of her greatness; her ability to transcend time and place when her contemporaries are left in the dust. Sir Walter Scott, who wrote during the same period as Austen (and gave her an endorsement quote in the time-honoured publishing tradition), was the international literary superstar of his age, yet nobody goes on a Scott-themed river cruise these days, or meets fellow fans dressed up as Ivanhoe, or creates a Bollywood *Rob Roy* film.* Something feels so relatable about Austen that adapters keep turning to her. What is it?

Firstly, many think she was the first novelist to create 'modern' personalities; not just types, but complex, changing beings with inner lives and social self-awareness, 'that flow of anxieties and fears' Anne Elliot feels in *Persuasion*. The critic James Marriott describes the change as like being in an art gallery:

> By the end of the 18th century the portraits in our gallery of literature are becoming more distinct, the faces more modern. And then you turn into the room marked 'Austen' and it's as if somebody has invented perspective, three-dimensional space, chiaroscuro and how to draw hands all at once ... Right here in front of your eyes, modern consciousness – bright and definite and familiar – emerges from the murk of history.

Secondly, she wrote about things that are never going to go away: our need to love and be loved, how to be good in a bad

* She has a global reach comparable perhaps only to Shakespeare. According to the convener of the Jane Austen Society of Pakistan, her novels chime in South Asia because so many Regency social conventions are found there today, notably the importance of making a good match.

world, families and money – what Auden bridled at as 'the amorous effects of brass', but what we know was a terror of sliding into poverty when women could not own property.* It's only the rich who claim money can't buy happiness anyway – as Gaby in *Desperate Housewives* says, 'That's just a lie we tell poor people to keep them from rioting.'

The third reason is adaptation itself. By 'adaptation', I mean 'Colin Firth in a wet undershirt', naturally. Andrew Davies's 1995 *Pride and Prejudice*, six hours of perfect television, not only identified sex as what he called 'the driving energy' of the story, shaping all subsequent screen versions and sending the nation into a collective hot flush, but also inspired the greatest tribute of them all: Darcy in the Bridget Jones novels. At the fever pitch of what was known as 'Austenmania', with Ang Lee's *Sense and Sensibility* storming the Oscars, Austen seemed to capture something about the minefield of post-feminist 1990s dating, where everybody read self-help tomes like *The Rules* (*Time-Tested Secrets for Capturing the Heart of Mr Right*) and negotiated the 'social hoops you have to go through in order to get off with someone', as Helen Fielding observed.† Ever since, Austen's

* Gill Hornby, author of *Miss Austen*, said, 'We pigeonhole her as a romantic novelist and read her books as love stories but … apart from *Emma*, the women are in peril. Your Georgian woman would have read the opening page of *Pride and Prejudice* and thought: "They have an entailed estate and five daughters? Oh my God, this is a horror story."'

† In *Bridget Jones: The Edge of Reason*, Bridget and her friends watch the wet shirt scene endlessly, and she interviews the actual Colin Firth, hilariously: 'CF: I think it was very important to Andrew Davies that Mr Darcy had the most enormous sex drive. BJ: [Gasps]. CF: At one point Andrew even wrote as a stage direction, "Imagine that Mr Darcy has an erection." [V. large crashing noise].'

book sales have continued to rise, even among Gen-Z readers – so much so that the publishing industry should probably erect some kind of monument to Firth's nipples.* Adaptation becomes a virtuous circle, with each new version keeping alive, and strengthening, the power of the original.†

Then there are the plots. As Fielding said of stealing *Pride and Prejudice* for her first Bridget novel and *Persuasion* for her second, they 'really do make you turn the pages. Plus, you know, Austen's dead, so I thought she wouldn't mind.' A lot of people have written about film being 'the revenge of story', the thinking being that, as the twentieth-century novel became more experimental and less reliant on plot, film took up the mantle of narrative instead (later TV). As Karel Čapek wrote:

> We speak of the democratization of literature, about the need to popularize the book. But try to find where the people are. They sit in movie theatres, because something's going on there, and because it thrills them ... basically the same as those who twenty-five centuries ago sat by the fire around the Homeric bard ... For film, despite all its flaws, has one primitive advantage: that it is epic, that there is always something going on.

* I enjoyed hearing that Lyme Park, where the wet shirt scene was filmed, has seen a visitor boom ever since; almost as much as I enjoyed Depression Barbie watching the scene in the *Barbie* movie, to which the BBC responded with a social media post saying, 'He swam so Ken could Beach'.

† In *A Theory of Adaptation*, Linda Hutcheon describes stories: 'like genes, they adapt to those new environments *by virtue* of mutation – in their "offspring" or their adaptations. And the fittest do more than survive; they flourish.'

Even though the modernists, like James Joyce, soaked up the impressionistic techniques of cinema in their writing, the screen has always been more at home with those classic realist nineteenth-century novels, due to their rich characterisation and solid storytelling – and, of course, the chance to make beautiful prestige costume dramas, or as my mother jokingly calls them, 'Mum films'.*

Austen's plots of love impeded, as pure as Shakespeare's comedies, are like templates that can be dressed up in the clothes of any age, just like the computer template Cher Horowitz uses to plan her outfits at the start of *Clueless* – the *ne plus ultra* of free-handed Austen adaptations. You could make each one a Hollywood pitch, or 'logline' as they're known: Two exes are thrown together again! She loves matchmaking but she can't find a match herself! Austen's novels contain the DNA of all rom-coms, just as *Robinson Crusoe* is found in *The Martian*, Dumas's books in the action-adventure movie, the gothic novel in horror or *A Christmas Carol* in all Christmas movies.

And this is why we have Emma reinvented as a rich 1990s valley girl, *Lady Susan* transformed into Whit Stillman's scabrously hilarious parlour piece *Love and Friendship* (starring a never-better Kate Beckinsale), or *Pride and Prejudice* with zombies, on Fire Island and as a murder mystery.† In fact, the raw material is so strong, and so durable, that you'd think it almost

* They also offer cultural capital. As the legendary film critic Pauline Kael noted, 'This is such an easy way to show off some kind of fake erudition: even newspaper reviewers can demonstrate that they've read a book by complaining about how different the movie is from the novel.'

† I have learned that the first line of *Pride and Prejudice* is now so overused it is banned from many newspaper and magazine style guides.

impossible to do a really bad adaptation of Jane Austen. Which brings us to the 2022 Netflix film *Persuasion*.

*Persuasion*, Austen's last completed novel before she died, is a bittersweet story of missed opportunities, heartbreak and regret in which Anne Elliot, the put-upon middle sister in a monstrous family, is persuaded by a well-meaning friend to turn down a marriage proposal from Frederick Wentworth because he's poor. Eight years later, he comes back into her life, a rich naval captain, and they are given a second chance – although neither can speak their true feelings.* There is a quiet undertow of pain that makes the delayed gratification of their eventual, hard-won happiness all the sweeter, yet still haunted by 'if onlys'.

The Netflix adaptation became notorious for turning the silent yearning into smug gurning, with Dakota Johnson playing Anne as Bridget meets Fleabag, smirking to camera with an 'amiright' wink (Johnson's eyebrows act even harder than Roger Moore's), drinking wine from the bottle, crying in the bath and famously saying things like 'He is a 10. I never trust a 10' and 'We're strangers. Worse than strangers. We're exes', lines that then became memes, presumably the intention when the entire aim of a film is to get clicks. The reviews were exquisitely bad, with highlights including: 'more wrong notes than an inebriated squadron of harpists' and 'everyone involved should be in prison'.

Could the film really be as bad as they said? Maybe it was fun-bad? Or even good-bad? Alas no, it was just bad-bad. I'm no purist – as we'll see throughout this book, often the best

* We know what's going on in their heads through Austen's innovative mastery of 'free indirect style', where she uses the third person to express her characters' consciousness. It's commonplace now, but she was the pioneer.

adaptations are faithless ones. As Vladimir Nabokov noted, 'A completely faithful cinema reproduction of a novel would mean filming one after another all its printed pages turned by an invisible hand at the rate of a three-minute pause.'

Anachronisms can work brilliantly in a period drama, such as the cordless phone in the original cut of Peter Greenaway's Baroque-era *The Draughtsman's Contract* (or the breakdancing in *The Favourite*, a kind of less good *Draughtsman's Contract* for reception pupils). Breaking the fourth wall had already been done in the 1999 *Mansfield Park*, and clever additions to Austen's words can be a sparky joy, as Emma Thompson's award-winning *Sense and Sensibility* script showed.*

*Persuasion*'s script, however, does not just gild the lily, but spray-paints it and sets it on fire. In fact, you could see the entire film as a step-by-step guide in how *not* to adapt a classic:

1. Decide that subtext is for cowards.† Instead, explain everything to your audience as if they are simple. If the title isn't enough of a clue, have Anne say, 'I am angry with myself for being persuaded.'‡ Throw in some feminist-lite homilies, such as 'Marriage is transactional for

* When Thompson won a Golden Globe, she made her acceptance speech a letter from Austen about the awards, 'thankfully there were no dogs and no children ... the gowns were middling'.

† From the TV comedy *Garth Marenghi's Darkplace*.

‡ To be fair, there are a couple of clunking lines in the otherwise excellent 1940 *Pride and Prejudice*, where Elizabeth says, 'At this moment it's difficult to believe that you're so proud', and Darcy responds with 'At this moment it's difficult to believe that you're so prejudiced.' This American version also made Mr Collins a librarian because the Hays Code forbade criticism of men of the cloth!

women, our basic security is on the line' – why show when you can shout? Then add some inspirational Insta-memes at the end: 'Don't let anyone tell you how to love, or who to love.' I was genuinely surprised Anne didn't follow this up with 'Dance like nobody's watching'.

2. Change your heroine's character entirely. The novel's spine is the Cinderella story, otherwise known as virtue rewarded. Anne, having lost her bloom at the ripe old age of a 'haggard' twenty-seven, remorseful at having denied herself happiness, has learned to fit herself into the spaces around other people's lives. As she hides her agony while Wentworth flirts with a pretty young thing, I'm reminded of Kurt Vonnegut's dictum, 'Be a sadist. No matter how sweet and innocent your leading characters, make awful things happen to them.' Anne thrums with repressed emotions. Cut to 2022, however, and here is 'quirky klutz' Anne talking to a pet rabbit, recounting a dream where an octopus is sucking her face and falling over a lot, as if somebody saw *Bridget Jones* without the sound on and thought the pratfalls were the funny bits.
3. Make Austen's best hero really dull. My favourite Austen leading man (Darcy, let's face it, is a bit of an arse until he gets fixed) is a toss-up between Knightley in *Emma* because he's such a grown-up, and Wentworth in *Persuasion*, because of his small acts of kindness for Anne, such as silently removing a small nephew who has climbed on to her back, and his recognition of her innate worth, culminating in the most romantic letter in literature: 'I can listen no longer in silence. I must speak to you by such means as are within my reach. You pierce my

soul. I am half agony, half hope. Tell me that I am not too late'. He is also a man of action, always on the move, delighting everyone he meets. This film seems to have mistaken him for sour-puss Darcy. He's so stiff and vapid that the love letter scene is botched, and when he and Anne eventually get together, I thought of Gore Vidal's phrase about the marriage of two Broadway stars, 'the rocks in his head fit the holes in hers'.

4. Make it for Netflix, where 'Regency' equals 'Bridgerton' candification. Use so much desaturated colour that everything has the unreal, honeyed glow of *Teletubbies* and all the stylistic flair of a Sanatogen ad. What is it with the Netflix sheen, which makes so many of their productions, from *The Thursday Murder Club* to their terrible *Rebecca*, look flat and cheap even when they cost millions? According to people who know more than me, it's because the channel has strict technical rules, even down to which cameras can be used, resulting in a uniform look that consumers (for that read algorithms) like.*

Austen's novels should be perfect for the screen because, to quote the French film journal *Cahiers du Cinéma*, they have 'physical adventure' – young people going places, boisterous dancing – and memorable locations, such as the Cobb in Lyme Regis. As Conrad famously said of his aim in writing, they 'make you see'. The trick is to balance this with

* It's also due, apparently, to an increase in close-ups and less background detail so it doesn't look weird on phone screens; high-res images jammed into a TV format; and most of the budgets spent up front on big names as they don't get a share of the profits – leaving less cash for production values.

visually expressing the characters' inner lives. Otherwise, you end up fulfilling Virginia Woolf's fears surrounding cinematic adaptation:

> So we lurch and lumber through the most famous novels of the world. So we spell them out in words of one syllable, written, too, in the scrawl of an illiterate schoolboy. A kiss is love. A broken cup is jealousy. A grin is happiness. Death is a hearse … the brain knows Anna [Karenina] almost entirely by the inside of her mind – her charm, her passion, her despair. All the emphasis is laid by the cinema upon her teeth, her pearls, and her velvet.

This *Persuasion* is all teeth and velvet and no heart, or brain for that matter. It's Tin Man Austen.

For those wishing to cleanse their souls with a truly good adaptation of the novel, I recommend the gritty, naturalistic, almost spartan film made for BBC Screen Two in 1995, somewhat overlooked at the time compared to you-know-what. Director Roger Michell shot everything in natural light and chronological sequence, so that we see Anne, played with subtlety by Amanda Root, bloom and grow in confidence before us, as she does in the book. Michell followed Ingmar Bergman's dictum that 'the human face is the most important subject of the cinema', with Root's unusually expressive eyes saying what words can't in Nick Dear's clever, pared-back script. It's almost like a silent movie in places.*

* Nick Dear said his watchwords were sincerity and realism, subtly updating Austen's language so that it feels natural, although it isn't quite the same as the original. It's more 'Austenesque'.

Ciarán Hinds in his chiselled pomp is Wentworth, a living embodiment of Clive James's comment that the screen is 'a way for the human race to worship itself in ideal form'. The film also visualises Austen's concern with class: the upstart naval officers thrusting themselves forward in marvellously big hats while the aristocracy decays; the disgruntled faces of the vile Sir Walter's servants.

This *Persuasion* is sincere and heartfelt, a far cry from the comedic, cosy, sugar-coated bonnets and breeches caricatures. It also gives the lie to the claim that classics ultimately have more 'room to breathe' as long-form TV series (although 1994's *Middlemarch* is unparalleled). Hitchcock once said that to fully convey a novel like *Anna Karenina* in cinematic terms, 'one would have to make a six to ten-hour film. Otherwise, it won't be any good.' But film *can* do the classics justice, such as Tony Richardson's ribald 1960s romp *Tom Jones*, Stanley Kubrick's exquisite, otherworldly *Barry Lyndon*, Terence Davies's *The House of Mirth* (a painterly mood piece, like his masterpiece *Distant Voices, Still Lives*) or *The Wings of the Dove*, which screenwriter Hossein Amini reinvented as 'noir in costume'. A good adaptation isn't a hollow greatest hits album. As Amini noted, it should recapture 'that first, unique, individual reading experience', when 'nobody else in the world understood or experienced that book exactly like I did', but then leave it behind to follow new adventures.

# 2

# THEY DESTROYED MY CHILDHOOD: *THE DARK IS RISING* AND OTHER TRAUMAS

'A children's book is a beating heart in paper covers'

Katherine Rundell

Whether we enter their worlds through a wardrobe or a chocolate factory, the books we read as children become part of us. If you cut me open, I would bleed Ladybird, Roald Dahl and Enid Blyton, along with some later Judy Blume and the long-forgotten, eccentric ballet stories of Lorna Hill (which I adored even though I was far too galumphing ever to take to the stage). Every reader has their own make-up. There's an all-consuming intensity to childhood reading, which we gradually forget as we grow up, like Susan in the Narnia books. When I watch my ten-year-old niece read, she falls into a kind of trance. It's this sense of physical possession (the writer Francis Spufford describes himself as 'sucking the words off the page' as a child) which means that a good adaptation of a beloved favourite can stay in our hearts forever, and why a bad one can feel like a personal betrayal – or, even worse, a scarring trauma.

One of the earliest film adaptations of a children's book was Cecil Hepworth's 1903 *Alice's Adventures in Wonderland*, in which Alice was played by his secretary Mabel Clark, and the white rabbit by his wife Margaret, who, according to Hepworth Studios director Lewin Fitzhamon, 'couldn't act for nuts'.* It is weird and sinister, but it is nothing compared to the 1988 Czech adaptation of *Alice*, which combines live action with some of the most horrific stop-motion animation ever to exist. Described as 'a grotesque, child-unfriendly masterpiece' by the British Film Institute (BFI), this film is like the worst cheese dream you have ever had. It's got a bleak, end of days feel, akin to the nuclear war TV drama *Threads*, with bunkers, mud, cockroaches, a stuffed rabbit that disgorges sawdust, a steak that comes alive, as in *Poltergeist*, and jam with pins in it. My notes also say 'sock with teeth that looks like something out of Francis Bacon!' and 'enormous doll dragged along by two birds with skull heads!', but I am still too upset to remember it all clearly.

No child should ever watch this film, and if they do, they should see a counsellor afterwards. It reminded me that, with a few notable exceptions – *Paddington 2*, the greatest family film ever made™, *Mary Poppins*, practically perfect in every way, *Willy Wonka and the Chocolate Factory* (not the Tim Burton travesty) and, above all, Lionel Jeffries's peerless *The Railway Children*, famous for its tear-jerking 'Daddy, my daddy!' platform scene as well as Jenny Agutter making a lot of teenage

* I was charmed to learn from Matthew Sweet's excellent book on British cinema, *Shepperton Babylon*, that Fitzhamon was a louche divorcé who lived with a guardsman, kept an aviary in his garden and had trained a pig to follow him around as a child.

boys feel rather funny – many films of children's books are deeply wounding.*

The film critic Tim Robey calls these types of movies 'family films that might require therapy even for the adults watching', and he places Nicolas Roeg's *The Witches*, described by reviewers as 'remarkably sadistic' (Dahl hated it too) into this category. I would also add the harrowing animation of Richard Adams's *Watership Down*, which features rabbits being run over, suffocating to death and having their throats ripped out; the film of Henry Williamson's red-in-tooth-and-claw *Tarka the Otter*, whose ending, as Tarka is killed by a hunting dog ('there was a third bubble in the waters, and nothing more'), haunted my dreams; and *The Water Babies*, which is half trippy Polish cartoon and half Victorian Ken Loach.† Even 1968's *Chitty Chitty Bang Bang*, the glorious musical based on Ian Fleming's story, decided to introduce the figure of the Child Catcher for the film, played by ballet dancer Robert Helpmann, presumably with the sole aim of giving young viewers night terrors. Oh, and I would also include *any* version of Carlo Collodi's disturbing *The Adventures of Pinocchio* in this list – the Disney one features a place called 'pleasure island', where boys get sick from smoking and booze.

* Dahl hated *Willy Wonka*, and Travers hated *Mary Poppins*, only handing over the rights because she was short of cash, and reportedly telling Walt Disney, 'The first thing that has to go is the animation sequence' after the premiere, to which he answered, 'Pamela, that ship has sailed'.

† I was obsessed with the songs in this film as a child, listening to them incessantly on a record ('High Cockalorum!') but recently tried to rewatch it and was just terrified by Billie Whitelaw as Mrs Doasyouwouldbedoneby and James Mason as a sadistic tyrant who actually *beats a donkey*.

In most cases, these films are based on sources that are also dark and gruesome (in the original *Pinocchio* the talking cricket is murdered with a hammer moments after his first appearance). As Katherine Rundell said of Tolstoy's little-known, epically bleak stories for children, they 'summon up the same feelings of delight and warmth that you find in Anna Karenina's suicide scene'.

The worst offenders in a rogues' gallery of highly triggering children's adaptations, however, are those that take a charming, innocent source and then proceed to trample all over it, destroying countless childhoods on the way. Take the hilariously terrifying *Babe: Pig in the City*, which erases all happy memories of the first, loveable movie featuring author Dick King-Smith's beloved sheep-pig. Babe's second cinematic outing involves, among other things, strip searches, the farmer maimed after falling down a well, drowning dogs and a dying goldfish: reviewers described a constant background noise of clattering seats as successive distressed children were hurried, ashen faced and weeping, out of the cinema.

Or there is the doomed 2003 adaptation of Dr. Seuss's book *The Cat in the Hat*, which has passed into box office poison legend, not just because of reports of diva behaviour from Mike Myers, giant props being stolen from the set, or the fact it bombed so badly Seuss's widow cancelled future adaptations. It's also because it received some of the most enjoyably creative bad reviews I've read, including 'dog food' from the *Evening Standard*, 'Like being run over by a garbage truck that backs up and dumps its load on top of you' (*Slate*), 'Take someone you hate' (*Newsday*), 'Cruelty to classic works of children's literature' (*New York Times*) and, romping home with the prize, 'Asshole in Fur' (*Dallas Observer*).

Another close contender is the 2018 Hollywood version of *Peter Rabbit*, which turned Beatrix Potter's sharp-edged sweetness rancid and transformed Peter, as voiced by James Corden, from a naughty, curious young child – as he clearly is in the books – into, frankly, a little shit. Mark Kermode earned the wrath of Corden's dad by noting the star's 'almost instantly irritating voice', opining that 'If you've read the books, you will be appalled,' and adding, 'If you can read, you're likely to be appalled.'* The sequel, *Peter Rabbit 2*, makes fun of this, with some knowing jokes about Corden's voice, and grating meta-gags about a children's book written by Rose Byrne's Bea being optioned ('I'd be spinning in my grave if it was ever adapted into some sassy hip-fest purely for commercial gain, probably by an American').

But now we come to the worst childhood betrayal of all: the 2007 Hollywood adaptation (desecration would be a better word, or perhaps violation) of *The Dark is Rising*, Susan Cooper's beloved 1973 fantasy novel. Compared to this, the previous abominations I've mentioned seem as harmless as *Bagpuss*.

First, the book. *The Dark is Rising*, the second in a sequence of five novels (the first is *Over Sea, Under Stone*, the others *Greenwitch*, *The Grey King* and *Silver on the Tree*) is one of those books that feels like discovering a special and secret place. Reading it still gives me that tingly sensation you get when you wake up and it's snowed overnight. It feels like yours alone, and so it's a bit of a shock to discover that millions of other people feel the same – there's even a worldwide readalong called 'The Dark is Reading'. Superfan Robert Macfarlane hits the nail on

* Bizarrely, the film was also criticised for 'allergy bullying' due to a scene in which the rabbits pelt Mr McGregor with blackberries.

the head: 'As is often the way when you encounter art of huge power, I at first felt absurdly possessive of *The Dark is Rising*. I was jealous of other people who'd read it – don't you know this is *all mine*?!'

The story (as does the readalong) begins on Midwinter's Eve. Will Stanton, who lives with his large family in a ramshackle farmhouse, is about to turn eleven. The opening pages are like the start of a horror movie, slowly building dread and unease. The animals are jumpy. The sky is dark with wheeling rooks. A storm is predicted. Will spies a strange old man who scuttles off. 'The Walker is abroad,' the farmer tells Will. 'And this night will be bad, and tomorrow will be beyond imagining.'

So it goes. Will wakes up the next day to find the land blanketed with snow and, as it once was in centuries past, covered with trees; his family in a deep sleep from which they cannot wake. He ventures out alone and eventually discovers that he is an 'Old One', tasked with keeping the forces of the Dark at bay in a primordial battle between good and evil. But he is helped in his task by allies, including Merriman Lyon (Merlin), who appears in all five books, by the magical signs he must collect, and by the powers of ancient pathways, which are hidden in plain sight and offer protection from evil.

There is so much to say about all five books in *The Dark is Rising* sequence, but two seem to me to be the most important – and the things the film completely missed.

The first is that it is resolutely British. I don't mean this in a jingoistic sense, but because Susan Cooper is part of a tradition of 1960s and 1970s children's fantasy writers, including Alan Garner and Diana Wynne Jones, who drew richly on what Ursula K. Le Guin called 'sources high in the mountains of Myth' – folk and fairy tale, Arthurian legend, Norse sagas, classical epic – to portray a contemporary world touched by magic. In *The Dark is Rising*, there is a sense of deep time and place, a continuum between ancient landscapes and the present; as Will says, 'two kinds of Time at once'.

The second is that the novel is distinctly un-cosy, rejecting neat oppositions between good and evil. Sometimes Merriman will sacrifice a flawed human – such as the heartbreaking Hawkin – for the struggle. Robert Macfarlane compared it to the Cold War, 'a conflict fought in the shadows, in which no one is clean'. An old, amoral, 'wild magic' is unleashed to defeat the darkness, as embodied in the terrifying figure of Herne the Hunter. With the antlers of a stag and 'strange tawny eyes, yellow-gold, unfathomable, like the eyes of some huge bird', Herne summons ghost-white, red-eyed hounds to chase down and destroy the forces that have been pursuing Will – at least, until the next novel.

There is no Herne and no Wild Hunt in the Hollywood adaptation, which was initially called *The Dark is Rising*, then *The Seeker*. No Walker either. No sense of deep time or place. I'm not sure what there is. It clearly hoped to ride on the coat-tails of *The Lord of the Rings* and the *Harry Potter* movies, but in doing so it lost everything that makes Cooper's novels special. (The *New York Post* went as far as to title its review 'Bad Harry Day').* Presumably because it was made by the Christian production company Walden Media, it obliterated the novel's

* The review jokingly noted that 'In today's England, a teenage boy is instructed by grown-up mentors in the use of magical powers while a dark lord who comes in many formats promises an epic battle. The movie is based on a 1973 book by Susan Cooper, who must be trembling in fear of being sued for ripping off J. K. Rowling's ideas and publishing them 20 years in advance.'

pagan, mythological roots, instead portraying a simplistic, Manichean struggle, where nothing is at stake and Will's quest becomes, in the words of one reviewer, 'as arbitrary as Sonic the Hedgehog collecting coins'.

It gets worse. The film also makes Will American, about to turn fourteen rather than eleven, and a mouth-breather who says things like 'Awesome!' and 'I'm supposed to save the world? I can't even figure out how to talk to a girl!' and occasionally does some kickboxing. The whole thing is shoddily made: it looks as if the set designers have transplanted some vaguely English-looking things (telephone boxes! Bobbies on the beat! A road sign saying Slough! An ... onion-domed church?) into a Romanian village, which is, in fact, exactly what they did.

I felt many things rising while suffering this film: anger, bitterness, sadness, bile, but definitely no dark. Susan Cooper was valiantly diplomatic when interviewed about it on NPR, saying that 'You do have to do violence to a book to make it into a screenplay ... but the alteration is so enormous in this case. They're just ... different.' The interviewer goes on to tell us that 'Cooper is waiting for the movie, but with a certain sadness. She says she sent a letter requesting changes to the film's script, but she's not sure any alterations were made.'

I hope Cooper was cheered slightly by BBC Radio's 2022 dramatisation, co-adapted by Robert Macfarlane, with a stellar cast including Toby Jones and Harriet Walter, and original music by actor and folk singer Johnny Flynn.* It is a thing of wonder, and a work of love – which is what's missing from the

* Further music inspired by the novel includes a 2019 electronica album by Handspan, composed as the soundtrack to an imagined 1970s children's TV adaptation that, sadly, never existed. Have a listen, it's great.

movie. When interviewed, screenwriter John Hodge admitted he didn't even like fantasy. That's his bailiwick, but it does make one question whether he was the right person for the job. I wonder if he, like many critics of the genre, assumed it is all about magic and monsters, a refuge for child-people who have never quite grown up. Fantasy may contain impossible things, but it exists (and has always existed, ever since the mythical creatures of *Gilgamesh*) to show us things about the real world: power, deception, endurance, hatred, regret, the true meaning of heroism. Katherine Rundell calls it 'philosophy's more gorgeously painted cousin'. She also, beautifully, describes it as 'an ancient song that each generation has heard, tuned to their own voice and sung onwards' to a new generation, retold, reshaped but always there. As C. S. Lewis said, fantasy is not a hiding place, but a seeking place. That is why it continues to matter, and why the film of *The Dark is Rising*, although bad beyond imagining, will become a distant memory while Cooper's novel continues to be sung ever onwards.

# Coda

## FROM BOOK TO SCREEN AND BACK AGAIN

Perhaps because it's dedicated to the pleasure principle – a story *has* to grip, to lure – or maybe due to its roots in oral folk and fairy tales (they're getting their own chapter later because: Angela Carter), children's writing is especially durable and malleable, ideally suited to being retold, repurposed and reinvented. These books are almost impossible to contain within their covers. As Sam Leith notes in *The Haunted Wood*, they exist on 'a continuum with other forms of entertainment and media'. There are, of course, commercial reasons – the merch! But, according to Leith, it's the nature of the beast too:

> From the bottom-up, child's eye perspective, it's completely natural: stories spill over. When you're playing with an action figure, you're writing a story. Children are omnivorous: they see a natural continuity between the books, the comics, the videogames, the TV show, the feature film, the action figures, the dressing-up costume.

In the golden age of children's literature, the stories spilled over into theatre, leaping into a different medium like the Darlings flying out of the nursery window ('The stage has always cheerfully swiped whatever good stories were going,' noted Philip Pullman). *Peter Pan* was a stage play and then a novel before it became a Disney film, which softened the malevolent edges of Peter and 'shoot the Wendy' Tinkerbell (and then, much later, became one of the worst box office bombs ever, Joe Wright's appropriately panned 'origin story', *Pan*).* And well before its eye-popping MGM musical incarnation and the later world of *Wicked*, L. Frank Baum's 1900 *The Wonderful Wizard of Oz* was a multimedia phenomenon, with the author writing spinoff books, stage musicals and comic strips inspired by his imaginary universe – he even presided over an elaborate touring spectacle involving dozens of actors, a full orchestra, slide show and film clips.† The term 'brand leverage', while being a frightful twenty-first-century coinage, is nothing new.‡

During my childhood, the medium of choice was the TV drama series. Roald Dahl warned us that it would give us a pain in the neck and an IQ of three, but some of my happiest childhood memories are of those sacred hours post-school,

* J. M. Barrie said he didn't like the statue of his hero in Kensington Gardens because 'it doesn't show the Devil in Peter'. But he did stipulate that all royalties from direct *Peter Pan* adaptations be paid to Great Ormond Street children's hospital – which the makers of *Pan* tried to bypass, making its failure seem karmic.

† A more unfortunate spinoff is 1985's scarring *Return to Oz*, in which young Dorothy is strapped to a gurney in a psychiatric clinic to have her memories of Oz obliterated, while 'damaged patients' scream in the basement.

‡ There's even 'musical to book' now, with LW Entertainment, which manages Andrew Lloyd Webber's body of work, expanding the *Phantom of the Opera* franchise into a new worldwide publishing programme, beginning with the 'YA reimagining' *Our Strange Duet*.

kicking back in front of the box with a Ribena in hand, like a tiny business executive relaxing with a martini after a hard day at the office (no one ever talks enough about how *exhausting* school is, for both pupils and teachers). I'm sure the kids are still all right, and I don't want to get all 'in my day', but I feel lucky to have grown up in a pre-streaming age when not only was your favourite programme a regular, shared pleasure, but books and television felt closely intertwined, with huge numbers of children's classics being adapted and programmes like BBC1's *Jackanory* (where an actor like Kenneth Williams sat in an armchair and read a book aloud: I *know*, but there really wasn't much other entertainment) often introducing young viewers to a story for the first time.

Every generation has its beloved, and my favourite teatime dramatisations were *Black Beauty*, whose theme tune it is impossible to listen to without wanting to gallop around the room, *The Phoenix and the Carpet* and, slightly later, *The Box of Delights*. I also experienced the strange 'patting your head while rubbing your tummy' sensation of trying to watch the dubbed foreign series that came our way at this time, most notably the Swiss/German *Heidi* (cue more Proust's madeleine music), where I mostly remember our curly haired heroine spoke a lot to her grandfather about bread rolls, and a rerun of the French-German *Robinson Crusoe*, whose fantastic theme tune sounds as though it could have been composed by John Barry. I genuinely think these series helped keep classic fiction, which might otherwise have been forgotten, alive in our minds. I also wonder if, sometimes, books for small people perhaps work better on the small screen, with that direct, intimate, almost cosy relationship that's akin to reading (and, unlike the cinema, doesn't require you to *leave the house*, thankfully).

It works in the other direction too. Before the age of video and on-demand, there was no way for you to cling on to the worlds you'd experienced on television or at the cinema, so popular shows and films gave rise not just to annuals (*The Goodies* was my favourite), action figures, sticker books, audiobooks and board games, but also morphed into book form with the rise of the novelisation.

'The book of the film' is as old as *King Kong* (it was the first official novelisation, in 1933), but they reached their zenith in the late 1970s and 1980s, with mega-selling books of *Star Wars*, *E.T.*, *Raiders of the Lost Ark*, *Clash of the Titans*, *Ghostbusters* and the prolific Terrance Dicks's *Doctor Who* series being the most popular. They were bought by adults too – *The Omen*, by the film's screenwriter David Seltzer, and *Alien*, by Alan Dean Foster, shifted millions – but the prime audience was a young readership.* One of my prized possessions was the 1981 hardback *Raiders of the Lost Ark Storybook Based on the Movie*, which featured colour stills from the film and Indy on the front cover, about to locate the Ark's resting place using the staff of Ra; heady stuff.†

As Alan Dean Foster, acknowledged King of the Novelisation, has noted, most of these books were produced from shooting scripts rather than the finished movie, meaning that on-set rewrites and ad libs were missing, and sometimes more.‡ When

* So much so that Ripley's most famous line in *Aliens*, 'Get away from her, you bitch', had the 'bitch' removed for Foster's novelisation.

† Even at the end of *Indiana Jones and the Last Crusade* I noticed the credits said, 'Novelisation from Ballantine books' – these things were big marketing tools.

‡ Or they were a completely different story, as with Christopher Wood's *The Spy Who Loved Me* novelisation, which bore no resemblance to the original Ian Fleming short story (in fairness, that's because the film didn't).

Foster worked on the *Alien* novelisation, 20th Century Fox, fearful of security breaches, refused to show him a single image of the creature, so 'I had to write the book without knowing what the alien looked like.' He's admirably defensive of his particular brand of adaptation, saying, 'It's always amusing to me, you take a book, say, *To Kill a Mockingbird*, throw away three quarters of it and win an Academy Award for best adapted screenplay. But if you take a screenplay and add three quarters of original material to it – which is a much, much more difficult piece of writing – well, that's by definition "hackwork."'

He also honours the role of fandom, saying that 'When I'm doing novelisations, I'm a combination of professional writer and 14-year-old kid sitting in the back of the theatre with his friends loudly criticizing the bad special effects.' This is why novelisations continue to live on today, but are now firmly ring-fenced in the science fiction and fantasy realms. When I asked one publisher about it, he recalled the glory days when there was fierce competition to acquire all kinds of novelisations, with special LA offices dedicated to the process, but said that the market is now 'completely atomised' because of 'the huge commitment from a passionate core of science-fiction fans, who want everything, and will pursue a story down any given rabbit hole'.* This genre is all about the world-building, and so any way to relive a particular universe, or immerse yourself

* He also remembered publishing a novelisation of *A Life Less Ordinary*, for which screenwriter John Hodge dictated the whole thing into a Dictaphone, which was then typed up, and, thrillingly, recalled getting an email from James Cameron no less, after the director was sent the manuscript for Stephen Baxter's unofficial *The Science of Avatar* and liked it so much he brought it into the official tie-in publishing programme.

in a continuation of it, succeeds, whether it's dressing up as Xena Warrior Princess at Fantasycon, writing fan fiction, seeing a *Stranger Things* musical or reading a *Stranger Things* novelisation.

These books still sell – the 2014 *Godzilla* novelisation was a *New York Times* bestseller – and they have always been more than hackwork. Arthur C. Clarke's *2001: A Space Odyssey* was developed alongside the film script and published a few months afterwards with contributions by Kubrick, and it's a truly classic book: less enigmatic than the film, but offering its own verbal poetry. Douglas Adams adapted *The Hitchhiker's Guide to the Galaxy* from his radio series into a phenomenal bestseller that has outlived its origins, and become adapted again in turn.

As the author David Barnett has said, 'these screen-to-book stories drew me further into sci-fi – as well as many authors working today'. He went on to observe how 'the best novelisation writers add depth, backstory and extra dimensions to what we see on the screen, flesh out ideas and sub-plots that are wrapped up in a pithy one-liner in the movie, or end up on the cutting-room floor. They can enrich fictional universes.'

It's the fictional universes that really matter. And yes, undoubtedly these novelisations, tie-ins and other extensions of the universe are created to sell us stuff. But they also acknowledge that the young reader or viewer, often a pallid, indolent, indoors kind of child who is half-heartedly encouraged to 'go and get some fresh air' every now and then, knew that we rarely needed to go out, because the best worlds were inside our heads all along. All we wanted was an excuse to linger in those worlds a while longer.

# 3

# THEY SEXED IT UP! *WUTHERING HEIGHTS*

*Harry*: That's it? A faceless guy rips off all your clothes, and *that's* the sex fantasy you've been having since you were twelve?
*Sally*: Well sometimes I vary it a little.
*Harry*: Which part?
*Sally*: What I'm wearing.

FROM *WHEN HARRY MET SALLY*

I thought of Sally Albright's recurring adolescent dream when I was watching "*Wuthering Heights*", in which director Emerald Fennell gave the world the sex fantasy *she'd* been having since she was a teenager, complete with costume changes. Her pretty film about pretty people (like *Saltburn* but a little less fun) may have had lovers of Emily Brontë's novel seething with anger – one even railed that 'our modern literacy crisis has found a new figurehead'* – but, in her defence, Fennell was refreshingly open

* One of the funniest bad reviews said, 'Emily Brontë died of tuberculosis 177 years ago yet this adaptation is still the worst thing that has ever happened to her.'

about her free-handedness with the source material, saying that she'd added her 'it's just an interpretation, yah?' quotation marks around the title because it was 'a version that I remembered reading that isn't quite real … You can only make the movie that you sort of imagined yourself'. In fact, she said, all adaptations should have quotation marks around them. Like any adapter, she was merely transferring the pictures from her own head to the screen (although I'd hazard a guess that coming from a multimillionaire family probably didn't hinder her chances of success in the film world).

The result was a kind of *Magic Mike* on the Moors, with a strapping, sweaty, topless Jacob Elordi saying 'Ah loov yer' in his best Brian Glover-style Yorkshire accent, while, with the hardest-working tongue in Hollywood, mostly licking Cathy and every other available surface. (I hope there were plenty of anti-bacterial wipes on set.) Yet, for all its wet mouth action, fish-fingering, kinky latex, dog collars and skin walls, I found Fennell's doggedly 'outrageous', playing-in-the-dressing-up-box take much more of a traditional, by-the-rules *Wuthering Heights* adaptation than I'd anticipated, for several reasons.

For a start, it follows the well-worn convention of framing this unhinged book – which Daphne du Maurier described as containing 'more savagery, more brutality' in its pages than any other nineteenth-century novel – as a love story. Indeed, 'The greatest love story of all time', according to the *Gone with the Wind*-inspired movie posters and the back cover of the tie-in edition. It's been the same ever since the trailer for William Wyler's smash hit 1939 Hollywood movie trumpeted it as 'The greatest love story of our time – or any time!'

*Wuthering Heights*, I think it's uncontroversial to say, is not a love story. It's not a sex story either, I'd wager. I would define it as a necrophiliac, semi-incestuous, sadistic, gothic revenge horror, full of shocking levels of violence against women, children and small animals, deeply unhealthy and obsessed by death (and property). Reading it again made me think of the deranged world of Jacobean tragedy, or a high opera, all heightened emotion and hysteria, nearly everyone dying before the storm passes and order is restored. The spicy French writer Georges Bataille said, 'It's not a normal novel ... It's unfathomable and ghastly' – and this is coming from the man who wrote a story where someone puts a boiled egg up their bottom.

The poster for the now-lost 1920 silent film "*Wuthering Heights*" (even those quotation marks aren't new) features a grim Heathcliff and the tagline 'Emily Brontë's tremendous Story of Hate', which seems fairer. But ever since Wyler's 1939 film transformed California's San Fernando Valley into the Yorkshire moors, and turned a troubling, multigenerational novel into a passionate romance between Merle Oberon and a strapping, nostril-flaring Laurence Olivier, 'sexy Heathcliff' has very much become the default. According to Lauren Livesey of the Brontë Society, the 'cruel but phwoar' stereotype was cemented by Olivier's turn a year later as Maxim de Winter, another dominating brute ('I'm asking you to marry me, you little fool') in *Rebecca*. 'Damn you, Laurence Olivier,' joked the journalist Samira Ahmed, '*Fifty Shades of Grey* is all your fault.'

I can't think of another book whose adaptations have given us such a skewed view of its story, which, yes, is about the foundling Heathcliff and his fierce attachment to his sort-of-stepsister Catherine, who betrays him by marrying the rich Edgar Linton (and later by dying), leading Heathcliff to wreak revenge on everyone, ruining Edgar's sister Isabella in the process. But it is also about their offspring, who, in the book's second half,

Heathcliff psychotically torments and degrades, stealing their inheritance until, not long after opening up Catherine's coffin in his longing to be with her corpse, he dies. An abused, brutalised child becomes a brutal abuser as an adult – Larkin's 'They fuck you up' seems a good moral.

Wyler's version, however, began the now-common trend of cutting the second half of the book, focusing solely on Cathy and Heathcliff and even, at the behest of producer Samuel Goldwyn, showing their ghosts happily reunited on the moors.* And if, as David Lean said, directing is '99% casting', then most filmmakers ever since seem to have had the sole aim of making women horny by serving up a roster of fanciable actors to play Heathcliff. One of my favourites is a lanky, young Timothy Dalton (he would later become James Bond), playing the role with lupine, sulky magnetism, even though he has a bowl cut that makes him look slightly simple. With a dreamy Michel Legrand score, this 1970 film also cuts the action halfway through but, intriguingly, hints that Heathcliff may be Catherine's half-brother. It is mostly, however, in the cinematic tradition of classic novels as bucolic romps, such as *Women in Love* and *Far from the Madding Crowd*, with Heathcliff at one point asking Isabella, 'Do you fancy a tumble then?'

Enter the 1992 film from *Wolf Hall* director Peter Kosminsky (one of the few adaptations to tell the whole tale),† and it's the

* I learned from David Niven's charming memoir of a (mostly) charmed life in Hollywood, *The Moon's a Balloon*, that 'forty-take Wyler' was an exacting sod, telling Niven his performance of the 'actor's nightmare' role of Edgar Linton was too comic, and saying to Olivier after numerous takes, 'Just ... just be *better*'.

† Another is the bleak 1988 adaptation from Japanese director Yoshishige Yoshida.

turn of Ralph Fiennes to play Heathcliff, all flashing eyes, elegant bones and flowing black mane, like a highly strung show pony, with a poorly cast Juliette Binoche as Catherine and her daughter Cathy, whose English accent makes her sound weirdly like Joyce Grenfell. I had never really thought of Fiennes as being sexy until I saw this film. Even Tom Hardy, who I know gets a lot of women frisky, has never really appealed to me, but put him in a wig on a crag, and bingo. In a review of the 2009 TV adaptation, Kathryn Flett described Hardy as 'entirely capable of making even careworn middle-aged women rend their garments, tear their hair and head for both the moors and the HRT'. From this, it seems like a natural leap to Margot Robbie's description of her girlfriends at a screening of Emerald Fennell's "*Wuthering Heights*", 'frothing at the mouth … like rabid dogs … I was like: if Jacob Elordi walked in right now, I think they would eat him.'

The casting of the genetically blessed Elordi as hot Heathcliff, and the equally blessed Margot Robbie as hot Cathy, however, has been hugely controversial, and not just because they're too old and too Australian. It's also been seen as continuing yet another screen custom: that of whitewashing Heathcliff who, it's now acknowledged, may be mixed race or at least of uncertain origins, described in the novel as 'a dark-skinned Gypsy' and a 'lascar' (a South Asian sailor). The presenter Anita Rani remembered that when she fell in love with the novel, 'I read Heathcliff as not being white. For me, he could have been Indian, he could have been mixed race, but screen adaptations made me believe otherwise.'

Screenwriter Olivia Hetreed said, of adapting the novel for Andrea Arnold's 2011 film, 'I think it's a story about a black boy, suddenly finding himself in a white world and a bunch of white people suddenly finding a black boy in their midst. When I look at the other film versions of this, I don't see that story, but then I look at the book, that's the story I see.' James Howson was cast as Heathcliff, the first time a Black actor would play the role, and the resulting film, a kind of tone poem rather than a literal adaptation, is, for my money, one of the best. It still presents us with a love story ('Love is a force of nature', says the poster), but it also creates a raw, unvarnished portrayal of childhood pain and exclusion, stripped back and thrilling in its elemental starkness. It's less bodice-ripper, more Beckett.

The worst Heathcliff? Why, arise Sir Cliff Richard, purveyor of Christian rhymes, who, in 1996, made the unusual decision to create and cast himself in the soft-rock opera-musical *Heathcliff* – maybe because they share half a name? It is as bad as it sounds. I made myself watch the 'special video version' on YouTube (according to the ad, it 'features exclusive footage of Cliff Richard shot on the Yorkshire moors' – I mean, I know he's not so popular these days, but still), and oh the horror, the horror. Sir Cliff strikes many poses in a beard that looks as though it's been drawn on with a marker pen, against a screeching backdrop of synth and electric guitars, a set consisting of revolving crags and a lot of people standing solemnly in dry ice – plus some hallucinatory scenes involving tribal masks. Compared to this, *Phantom* is like *Parsifal*.* As one reviewer said, 'At times, I felt embarrassed for him, but you could tell he was enjoying himself and so too were the middle aged ladies in the

* It made me think of the genius spoof musical of *The Elephant Man*, *Elephant!*, which is the highlight of the underrated comedy film *The Tall Guy*, and has far better songs.

audience.' When at the end, Heathcliff says, 'Death it beckons,' I thought, yes, please.*

As if to prove Noël Coward's maxim about the potency of cheap music, it broke box office records, but the reviews were so bad ('Living dull') that Cliff decided, pottily, to use them as an advertising campaign for the musical, featuring quotes such as 'This Wretched Show', 'The Bad-Taste Theatre Event Of The Decade' and 'It Was Like Watching The Pope Smoke Dope', with the line 'When Reviews Aren't Good Audiences Know Better'.

One thing the show did get right is a song called 'A Misunderstood Man', which Heathcliff is, but perhaps not in the way this musical thinks. He's not tragic or romantic. To be fair, he waves enough red flags himself, recalling Isabella's delusion in 'picturing in me a hero of romance', hanging her little dog on their wedding day, and saying things like 'I have no pity! The more worms writhe, the more I yearn to crush out their entrails!' *Caveat emptor*, ladies. Yet the brooding, fiery stereotype of Sylvia Plath's brute, brute heart persists.

I think I should just accept that Heathcliff is a kind of *tabula rasa*, upon whom everyone in the novel, as well as readers and adapters, puts their own stamp. He has broken free from the literary source entirely, with a life of his own: one of those characters that everyone has heard of, and has an image of, even if they've never read the book – just as the word 'Byronic' is used as Heathcliff shorthand by those who haven't opened a volume of Lord Byron's poems.

* There was also, I discovered, a far less offensive 1994 musical, recorded with Lesley Garrett singing the part of Cathy and Bonnie Langford as Isabella, as well as an opera composed by Bernard Herrmann, he of Hitchcock fame.

French film theorist André Bazin noticed this about classic novels when he said that 'Alexandre Dumas and Victor Hugo simply serve to supply the film-maker with characters and adventures largely independent of their literary framework. Javert or D'Artagnan have become part of a mythology existing outside of the novels.' Whether it is James Bond, Sherlock Holmes (whom Conan Doyle had to resurrect following an outcry when he killed him off), Miss Havisham or Harry Potter, some heroes or villains are so big that their stories become greater than their origins, unmoored from their creator and immortalised as myths – universal tales to be retold and disseminated around the world. It makes them perfect for adaptations.

Heathcliff definitely has this mythic quality; as Philip Larkin opined, 'a sort of sprite of the bergs, a cousin to Mary Shelley's monster, a creature of the northern mists, a gnome'. If you look at him as a gothic monster – part sexy-death Dracula, part rejected Frankenstein offspring – then the Heathcliff myth makes more sense. Emily Brontë's imagination was marinated in gothic fiction from a young age, and this most shape-shifting of genres, a kind of sex-fear-death-blood-monsters-evil-corruption free-for-all, is almost overripe for adaptation. There have been literally hundreds of *Dracula*s and *Frankenstein*s; both Bram Stoker and Mary Shelley saw theatre productions of their works in their lifetimes and, with the advent of cinema, adapters had even more opportunity to juice them. (Perhaps because gothic is an essentially un-humorous genre, my favourite *Frankenstein*s are the comic pastiches *Carry on Screaming* and Mel Brooks's *Young Frankenstein*, or should I say Fronkenshteen? I didn't love Guillermo del Toro's overstuffed Netflix passion project, featuring Jacob Elordi as *another* sexy beast, although in its favour it did keep the hoary old seadogs and, accurately, made the monster talk – in the book he never shuts up!)

The undead, it seems, won't die. According to the trend website It's Nice That, 'Gothic is having a moment'. Perhaps it's dark tales for dark times, or perhaps capitalism just wants to sell us things at Halloween, but there's something in those ruins and spiky letters that continues to grip. This is why, even though reviewers didn't know what to make of *Wuthering Heights* when it first appeared, Emily is now the most read and the most adapted of the three 'weird sisters', as Ted Hughes called the Brontës, even outstripping Charlotte's own gothic tale of taming the beast, *Jane Eyre*.* The Brontë myth – the grim Haworth rectory, the fictional fantasy kingdoms, the early deaths, the alcoholic brother – seems strongest in her, perhaps because the least is known about her.†

You could almost call it a cult – especially at the sight of crowds of enthusiastic women in red dresses waving their arms around to Kate Bush on 'The Most Wuthering Heights Day Ever', held around the world annually.‡ It was a cult created, in part, by Emily's own sister Charlotte who, troubled by the novel's savage reviews ('Coarse', *Spectator*; 'Repellent', *Eclectic*

* Like Heathcliff, that gothic Bluebeard/Beast Mr Rochester also dominates imaginations, and adaptations, more than Jane – my favourite is Michael Fassbender.

† The best portrayal of the sisters is in the sitcom *Psychobitches*, where women from history are analysed in the psychiatrist's chair by Rebecca Front. The Brontës are tiny, squabbling, randy northerners, Charlotte saying of Emily, 'She's got a nasty streak ... she beat up her own dog.'

‡ Bush was inspired by a 1967 TV adaptation starring a wolfish Ian McShane. Her song in turn spawned the brilliant *Not the Nine O'Clock News* sketch in which Pamela Stephenson sings about 'my leeeotaard'.

*Review*; 'How a human being could have attempted such a book as the present without committing suicide … is a mystery', *Graham's Lady's Magazine*), added a preface to the 1850 edition that cast her sister as something otherworldly: 'a native and nursling of the moors'.

I first read *Wuthering Heights* at university, and I remember being very impressed with the novel's ingenious Russian doll structure of narrators within narrators – or, as Jeremy in the sitcom *Peep Show* says, 'The story's told by a man and then a lady and then no one!' I also wrote a lot about female rage (my favourite work of literary criticism was called *The Madwoman in the Attic*, which began with the line 'Is a pen a metaphorical penis?') and I went to a lecture by the Marxist Terry Eagleton, who thought Heathcliff was Irish and it was all about the Famine. Today I'm still taken aback by the novel's sheer levels of physical violence, including young Heathcliff being beaten until his arm turns black, then later beating his wife; poor old Nelly Dean the nursemaid being slapped so hard her eyes water, and having a knife put in her mouth; and the narrator dragging the wrist of Catherine's ghost over a broken window pane until it bleeds. People are frequently attacked by savage dogs with names like Gnasher, Throttler and Wolf. Everyone behaves like a tyrannical, authoritarian child. It is *sui generis* in its raging madness.

I never found it erotic, however, even though it features a crag called Penistone. The bond between Cathy and Heathcliff, as many, including Daphne du Maurier, have said, is completely sexless. According to literary critic Elizabeth Hardwick, '*Wuthering Heights* is a virgin's story. Cathy is as hard, careless, and destructive as Heathcliff. She too has a sadistic nature. The love the two feel for each other is a longing for an impossible completion.' All the 'I am Heathcliff' is fevered and restless, a constant seeking of something unreal. It's also slightly wrong, as the two have grown up as siblings, and, according to many, the novel desecrates two sacrosanct taboos: incest and necrophilia (what with all that grave-bothering). No wonder Emerald Fennell was drawn to it, even though, sadly, she eschewed the ghosts and the horror.

I'll leave the final word on the novel to *Peep Show* again. Jeremy is rashly hosting a book group and can't get on with *Wuthering Heights*:

> I've been on the same four pages for three hours ... [close to tears now] I can't do it, Mark, it's 372 pages long ... so what I was thinking was, could you read it for me, the stupid olden days book?

Mark agrees, and at the meeting, when a bespectacled twat opines that 'It's not a fucking love story, it's a fucking fuck story, it's about animal lusts and earth and dirt and fluids ... an ode to dark passions', he socks it to him: '*Wuthering Heights* clearly isn't a hymn to lust and passion ... it's about how finite and shallow all that gothic nonsense is, and how it inevitably has to give way to real life, and real love.'

Well said, Mark.

# 4

# DID THEY ACTUALLY READ THE BOOK? *IN A LONELY PLACE*

I have a confession, one that would probably get me thrown out of film school if I were ever to attend one. I don't really enjoy classic film noir.* If that's not bad enough, I don't particularly like westerns or French New Wave either. I may as well tear up my BFI membership card now. I realise these are the genres you are meant to worship if you are Serious About Films.† I suppose everybody has their blind spot. For a lot of people, it is musicals, but then those people are insane.

When it comes to noir, I'm more a fan of those grubby British-set thrillers you could class as 'bedsit noirs', into which category I would place films like *Brighton Rock*, *Night and the City*, *Séance on a Wet Afternoon*, *It Always Rains on Sunday*

* The only exception is *Sunset Boulevard*, because it has such a strong sense of camp.

† What's worse, even those Howard Hawks screwball comedies like *Bringing Up Baby* don't do it for me. They just seem to me to be *people talking really fast*. I know this makes me sound like a granny in the 1960s saying the Rolling Stones are 'just noise'. I feel bad, I really do.

and *Payment Deferred*, based on the cracking crime novel by *Hornblower* author C. S. Forester. They seem far more exciting and scary to me, perhaps because, as the veteran critic Pauline Kael said of kitchen sink dramas, 'These films ... share a true horror – the people live without grace. They live in ugly little rooms, and they get on each other's nerves. The main difference between the English working class and the American working class experience may be the miracle of space.' I also relish a glossy neo-noir like *The Grifters*, *LA Confidential*, *The Last Seduction* or *Basic Instinct* (the latter mostly for its sweetly naïve belief that the sight of a middle-aged man in a nightclub wearing a V-neck pully with nothing underneath is enough to give a woman of Sharon Stone's calibre a seemingly instant orgasm).

For many, however, the American 1940s and 1950s film noirs *are* cinema – if you say 'the movies' to a certain generation, it conjures up an instant image of Bogie in his trilby.* Maybe they leave me cold because, as a filmgoer, I like to stuff my greedy little face with beauty, and while the dames in these films are knockouts, the men generally aren't (Humphrey Bogart was described as 'the very image of our condition. His face was a living reproach'), apart from Elliott Gould in *The Long Goodbye*, mmmm. Perhaps it is because of the fear and mistrust of women that's always lurking in this cynical, world-weary postwar genre. It's certainly the reason why I think *In a Lonely Place*, Nicholas Ray's acclaimed 1950 film of Dorothy B. Hughes's 1947 novel, is one of the worst betrayals of a book I can think of. Not an artistic or narrative betrayal (far more acceptable), but a moral one.

* The term 'film noir' was coined by French critic Nino Frank in 1946 to describe both a mode and a mood; his nation loved noir's pessimistic, existential sense that 'men make plans and God laughs', as the saying goes.

First, the book. I can't believe it isn't more famous. I suppose it's been overshadowed by the film, but it needs to be better known. I feel quite evangelical about the fact that everyone should read it (although I know there's nothing easier to resist than someone telling you something is a 'must read'. *Is it, really?*). The first reason everyone should read it is that it contains the seeds of every subsequent 'inside the mind of a serial killer' novel, from *The Killer Inside Me* to *American Psycho* and all the lesser imitators that now clog up our screens and bookshelves (I'm looking at you, *You*). The second is that it's one of the most chilling portrayals of toxic masculinity I've ever read, a feminist anti-noir that completely turns the genre on its head. And the third, in case that makes it sound like a worthy work of critical theory by 'Germaine sodding Geer' (copyright Bridget Jones's mother), is that all these subversive ideas are smuggled in via the guise of a short, sleek, fast-paced thriller with a white-knuckle grip and the kick of a very strong martini.

The novel's unforgettable opening takes us into a strange, otherworldly nocturnal LA of darkness and fog, of rolling ocean and deserted beaches. The narrator, former Second World War pilot Dix Steele (paging Mr Freud), is watching a young woman get off a bus, and starts to follow her, enjoying her fear. Dix is fascinated by women, and he hates them ('They were all alike, cheats, liars, whores. Even the pious ones were waiting for a chance to cheat and lie and whore.'). And, we soon come to realise, he kills them, in order to recapture 'that feeling of power and exhilaration and freedom that came with loneness in the sky' – we never see the murders, but they are there, between the lines, infecting the pages.

When Dix catches up with an old war comrade, Brub, now a detective hunting the killer who's been strangling women across the city, he amuses himself by gaining an insight into the investigation. But gradually he loses control, and two women – Brub's wife Sylvia, and Laurel Gray, with whom Dix has begun a relationship – outwit him. Eventually, he breaks down and confesses. The book's original blurb calls it 'A latter day *Crime and Punishment*, told from the killer's point of view', and, like Raskolnikov, Dix thinks he's a superman, a Napoleon. In reality, he's pathetic, like a prototype incel. He pretends to work as a writer while surviving on handouts from his uncle. He soothes his red rages with drink and food (the wonderful descriptions of eating in this book rival Ian Fleming's, with huge sandwiches, steaks, burgers, French fries, shrimp cocktails, 'man-food').

Using an intimate third person, Hughes takes us right inside the sour brew of self-pity and self-delusion that is Dix's head, as he crafts his own mythos surrounding his failures: 'He'd been hounded all his life by idiot fate. He'd had to smash it in the face to ever get anything good.' According to the writer Megan Abbott, this was Hughes's *modus operandi* – 'her abiding interest in the psychology of difference, in taking on the perspectives of those unlike herself: from street punks to political prisoners.' And here, a man who hates women.*

By the time Hughes wrote *In a Lonely Place*, the hard-boiled crime novels pioneered by Dashiell Hammett, Raymond Chandler and James M. Cain, and their shadowy, chiaroscuro film counterparts, were already feeding into and shaping each

* According to Christine Smallwood in the *New Yorker*, 'Crime was never Hughes's interest – evil was. And to be evil for her is to be intolerant of others, of the very fact of the existence of something outside the self. With her poetic powers of description, she makes that evil a sickness in the mind, and a landscape to be surveyed.'

other. Book and film were closely linked, more than with any other genre. When he invented the morally ambiguous, sardonic gumshoe with Sam Spade, in his 1930 novel *The Maltese Falcon*, Hammett was adamant that 'I'm only going to write in objective and filmable form', making him one of the first writers not just to be influenced by cinema, but to be writing *for* cinema, focusing on scenes and exteriors rather than inner motivation.* (In a possibly apocryphal story, when *The Maltese Falcon* was adapted, it turned out to have been by John Huston's secretary, who just typed up the book in script form!)

All the California crime writers – 'the boys in the back room', as Edmund Wilson called them – were enmeshed with Hollywood, and in a further loop in the game of adaptation cat's cradle, Raymond Chandler not only had his novels adapted for the screen, but also adapted other authors' works, including James M. Cain's *Double Indemnity*, which he and director Billy Wilder just made more like the jazzy 'badinage' dialogue of his own wisecracking fiction, as well as smoothing the structure.†

When you read the novels that inspired film noir, it's like having a film beamed directly into your head (I had the same experience reading the original *Vertigo*).‡ I suppose this is why,

* It was originally serialised in *Black Mask* in 1929. My first introduction to the story, however, was a children's book called *The Falcon's Malteser*. Dorothy Parker was in such raptures over Sam Spade she described herself as 'mooning about in a daze of love, such as I had not known for any character in literature since I encountered Sir Lancelot'.

† Of structure, Wilder said, 'A screenplay is a mixture of poetry and architecture. If you don't have the architecture the fucker will collapse on you.'

‡ It's the same with that Southern gothic masterpiece *The Night of the Hunter*, which, author Davis Grubb said, 'I had been filming in my head as I wrote it'.

about halfway through *In a Lonely Place*, I started to realise, *Dix thinks he's in a noir movie*. He thinks he is the lone wolf antihero, and he thinks Laurel Gray is the femme fatale, that (so the theory goes) smoke-wreathed, vampish, castrating embodiment of male fears about women gaining independence during the Second World War. Look at his description of meeting her:

> She stood in his way and looked him over slowly, from crown to toe. The way a man looked over a woman, not the reverse. Her eyes were slant, her lashes curved long and golden dark. She had red-gold hair, flaming hair, flung back from her amber face, falling to her shoulders. Her mouth was too heavy with lipstick, a copper-red mouth, a sultry mouth painted to call attention to its promise.

She's Barbara Stanwyck in *Double Indemnity* or Ava Gardner in *The Killers* or Lana Turner in *The Postman Always Rings Twice*: treacherous, irresistible, there to lure men to their doom. 'He'd known what she was the first time he'd looked at her,' he asserts. 'Known he couldn't trust her'. But, of course, *everything* Dix thinks is wrong. He is the threat. And it is Laurel and Sylvia who are the detectives. It's audacious, and brilliant, turning all the book and film clichés on their heads. There's nothing else quite like it.

*This* is the reason I can't stomach Nicholas Ray's celebrated film adaptation. It takes Dix on his own terms and not the novel's. Not only does it make him innocent of the murders, it turns him from a whiny, self-pitying creep into a whiny, self-pitying 'tortured artist', whose violence (breaking a woman's nose, beating up a stranger, almost strangling Laurel because she is going to leave him) is excused and even venerated by those around him. He's no longer self-aggrandising because the movie aggrandises him. He's no longer pretending to be a writer; he *is* one – a Hollywood screenwriter, who we know is supposed to be an intellectual genius because he says words like 'thespian' but is trapped by the movie system around him. He's, haha, adapting a trashy novel for the screen ('All you have to do is follow the book,' he's told by his agent).

The script turns a study of misogyny into a 'paranoid women's film', like *Rebecca* or *Suspicion*, when Laurel starts to suspect that her beloved may be a monster. It is also a 'writer chewed up by the Hollywood system' film, a cinematic trope found in movies like *Sunset Boulevard* – of course it is, industries are obsessed with seeing themselves. It reads like a list of excuses made for violent men. 'He's exciting because he's not normal,' Brub says at one point. Later, when Laurel confides her fears about Dix to his agent, he chastises her: 'You knew he was dynamite. He has to explode sometimes ... You've got to take all of it, the bad with the good ... You can't hurt him like this ... He can't take defeat.' God spare me.

It's very much played in the tragic romantic key, as a love affair between two cynical, wary people who become poisoned by suspicion and violence. It ends when Laurel tells Dix that she can't live with a maniac anymore, and he starts to strangle her ('I'll never let you go'), until a phone call from Brub saying the real killer has been arrested saves her life. It's too late; Dix has shown the potential murderer inside. We're clearly meant to think this is very sad. 'I was born when she kissed me; I died when she left me; I lived a few short weeks while she loved me', goes the end of Dix's script, and the film's.

There are, admittedly, some great lines in the film. When Dix tells Laurel they're going to have dinner that night, she retorts, 'We *are* going to have dinner. But not together.' Gloria

Grahame, only twenty-seven, is magnificent, and Humphrey Bogart is genuinely creepy and sinister. The exquisite, sombre cinematography emphasises this: in one scene re-enacting a murder ('Squeeze harder, harder, squeeze harder, it's wonderful to feel her throat crush under your arm'), the lighting transforms him into a ghoul from a horror film.*

The sourness at the film's heart is clearer when you learn how it was made. Director Nicholas Ray was married to the much younger Gloria Grahame and the couple were secretly in the process of separating.† So Ray drew up a contract stipulating that he could monitor everything she did: 'my husband shall be entitled to direct, control, advise, instruct and even command my actions during the hours from 9 AM to 6 PM, every day except Sunday ... I acknowledge that in every conceivable situation his will and judgment shall be considered superior to mine and shall prevail.' She was also forbidden to 'nag, cajole, tease or in any other feminine fashion seek to distract or influence him'. Ah, those feminine wiles.

So Grahame was dominated by a control freak on screen and behind the camera. Some people have noted that Bogart too was married to a much younger woman (Lauren Bacall), and even spotted similarities between him and Dix in the film. As Louise Brooks (yes, that one) wrote in *Sight and Sound* magazine in the 1960s, '*In a Lonely Place* gave him a role that he could play with complexity because the character's pride in his art, his selfishness, his drunkenness, his lack of energy stabbed with lightning strokes of violence, were shared equally by the real Bogart.'

* As Peter Bradshaw puts it, 'he becomes wizened and rat-like and his crooked teeth protrude gruesomely'.

† In an unexpected twist, Grahame later married Ray's son!

The film was made by Humphrey Bogart's own production company, Santana Productions (named after his beloved yacht), which he'd set up after leaving a bruising relationship with Jack Warner's studio system. And when the initial actor hired for Dix, John Derek, was dropped for Bogie himself, there was no way he could be a serial killer, so, for solid commercial reasons, the murderer's identity was changed. Hughes was phlegmatic about this, saying, 'who am I to criticise the experts in their fields?' As Graham Greene, whose novels were fodder for dozens of films, acknowledged, 'When you sell a book to Hollywood ... The film producer can alter anything. He can turn your tragedy of East End Jewry into a musical comedy at Palm Springs if he wishes. He need not even retain your title, though that is usually almost the only thing he wishes to retain.' (Although when her novel *Union Street* was made into the film *Stanley & Iris*, Pat Barker quipped that she'd written a book about seven working-class women and yet it became a movie starring Robert De Niro – all they'd kept was one character's name!)

The title and character names really are all that's left of Hughes's work. This is nothing new, I realise. *I Am Legend* springs to mind as a prime example of a movie missing the bloody point of a book's title by making the 'legend' a lone hero who saves humanity, rather than the distant memory of an extinct race, as he is in the novel.* The most recent, Oscar-winning adaptation of *All Quiet on the Western Front* seemed to misunderstand the book's title (where Paul is killed on a day

* *I Am Legend* was also filmed as *The Last Man on Earth* and *The Omega Man*, leading the author Richard Matheson to ponder, 'I don't know why Hollywood is fascinated by my book when they never care to film it as I wrote it.'

when, ostensibly, nothing happens), with one German critic saying, 'you have to ask yourself whether director Berger has even read Remarque's novel'.

*In a Lonely Place*, however, feels less like an interpretation and more like a kick in the teeth from a big male boot. It's a bully of a film. Unlike Laurel and Sylvia, everyone who made it seems to have been hoodwinked by Dix's view of himself. The reviewers were taken in too. Ray, who also directed *Rebel Without a Cause*, was one of the directors fetishised by French critics, who saw him as a nonconformist genius: 'The cinema is Nicholas Ray,' said Jean-Luc Godard. According to one, Jean Wagner, Ray's heroes were like Camus's Meursault in *The Stranger*, and Dix deserved more sympathy than the murderer's victims because of his special, precious nature as somebody who sees through phonies, a 'magnificent fool'. Even the otherwise excellent BFI Modern Classics guide calls it 'One of the cinema's most intense dissections of the violence of romantic relationships'. I think that should say 'of the violence of violent men'.*

It makes me cross. Perhaps not Norma Desmond meltdown or Peter Finch 'I'm as mad as Hell and I'm not going to take this anymore!' levels, but extremely put out. Everyone else seems to venerate this film, however. It's always in those Top 100 Movies of All Time lists.†

* Incidentally, one contemporary ad for the film shows a close-up of Bogart's eyes and asks the male spectator, 'Are you a man of violence?' The women are asked to suspect if the men in their lives are violent. 'Look deep into Bogart's eyes – is it love, hate, or murder?' Sigh.

† And in the 1986 pop song 'In a Lonely Place' on the album *Especially for You* by the Smithereens (no, not Kylie and Jason, sadly), which incorporates lines from the film into its lyrics.

The filmmaker Robert Bresson, when talking about adaptation, said that it should not necessarily mean fidelity, and that the 'literary form must not enter into the cinematographic work'. But he also said in an interview that 'if you love a work, you adapt it much more easily. To love a work also means to feel it.' Ultimately, the film of *In a Lonely Place* seems to me to be born not out of love, but something far nastier.

# 5

# THEY SANITISED IT: *THE COLOR PURPLE*

Once upon a time, around the middle of the eighteenth century, large numbers of people started reading – and it was considered dangerous. It was described as a craze, an epidemic. Many people think the French Revolution wouldn't have happened without it. Elites were appalled at the idea of books somehow getting *into the wrong hands* (famously echoed centuries later by the prosecutor in the 1960 *Lady Chatterley's Lover* obscenity trial, who asked whether it was a novel 'that you would wish your wife or your servants to read').

Well, *plus ça change* and all that. The humble book, 'a flat object made from a tree with flexible parts on which are imprinted lots of funny dark squiggles', as Carl Sagan put it, is still deemed to be about as safe as a stick of nitroglycerine by authoritarian regimes all over the world, which, at the time of writing, includes the United States of America. In the last couple of years, banning books – often more euphemistically referred to as books being 'withdrawn' from public school libraries – has increased at an alarming rate in the US, mostly as the result of a concerted anti-diversity, equity and inclusion campaign targeting works about race or sexuality. PEN America, which is dedicated to free expression in literature, said it has seen nothing like it 'since the Red Scare McCarthy era of the 1950s'.

The banned list is a mixture of newcomers and perennial offenders, and the reasons given show the banners are nothing if not literal. *The Witches*? Witchcraft. *Brave New World*? 'Anti-family' (yes, that's the point...). *The Grapes of Wrath*? For portraying 'Kern County, California, in a negative light'. Of course. *Nineteen Eighty-Four* for being both pro- and anti-Communist. *Fahrenheit 451*, whose title comes from the temperature at which books burn? Violence, negative portrayal of Christianity, offensive language and, the biggest sin of all, criticising firemen.* Margaret Atwood's novel *The Handmaid's Tale* is currently banned in sixty-seven US school districts (the PEN website's blurb tartly reads: 'In the near future, Offred is a handmaid in an authoritarian society who is not permitted to read. We'll let that sink in.') In Utah, Atwood's novel *Oryx and Crake*, if found on a pupil, must be sent to a warehouse in a special box marked 'sensitive materials'. Dangerous indeed.†

A glance at PEN's most banned books of 2024–25 (No.1 is *A Clockwork Orange*, No.6 is Judy Blume's *Forever*, which makes

* Ray Bradbury, the author of this incendiary work, had a bleaker view, saying, 'The problem in our country isn't with books being banned, but with people no longer reading. You don't have to burn books to destroy a culture. Just get people to stop reading them.'

† Angie Thomas's young adult novel about police brutality, *The Hate U Give*, has been pulled off many a shelf and recently made the headlines for being removed from a school in Dorset, in the UK. The author said in response, 'I wish more adults would put the same energy they have towards banning books into creating a world where things like racism and police brutality no longer exist.'

me oddly proud that these modern classics continue to annoy and offend) shows that Alice Walker's Pulitzer Prize-winning, multi-million-copy-selling 1982 novel *The Color Purple* is still up there. It was first banned in 1984, in Oakland, California – leading Walker to wonder in a subsequent essay 'how the banning was coming along', and it's been the same ever since, challenged constantly for its slang, swearing, sexual violence and, heaven forfend, lesbians.

Walker said that her mother never got past the first page of the book. If you haven't read it before, or for a while, or if you read it after seeing the film (as I did), this epistolary novel *is* shocking in its brutality. It follows the life of Celie, a Black girl in 1900s rural Georgia. On page one she is raped by her stepfather at the age of fourteen ('He never had a kine word to say to me. Just say You gonna do what your mammy wouldn't.'). On page two, she gives birth to a baby, and he takes it away to kill it. On page three we discover he's taken away another baby, a boy, possibly to sell it. He beats her, takes her out of school and marries her off to a man called Mr., who abuses her and sends away her beloved sister Nettie – she finds out years later that he has been hiding all of Nettie's letters from her. Celie is utterly deprived of love and affection.

Yet somehow, because of the rawness and insistent clarity of her voice, as she recounts her experiences in a series of letters to God, the book transcends the suffering. Love does arrive, first in the shape of Celie's fearless sister-in-law Sofia, and then in the shape of Shug Avery, the female nightclub singer who becomes her lover and opens up a world of sexual desire for her. It's a novel of resistance and sisterhood, and carving out some kind of joy. It's also deeply spiritual. Celie comes to realise that the 'old white man' she's been writing to isn't listening, but that divinity is around her, in a blade of corn, a purple field. She starts to write to her sister Nettie instead, and her very last letter is addressed 'Dear Everything'.

Walker said that she wrote the book in order to listen to her ancestors, and 'as a gift to the people. All of them. If they wanted it, let them fight to keep it, as I had to fight to deliver it.' It became a bestseller but the criticisms – mostly centring on the novel's 'folks' speech' and its portrayal of Black men – caused her huge pain.

Yet, as is so often the case when the verbal becomes visual, there for all to see, it was only when the novel was made into a Hollywood film that the controversy really ignited. The choice of two non-Black men (director Steven Spielberg and scriptwriter Menno Meyjes) to adapt a novel by a Black woman was criticised from the start, but then, as Walker acknowledged, she wanted to go mainstream in order to give her story to people who might not have read the book. And, as the actor Margaret Avery, who played Shug, said, the sad truth was that there were no Black directors whom the studios would trust with the project at the time.

The controversy surrounding the 1985 film's portrayal of Black men as violent thugs was even fiercer. One US TV show dedicated to a debate on it was dubbed 'purple rage'. For many, including African American civil rights organisation the NAACP, it was yet more Hollywood propaganda that had been reinforcing centuries-old stereotypes since *The Birth of a Nation*. Walker said years later that 'It's a book mostly about women, and what they're doing, and how they're carrying on no matter what the men are doing.'

As the writer Aisha Harris recently noted, 'A recurring thread in the controversy was the stark gender divide in reactions to the film's depiction of gendered violence, intergenerational trauma, and queer romance – many Black women felt seen on the page and screen for the first time; many straight Black men felt attacked and demonized for the hundredth time.'

Walker's own 2017 'Dear Reader' at the front of the UK paperback edition, in which she describes going to a recent packed-out screening of the film, is illuminating. She notes the differences between the book and the film, such as casting a large man, Danny Glover, as Mr., whereas in the text he's small, to show that 'size doesn't matter when it comes to terrorizing and dominating women'. She laments the neglect of the novel's spiritual side, and the way Celie's self-empowerment by making trousers ('folkspants') is reduced to a comic moment. She rails at the inaccuracies: 'I could barely stand the sight of all those cosmos blossoms at the beginning of the film. First of all, I'm not sure the cosmos is a flower that thrives in the South ... Who planted them?'*

And yet she laughs and cries too, along with the rest of the audience. Spielberg, on shaky ground as he may have been, did his job. The movie was a huge, mainstream, commercial hit. It fulfilled critic Roger Ebert's description of film as 'a machine for creating empathy' by deliberately universalising the story. But in doing so, it lost a lot. Looking at it now, there are mighty performances, notably from Whoopi Goldberg as Celie and Oprah Winfrey as Sofia, and scenes that jar. It looks too bright and glowing (Walker said it was like watching a cartoon); Quincy

* I agree, it is making the book's whisper of purple too obvious, but it's also a visually affecting scene: the young girls/children playing a game in the field have their bodies hidden by the flowers; when they are fully revealed, only then do we realise one of them is pregnant.

Jones's swelling score feels too sweet. Most importantly, Celie's sexual self-discovery as a gay woman is nowhere to be seen.

For Spielberg, this was to get a lower age rating, but he also admitted years later that 'I was shy about it. In that sense, perhaps I was the wrong director to acquit some of the more sexually honest encounters between Shug and Celie because I did soften those. I basically took something that was extremely erotic and very intentional, and I reduced it to a simple kiss.' He had always loved the book and 'wanted part of it to belong to me', but maybe it wasn't really his story to tell? Perhaps, just as others have tried, he was censoring the book, in his own way?

Fast-forward forty years, and we see Walker's story being sliced very differently, with the emphasis on positive empowerment. The PEN website's description of the book tells us that '*The Color Purple* writes a message of healing, forgiveness, self-discovery, and sisterhood to a new generation of readers … and carries readers on an epic and spirit-affirming journey toward transformation, redemption, and love.'

The 2023 musical film version of *The Color Purple* follows this uplifting pitch, turning up the joy to Prozac overdose levels. Written by Marcus Gardley, directed by Blitz Bazawule (co-director of Beyoncé's *Black Is King*), with Oprah Winfrey, Quincy Jones and Steven Spielberg on board as producers, it's based on the smash hit Broadway stage musical of the novel. As Taraji P. Henson, who plays Shug in the new film, put it, 'We don't wallow in the muck … We laugh, we sing, we go to church, we dance, we celebrate, we fight for joy.'

Many reviewers thought they'd over-indexed on the joy, however, with UK critics complaining that 'the songs, with their antiseptic polished sheen, seem fundamentally out of tune with the unforgiving grit of the plot'; that it 'sugars the pill and softens the blow'. The Americans, on the whole, were more positive, and perhaps, given the nation's long history of Black pain both on and off screen, that's not entirely unsurprising. The *New York Times* praised its 'gravitas and heart', but also acknowledged that 'to really tell Celie's story, you have to allow space for some unutterable atrocities that give heft to her later development. Hollywood movies are ill-suited to this kind of material, and the whole thing inevitably suffers as a result.'

I found watching it a slightly bewildering, exhausting experience, as I do so many modern movie musicals, which are all big, colourful spectacle, soaring numbers, relentless emotional climaxes (without the quieter moments that let the loud bits stand out), brassy-stampy-clappy tunes and frenetic, ceaseless movement, when all I want to do is keep still and look at the dancers' feet. But it does have a song dedicated to the clitoris, 'Push Da Button', so that's great.

The violence and horror are either eliminated or turned into a kind of slapstick, but I understand that showing misery was never the aim. I suppose my main disappointment is that, forty years after Spielberg's version, this new one still fails to do justice to Celie and Shug's spiky, sexy love affair. The first time Shug sees Celie in the novel, she drunkenly laughs and slurs, 'You sure is ugly!' That line made it into the Spielberg film, but it's eliminated here, along with all the contrary ambivalence of their relationship. Instead, most of the complexity, and the genuine tenderness between them, is transmuted into a kind of saccharine romance, with Hollywood dream sequences where the two of them are spun on a giant turntable. The relationship is so key to the book. It leads Celie to realise her body can bring her pleasure as well as pain, but also to recognise that she is worthy of love. Shug may be a capricious mistress (at one point she runs off with a nineteen-year-old boy!), but she holds Celie up, encouraging her to become an independent being, both emotionally and financially. I wouldn't say this film straight-washes, but it comes pretty close with its prettification of desire.

Straightwashing in Hollywood is nothing new; in fact, it could be described as the cornerstone of the industry, from gay stars trapped in lavender marriages to the expurgation of gay themes and lives under the Hays Code, a set of moral guidelines for US filmmakers that ended in 1968. In adaptation terms, this meant the unnamed queer narrator of Truman Capote's autobiographical novella *Breakfast at Tiffany's* becoming a straight man in the film, who falls in love with Holly Golightly. (Capote also lobbied for Marilyn Monroe to play the part of the damaged, lost-girl heroine; surely a far better fit than the fairy-like Audrey Hepburn.)* It meant the elimination of a gay relationship in the film of the play *Cat on a Hot Tin Roof.* And it meant the famous 'snails or oysters' bathing scene between Laurence Olivier and Tony Curtis being cut from Kubrick's 1960 film of the novel *Spartacus*.†

In the documentary *The Celluloid Closet*, Armistead Maupin praises the post-Code film musical *Cabaret* as 'the first film that really celebrated homosexuality'. For him, Michael York's

* I'm amazed when I ever see this in people's favourite film lists. Holly is incredibly annoying, and Mickey Rooney's performance as her Japanese neighbour, criticised even at the time, has made it unwatchable for years.

† *Spartacus* is interesting on a whole other level of censorship: Howard Fast wrote the novel in response to being imprisoned during Hollywood's anti-Communist witch hunts; screenwriter Dalton Trumbo, also blacklisted by McCarthy, worked on the script in secret but was given a screen credit as an act of solidarity from star and producer Kirk Douglas.

character was gay and treated as normal. For Christopher Isherwood, however, the author of the 1939 novel *Goodbye to Berlin* upon which the movie was based (after it had been a play, *I Am a Camera*, and an inferior, in my view, stage musical), it was another straightwash. 'In the film of *Cabaret*,' he said, 'Brian's homosexual tendency is treated as an indecent but comic weakness to be snickered at, like bed-wetting.' *Cabaret* is frequently ranked as the best movie musical ever made, and I agree, but the weakness of Brian's portrayal rings true.

In the spirit of mischievousness, really, I also note that there is a strong hint of homoeroticism in Ian Fleming's James Bond novels – so much so that Noël Coward wrote to him jokingly after reading the description of Honeychile Rider's boyish bottom in *Dr. No*: 'I know we are all becoming progressively more broadminded nowadays but really, old chap, what *could* you have been thinking of?' This was purged from our action man for the films – as well as smoothing the harder edges of the character, and changing the locations from boring old seaside castles, and Deal in Kent, of all places, to secret volcano lairs and space shuttles. (I also note that Amazon Prime, which recently bought the rights to the Bond franchise, got into trouble for stripping the guns out of the original movie posters, before quietly reinstating them.)

In so much I've read about adaptations, phrases like 'toned down', 'sanitised', 'sugar-coated', 'defanged' or 'watered down' are used when criticising them. Sometimes it's clearly to do with age ratings. Michael Crichton's original *Jurassic Park* novel is pretty violent, with a baby eaten by dino-clones in the first few pages, and the park's owner a psychotic megalomaniac who also gets eaten, whereas in the 1993 film, played by Richard Attenborough, he's Father Christmas with a Scottish accent.

Spielberg deliberately reduced the gore to make a kids' film, one I admire hugely, mostly for its star Jeff Goldblum's dedication to showing his bare chest in as many scenes as possible. Sometimes it's artistic – in Robert Bloch's original novel *Psycho*, Norman Bates is physically repellent; Hitchcock cast the good-looking, well-groomed Anthony Perkins as his villain to wrongfoot the audience.

Sometimes, however, the reason seems to be a failure of nerve, or a lack of political conviction, with hard-to-digest ideas made more palatable for a mainstream audience. When the first part of Philip Pullman's *His Dark Materials* trilogy was filmed, the novel's fierce criticism of organised religion was softened, leading the National Secular Society to accuse it of 'castrating it' (it didn't stop the Catholic League from demanding a boycott, however, because it feared the movie would send children to the books – those dangerous books again). Alan Moore, a fine hater of seemingly all adaptations of his graphic novels, accused the Wachowskis-scripted film *V for Vendetta* of whitewashing the original's specific theme of fascism and anarchism in the UK in the 1980s – he refused to take royalties because he loathed it so much. In fact, Moore is pretty much against cinema in every way, not just because, in his view, the accountants are in charge, but because 'There's something a bit bullying about screen entertainment. It doesn't leave room for the audience's own imagination.'

The word 'bullying' is interesting. With a book, we can go at our own pace; cinema tells us where to look, and when. As Stephen King put it, 'The imagination moves with its own tidal flow. Films, even the best of them, freeze fiction.' It made me think of a quote from Toni Morrison about the perception that a book can only, somehow, be perfected when we actually see it.

'I was always annoyed,' she said, 'when my students would ask, "When is there going to be a movie?" I told them that a novel is not what happens before the movie. Why can't it just be a book?'* Anthony Burgess observed too how 'Every best-selling novel has to be turned into a film, the assumption being that the book itself whets an appetite for the true fulfilment – the verbal shadow turned into light, the word made flesh … Because of the primacy of sight among all the human senses, the book is generally now regarded as a handmaiden to the film.'†

As Hitchcock said, they're called moving pictures not talking pictures, but I wonder whether, when satisfying the seemingly pathological determination to visualise what we've imagined in our heads, a filmmaker then can't quite go the whole way. *The Grapes of Wrath* ends with a woman breastfeeding a starving man; John Ford's 1940 film did not show this. Peter Jackson made an oddly saccharine, almost zany fantasy film out of *The Lovely Bones*, Alice Sebold's flawed but powerful bestseller narrated by a teenage girl who has been raped and murdered by a neighbour ('I felt like a sea in which he stood and pissed and shat' was one of the more horrible lines that stayed with me). But then who really wants to see all that? As David Cronenberg noted about making his experimental cut-up homage to William Burroughs's *Naked Lunch*, a direct adaptation would have been far too expensive and 'would be banned in every country in the

* She also had an excellent phrase about what happens when your book is made into a movie: 'stroke the author time', when the filmmakers are nice to you, before doing whatever they want.

† Veteran British filmmaker Peter Greenaway was even saltier: 'We don't need books to make films. It's the last thing we want – it turns cinema into the bastard art of illustration.'

world' (it's true; bringing a talking anus to life on screen is a challenge).

The phrase 'left to the imagination' seems apt. In fact, the only example I came across where the film is grittier and harsher than the book is another coming of age tale, Barry Hines's heartbreaking 1968 novel *A Kestrel for a Knave* (described as 'Yorkshire's *Moby-Dick*' by poet Ian McMillan), which was filmed by Ken Loach as *Kes*. Initially, the producers suggested some pretty wild changes to the story, including Billy Casper's mother getting murdered and Billy getting a job in a zoo, but as Hines said, 'we found that scenario quite easy to resist'. Book and film are both stunning, but on screen we lose Billy's rich, cinematic inner life, and with it the suggestion that, perhaps, he might be okay. Instead, the film ends on a bleak, downbeat note (well, it *is* Ken Loach).

*Kes* is the outlier. Cinema, especially mainstream cinema, wants to make us happy.* It is a crowd pleaser. We willingly suspend our disbelief and get played like a piano, to paraphrase Hitchcock – it's no accident that so many filmmakers use the language of lies when talking about film: 'lies 24 frames a second' (Stanley Donen), 'illusionist work' (Werner Herzog). In the words of Hilary Mantel, 'The cinema creates a mythic identity. We watch a film all together, in the dark. We engage in collective dreaming. And we eat – we eat with our fingers, cheap, gratifying, baby food – as if suspending adult life and adult judgement, sinking entirely into the story we are told. The image has taken reason prisoner.'

* According to the ever-quotable Pauline Kael, however, *all* cinema does this: 'the educated audience often uses "art" films in much the same self-indulgent way as the mass audience uses the Hollywood "product", finding wish fulfilment in the form of cheap and easy congratulation on their sensitivities'.

Maybe it's better that some pictures are left in our heads. It's why we read, after all. To quote Alice Walker's final verdict on her Hollywood adaptation, 'Thank the Goddess there is a book.'

# 6

# THEY RUINED THE ENDING: *THE LORD OF THE RINGS*

'Endings, frankly, are a bitch'

William Goldman

Being in the world of a great book or film is like a party you never want to end. Just one more song! Come on Eileen! Yet, inevitably, the music stops, the lights come on and, tired, drunk and sweaty, you have to leave the dance floor and go home.

The one consolation is that writers seem to dislike endings, or what was known in the trade as 'the wind-up', as much as readers do. George Eliot admitted that 'conclusions are the weak points of most authors' (although she still gave *Middlemarch* the greatest closing line in fiction); Hemingway apparently wrote thirty-nine different endings to *A Farewell to Arms*; later, Ian McEwan wavered over including his meta-twist at the end of *Atonement*.

Solutions to the ending problem have ranged from the *deus ex machina* (or marriage/big pile of corpses) of ancient drama to what Henry James sarkily described as the 'distribution at the last of prizes, pensions, husbands, wives, babies, millions, appended paragraphs and cheerful remarks' that winds up many Victorian novels, to the more open, uncertain conclusions of the modernists (E. M. Forster said it was effectively immoral for a modern author to close a story with a happy ending) and postmodernists.* Thomas Pynchon and David Foster Wallace even ended their novels mid-sentence – as the philosopher Jan Kott said, 'ancient tragedy is loss of life, modern tragedy is loss of purpose'.

But whether a story slips away with an enigmatic French exit or tries to make everyone happy with an Irish goodbye (when you stick around for hours hugging all and sundry), endings are artificial things. The screenwriter William Goldman described narrative as an endless piece of string in which the writer makes two arbitrary snips, at the beginning and the end. The snips create the illusion of purpose: as filmmaker Wim Wenders said, 'Stories give people the feeling that there is meaning, that there is ultimately an order lurking behind the incredible confusion of appearances and phenomena that surrounds them.'† This is why botched endings are one of our most common bugbears, especially those of long-running adaptations, where every series may be the last, or where the screen version runs ahead of the books, such as with *Game of Thrones*.

Ultimately, the real ending is when our little life is rounded with a sleep ('The only true ending is death': Roger Ebert),

* William Makepeace Thackeray said, 'The end of a novel, like the end of a children's dinner party, must be made of sweetmeats and sugar-plums' (although the endings of most children's parties are more akin to Shakespearean tragedy, strewn with the bodies of exhausted parents).

† My favourite movie open ending is that of *The Day the Earth Caught Fire*, in which Earth has spun off its axis towards the sun. As we wait to hear if crisis has been averted, a London newspaper prepares two different front pages: 'World Saved' and 'World Doomed'. We never find out which wins. This film also contains the most hilarious depiction of 1960s 'beatniks' I have ever seen.

and who wants to be reminded of that? According to André Bazin, cinema is 'a fundamental and psychical need to reverse the finality of death', and this avoidance of the *memento mori* is probably why so many book-to-film endings are softened, or made happier. Sometimes they even save dead characters, such as in the notoriously terrible 1995 movie of *The Scarlet Letter* (more on that travesty later) or the Hollywood remake of the original Dutch *The Vanishing*.* The CIA-funded 1954 cartoon film of Orwell's *Animal Farm* ended with the other animals overthrowing the corrupted pigs – they wanted to give the audience hope, they said, but also had to show that Communism could be defeated. In fact, the 'Hollywood ending' has become a film trope in itself, such as in the wicked satire on moviemaking, *The Player*, where a struggling screenwriter's depressing legal drama is betrayed with a tacked-on, upbeat finale and famous actors (Bruce Willis and Julia Roberts) in the lead roles. 'Cinema can fill in the empty spaces of your life and your loneliness', as Pedro Almodóvar noted, and happy resolutions comfort us with a lovely narrative panacea.

I think this is why, when he adapted *Great Expectations* in 1946, David Lean said that it was 'our intention to make a fairy tale', changing the ending so that Pip tears down the curtains of Satis House, letting in the light, and he and Estella leave hand in hand towards a bright future – one critic described it as 'pure movieland'. But then Dickens never knew how to end his story, obsessively rewriting it as if he were scratching an itch

* Based on the novella about a man searching for his missing girlfriend, *The Golden Egg*, the original Dutch adaptation ended with him being buried alive just like her; the English-language version concludes with a dramatic rescue, and a publishing deal.

and, on the advice of his friend Edward Bulwer-Lytton, arriving at a more upbeat conclusion than he had originally intended.* I wonder if he might have quite liked the way Lean's ending exorcises the dark ghosts and repressed childhood shame that soak the pages of the novel.

Sometimes there is a less deliberate reason for a new movie ending. When Stanley Kubrick adapted Anthony Burgess's novel *A Clockwork Orange*, he famously left out its realistic conclusion (where teenage thug Alex grows up and grows out of ultraviolence) because he had been working from the US edition, which omitted the last chapter. His Alex gleefully returned to his natural state of wickedness at the end, and the film became notorious for being banned by its own director after Kubrick read that it had inspired copycat crimes. Burgess ruefully said of this, 'The film made it easy for readers of the book to misunderstand what it was about, and the misunderstanding will pursue me till the day I die.'†

More usually, the enforcers of the Hays Code loomed during, or even before, a film was made. Hitchcock's masterly adaptation of Daphne du Maurier's novel *Rebecca* was forced to make Maxim de Winter an accidental killer rather than a cold-blooded one, which would have been 'a clear violation of the Production Code, since it apparently justifies and condones

---

* Edward Bulwer-Lytton, most famous for starting one of his novels 'It was a dark and stormy night', inspired the annual Bulwer-Lytton Fiction Contest to seek the worst fictional opening sentence possible.

† In 1987, Burgess adapted his novel for the stage, and included this telling stage direction: 'A man bearded like Stanley Kubrick comes on playing, in exquisite counterpoint, "Singin' in the Rain" on a trumpet. He is kicked off the stage.'

murder'.* Similarly, when the Boulting brothers filmed Graham Greene's *Brighton Rock* in 1948, they feared British censors would not allow its bleak ending, where Rose, the young widow of psychopath Pinkie, goes off to listen to the malicious voice recording he's made for her ('What you want me to say is I love you. Well here is the truth. I hate you, you little slut. You make me sick'). Instead, in a stroke of cinematic genius, the record gets stuck on 'I love you'.

Hitchcock said, 'Always make the audience suffer as much as possible' (although his adroit, almost comically sudden endings were mostly happy, and moral). Sometimes filmmakers clearly decide that viewers need a reward after the suffering. Frank Darabont's extra scene at the end of *The Shawshank Redemption*, showing Andy and Red reunited on the shore of the Pacific Ocean, had test audiences weeping and cheering because they were so uplifted, so, against his better judgement, he kept it in – as Tim Robbins said, 'You *need* that ending'.† I suspect a similar wish for some kind of emotional catharsis explains the bizarre decision to have Offred murder the Commander at the end of the largely forgotten 1990 film of *The Handmaid's Tale*. (Harold Pinter's script was reworked so much he requested his name be removed from the credits.) Flawed and trashy in places,

* Much to the annoyance of producer David O. Selznick, who railed that 'the whole story of *Rebecca* is of a man who has murdered his wife, and it now becomes the story of a man who buried a wife who was killed accidentally!'

† This ending doesn't appear in Stephen King's short story, *Rita Hayworth and the Shawshank Redemption*. Darabont made up for this saccharine addition with his later adaptation of King's *The Mist*, adding a famously heartrending finale that was far bleaker than the original; King loved it and said he wished he'd thought of it.

as if Paul Verhoven decided to direct *The Female Eunuch* (the poster shows Natasha Richardson scantily clad in red with the strapline, 'A haunting tale of sexuality in a country gone wrong'), this movie bankrupted its studio, but I have a soft spot for it, and not just because it stars 1980s dreamboat Aidan Quinn as Nick the chauffeur.* For me, its glossy made-for-TV visuals highlight the horror of Gilead more effectively than the in-your-face grimness of the recent Emmy award-winning Hulu series.

Cinema knows that humans are hopeless hope addicts, and I am a sucker for a happy ending (after all, *most* people's existences are fairly okay, *most* marriages survive, *most* lives don't end in abject misery). But one adaptation where I wish the filmmakers had cleaved more faithfully to a sad, downbeat conclusion is *The Return of the King*, the final part of Peter Jackson's blockbuster adaptations of *The Lord of the Rings*. Although I am extremely fond of these films, which are pioneering works of genuine love and dedication, they fail to acknowledge that Tolkien's vision, especially in the last book of his trilogy, is a tragic one – and they omit the Scouring of the Shire, which we shall come to later.

Tolkien was emphatic, when interviewed, that his overriding theme was 'Death, and the inevitability of death'. He resisted attempts to paint his work as an allegory, but he acknowledged the effects of the First World War trenches in its preface: 'I remember miles and miles of seething, tortured earth, perhaps

* Reviewers hated the film, with one saying director Volker Schlöndorff was 'as uncomfortable in this feminist nightmare as a man in a lingerie department', although I think most critics at the time took umbrage with the concept itself: 'paranoid poppycock – just like the book', not realising quite how on point it was.

best described in the chapters on the approaches to Mordor.' 'Anguish is, for me, the prevailing note,' wrote C. S. Lewis in his review of *The Lord of the Rings*. When he called it 'a book that will break your heart', I don't think he was just being nice about his friend's work.

Yet ever since it was published, there has been tension between the aims of Tolkien's tragic epic and the public's response to it. When the first volume of this earnest, self-consciously archaic English mythos, born of a deep knowledge of languages and ancient sagas, appeared in 1954 (followed by *The Two Towers* later that year and *The Return of the King* in 1955), it was an anachronism at a time of literary existentialism and angry young men.* Many critics derided it, such as Edmund Wilson with his brilliantly titled hatchet job 'Oo, THOSE AWFUL ORCS!'† Even now it's easy to mock its slight whiff of unwashed dungeons-and-dragons losers, who probably had the 'V' for virgin sign made at them in school.‡ In a *Friends* episode, Ross asks, 'Didn't you read *The Lord of the Rings* in high school?' Joey's response: 'No, I had *sex* in high school.'

However, Tolkien became hip in the tree-hugging 1960s, when an unauthorised one-volume US edition of *The Lord of the Rings* was adopted as a counterculture Bible by

* Tolkien worried the title of the final part gave the game away, but his publisher won the battle. He also agonised over his characters' names: at one point, Strider was going to be called Trotter!

† My favourite negative Amazon review of *TLOTR* says, 'This book is so boring!!! I think this is the most boring book in the world. I don't think this thing should be a book!' Did Trump write it?

‡ In Jonathan Coe's novel *The Rotters' Club*, Benjamin and his nerdy friends start a prog-rock band called 'Gandalf's Pikestaff'.

students – complete with badges saying 'Support Your Local Hobbit' and 'Gandalf for President'. Led Zeppelin dedicated a concept album to it, rock bands named themselves after its characters, the Beatles wanted to star in a film version (Paul as Frodo, George as Gandalf, John as Gollum and Ringo as Sam) and Tolkien mania reached its apotheosis, or probably nadir, with *Star Trek* legend Leonard Nimoy's 1967 single 'The Ballad of Bilbo Baggins', which makes his co-star William Shatner's recording of 'Lucy in the Sky with Diamonds' look positively understated.

The popularity of *The Lord of the Rings* has never waned since. It has now sold over 150 million copies worldwide, become a cultural touchstone – and a billion-dollar franchise.* Because of their roots in ancient myth, that sense, in Tolkien's words, of 'recording what was already "there"', his books have a sense of universality, and of portability – he called it 'applicability' – that makes them perfect for transplanting into other media, whether it is radio, TV, film or stage.†

At first Tolkien resisted a *Rings* adaptation, berating the 'sillification' of a 1955 radio version (he also loathed Disney), but a couple of years later he'd warmed to the idea of an animation, writing to his publisher that it was the one medium that could encompass his world, 'quite apart from the glint of money,

* Modern fantasy would not exist without him either. As Terry Pratchett said, 'Tolkien is a mountain you're either trying to write against, or realise that you're already standing on.'

† Including, I am sad to say, a valiant but doomed West End musical, which my sister called 'the worst experience of my life', and made a lot of people think of Tolkien's Inkling friend's response to one of his readings: 'Oh God, no more bloody Elves!'

though on the brink of retirement that is not an unpleasant possibility'. So, in 1969, he sold the film rights to United Artists for £104,000 (over £2 million in today's money). However, deemed 'unfilmable' by a succession of directors, including Kubrick, the project languished.

Then, in a mad turn of events, the esteemed British director John Boorman came on board with a script where, among other things, Frodo and Galadriel get it on ('his eyes wander over her body, drinking in its loveliness'); Éowyn experiences a magical orgasm; and the Council of Elrond becomes a rock opera featuring 'a character who is a combination of Mick Jagger and Punch'.* A small part of me would have liked to see this deranged vision made real, but audiences were spared the pleasure when United relinquished the rights, leading to the maverick director of filthy X-rated cartoons Ralph Bakshi taking on the project instead. I *think* I remember watching the resulting 1978 animated film as a child, and I definitely remember it as the start of my crush on Aragorn, who in this version sports a Playmobil-style bowl haircut and flaunts his manly thighs in a daringly short tunic.†

Like many people, my first life-changing encounter with *The Lord of the Rings* was an adaptation, in this case the outstanding 1981 BBC radio series featuring a dream cast of

* Who knows, perhaps Middle-earth porn could have become a thing (I note there is already a Finnish Tolkien film called *Hobitit* but I suspect that's not the same).

† Bakshi's Rotoscope technique, where animators trace over live-action film sequences, proved near ruinous, but his film was hugely influential on Peter Jackson, with several scenes, such as the Hobbits hiding from the Black Rider, recreated almost exactly.

British thespians: John Le Mesurier as Bilbo, Ian Holm as Frodo (who would step into his fictional uncle's shoes for Peter Jackson's films), Michael Hordern, his woody voice creaking like an old cello as Gandalf, and, best of all, a rakish Robert Stephens playing Aragorn as if he's just barrelled in from an all-day drinking session at the Prancing Pony. I used to listen to it with my younger sister at our granny's, who recorded it from the radio on to meticulously labelled cassette tapes. From the moment I heard the haunting, insistent strings of the series' theme tune, the hairy feet and preciouses and second breakfasts entered my soul.

The one adaptation to rule them all, however, is Peter Jackson's three-part mega-bucks mega-version, shot in one epic production over fifteen months in a heaven-sent New Zealand landscape. It is *huge*, a work of wholehearted passion and commitment to recreating Middle-earth (they even brought Tolkien illustrators, blacksmiths and Elvish pronunciation experts on board). There seems to have been an atmosphere of genuine, wholesome fellowship on set, and love for the books: Viggo Mortensen took the role of Aragorn because his son was a fan, Christopher Lee instantly accepted the part of Saruman because he reread them every year – and was the only cast member to have met Tolkien in real life.* Ian McKellen based his performance on the author, from his avuncular pipe-smoking to his mischievousness (apparently Tolkien would tease unwary shopkeepers by handing them, among a handful of coins, his false

* Over twenty years after the first film came out, the actors who'd played the four Hobbits made everyone's day on Twitter when they were spotted adorably having dinner together in a restaurant.

teeth).* The best film fact I discovered is that I share my fear of flying with my favourite Sheffield beefcake Sean Bean, who refused to be taken by helicopter to remote mountain filming locations and hiked up instead. (I also enjoyed learning that his much-memed 'One does not simply walk into Mordor' speech was only dreamed up the night before, so when he looks down in a tortured way, he's actually reading the script on his knee.)†

This version gets so much right: the look of Middle-earth, the vivification of Gollum by Andy Serkis via cutting-edge technology, the wise decision to bring Arwen and Aragorn's love story in from the appendices, the care and craft of the entire enterprise. I can overlook the CGI pewter sheen, and Legolas the teen-pleasing Elf surfing down the steps of Helm's Deep. I will even forgive it for axing the woodland spirit Tom Bombadil, who has been left out of pretty much every adaptation. RIPTB.

I'm not sure if I can forgive the excision of the Scouring of the Shire, though. This key event, which Tolkien planned right from the start, forms the penultimate chapter of *The Return of the King*. In it, Saruman has not been killed at Isengard, but released, and finds his way to the Hobbits' homeland, which he trashes purely out of spite. The valiant four return to find trees cut down, their neighbours enslaved, the land and streams

* However, he did not like giving lectures at Oxford, mumbling with his back to the students because he wanted to go off and write his book instead – one determined attendee who kept returning was the children's fantasy author Diana Wynne Jones.

† In further Bean/Boromir joy, the film *The Martian*, in which he stars, features a secret meeting codenamed 'Elrond'. Most pleasingly, Mars is also described as 'a barren wasteland' in the film.

polluted. As they vanquish Saruman and rebuild, Tolkien makes his Hobbits work for their happy ending. If we lose this, it feels, as many reviewers of the final film noted, as though nothing was ever really at stake:

> 'This is worse than Mordor!' said Sam. 'Much worse in a way. It comes home to you, as they say; because it is home, and you remember it before it was all ruined.'

The pleasure of *The Lord of the Rings* is the small things, such as a good meal – it's more swords and scones than swords and sandals – and what happens when those modest joys are threatened, as much as large-scale macho battles. In many ways Tolkien's story is about those who cannot cope with the masculine ideals of power.*

Instead, it is a book that honours suffering, grief and loss, and acknowledges that some wounds don't heal. I don't think it is an accident that my granny, who lost her husband in the Second World War and her only child (my father) when he was thirty-three, had such a deep love of Tolkien. I now have her carefully inked map of Middle-earth on my wall, and I think of the quiet way in which she dealt with her lot in life, and passed on her love of books, music and art to my sister and me, showing that through wonder we do not retreat from reality, we rediscover it.

The real heroes of Tolkien's world are the little people who keep buggering on with the daily business of living, sometimes

* Let us not forget that, in a book that features more named horses than named women, a female character still gets to give the killer blow: Eowyn, who rebels against her role in life and rides to battle, destroying the leader of Mordor and saving Middle-earth in the process.

against almost impossible odds, with the hope of returning to hearth and home. As Elrond says of the deeds that move the wheels of the world, 'small hands do them because they must, while the eyes of the great are elsewhere'.

# PART II

## What They Get Right

# 7

# FAITHLESS AND FABULOUS: *CHILDREN OF MEN* AND OTHER FUTURES

'The great mystery of adaptation is that true fidelity can only be achieved through lavish promiscuity'

David Hare

Do you need anything else when you've got Clive Owen in a trench coat? This is a serious question I started asking myself when rewatching *Children of Men*, the unfaithful film adaptation of P. D. James's dystopian novel, in which he stars. Sometimes an actor is so ridiculously beautiful I worry that, for me, the entire cinematic event is reduced to gawping at their impossible physiognomy, 'to the point where the aesthetic pleasures of bone-structure photographed over an hour or so are enough entirely to satisfy you'.'*

It doesn't help that this is Peak Clive, looking like a grubby, unkempt deity, dressed like a noir detective and striding around rangily like he owns the screen (he does).† Perhaps filmgoers are ultimately dirty little perverts, 'furtive, naughty dreamers,

* From Antonia Quirke's fabulous book *Madame Depardieu and the Beautiful Strangers*.

† I used to have a picture of him above my desk at work, until an unworldly editor asked if it was my husband and I felt guilty and took it down.

voyeurs in the dark'* watching unbelievably attractive people kill each other and have sex. Undoubtedly, but I also admire *Children of Men* because I think it's the perfect example of an adaptation that abandons the book to create something entirely new. It is a faithless, impure lover, and in adaptation terms those are often the best kind.

Both the book and the film (which removed the definite article from the title) have the same breathtakingly simple concept: a world without children, as if the Child Catcher in *Chitty Chitty Bang Bang* had taken them all away. The global population has been infertile for years, the planet is dying and Britain is a dictatorship. Theo Faren, our solitary, sardonic anti-hero, is enlisted by a gang of rebels who are hiding a secret: the only known pregnant woman on earth.

This is where the similarities end. P. D. James's 1992 novel *The Children of Men* is a cerebral, autumnal work, spiked with terror and weirdness. In this childless world the playgrounds have been dismantled and women parade lifelike dolls in prams, or get their pets christened. The last surviving generation, the Omegas, are beautiful and cruel, while the elderly die in mass ceremonies called the Quietus, and young foreigners ('Sojourners') are invited to the country to work. Life is nevertheless, in many respects, normal, with hotels, golf courses and trips abroad.†

Alfonso Cuarón's film, however, is a vision of shabby hell, or a Reform Party wet dream depending on your viewpoint. Britain's

* David Thomson, *The Big Screen*. Pauline Kael also alluded to this with her book title *Kiss Kiss Bang Bang*.

† James's detective novels featuring poetry-writing Inspector Dalgliesh, for which she is most famous, share this same mix of elegance and darkness.

borders are closed, immigrants are rounded up and deported, while posters shout JOBS FOR THE BRITS. Terrorist bombs go off with grim regularity on the rubbish-strewn streets of London, and the countryside is polluted. Theo is a hot mess, an alcoholic office drone rather than the book's Oxford don. It's the most depressingly realistic dystopia I've ever seen. If the world dies, this is surely how it will look.

But then, in some senses, *Children of Men* isn't a dystopia at all. This is not just because both the book's setting (2021) and the film's (2027) are now here – always a curious feeling, watching a vision of the future when it's become the past. It's also because crumbling infrastructure and armed guards are already a reality for millions of global citizens – just as Margaret Atwood said everything in *The Handmaid's Tale* had already happened to women somewhere. Cuarón told his set designers to 'make it more Mexican', and he made the mother of the secret baby a young Black 'fugee', showing that ageing societies can only be saved by the people some would like to chuck out. For him, it wasn't a prophecy at all.

When I saw the film at the cinema nearly twenty years ago, I found it exhilarating (I also found some of the acting by the rebel gang a bit 'school play', and still do) but also thought that the contemporary parallels with the War on Terror and the post-9/11 Patriot Act – immigrants being rounded up in cages, dressed in orange jumpsuits – were too on the nose.* Now, as US Immigration and Customs Enforcement agents are assaulting citizens on the streets at the time of writing, I feel like an idiot.

* The film's veteran anti-war activist Jasper is played brilliantly against type by Michael Caine, who said it was the first time he'd ever smoked weed or farted on screen.

The historian Francis Fukuyama claimed this film 'should be on people's minds after Brexit and after the rise of Donald Trump', and now, especially given the rise of the pronatalism movement, it's just too prescient for comfort. There is even a reference to a global pandemic, for heaven's sake. Peter Biskind calls our culture one of 'apocalypse porn', where not only do the extreme, grim scenarios of dystopian film and TV act as a black mirror for our deepest fears, they have also readied us for an age of nihilistic political extremism where man is wolf to man.* Naomi Klein dubs it 'end times fascism'.

It's true that we all read our own age's concerns in art. But by turning up the dial on race and populism, I think Cuarón tapped into something that isn't going away. In the film's finale, a refugee camp in Bexhill becomes a full-on warzone, captured in a visceral single-shot sequence, but a quieter scene stuck with me the most. When Clive Owen's Theo (with his perfect mouth) asks his wealthy cousin, who's hoarding priceless art for a non-existent future, how he copes, he replies, 'I just don't think about it.' Perhaps we have all become immune to suffering and have started to tune out as the world goes mad – it's easy to see why Marxist philosopher Slavoj Žižek called the film 'the best diagnosis of the ideological despair of late capitalism'. It ends not with a bang, but with a shrug.

P. D. James was definitely *not* a Marxist. She was a Conservative peer and a devoted Anglican, and her novel is deeply concerned with religion. God is omnipresent – its title is Biblical, two key characters are believers, and the miracle child

---

* In his book *The Sky is Falling! The Unexpected Politics of Hollywood's Superheroes and Zombies.*

is baptised at the end. The book's Theo is clear on the causes of society's slow death:

> Pornography and sexual violence on film, on television, in books, in life, had increased and became more explicit but less and less in the West we made love and bred children. It seemed at the time a welcome development in a world grossly polluted by over-population. As a historian I see it as the beginning of the end.

Does this mean that somehow Cuarón has betrayed James's bracing small 'c' conservative argument for social decay? Not according to the author, who acknowledged that it had created something new, saying, 'It's obvious that this film departed from the book, but I'm so proud to be associated with it.' Or maybe she just fancied Clive Owen. We are all human, after all.

Cuarón used the novel as a jumping off point, and then left it behind to follow his own interpretation. As the screenwriter William Goldman said of adapting, 'What's the story about? There is no right answer for this question.' The question he preferred to ask himself when adapting was, 'What must we cling to?' The answer: 'My emotional connection with the source material.'

Science fiction and speculative fiction are perfect for playing fast and loose with because they're high concept: the idea is what the adapter clings to. And because this genre is about the anxieties of its age rather than the imagined future, each book is a vessel into which a filmmaker's own preoccupations can be poured.

You can see this in Pierre Boulle's 1963 science-fiction novel *Planet of the Apes*, a meditation on humanity's treatment of other species, which features two fantastic twists at the end. The 1968 film (which added a 'The') is a different beast entirely, making significant story changes, adding a landmark, otherworldly score by Jerry Goldsmith and turning it into a chilling parable about humans nuking the world, culminating in *that* famous ending on the beach, for which a huge seventy-foot scaffold was built to allow the high-angle shot of the ruined Statue of Liberty.* It's a similar story with *Under the Skin*, Michel Faber's perfectly haunting novel of a female alien disguised as a human, who hitches around Scotland picking up men to be harvested for their meat. Director Jonathan Glazer, who would later win an Oscar for his loose adaptation of *The Zone of Interest*, took a whisper of this idea and ran with it, resulting in a deeply mysterious, ambient piece of arthouse guerrilla filmmaking about surveillance, the male gaze and human violence.†

Our species' self-loathing is also at the heart of Philip K. Dick's novel *Do Androids Dream of Electric Sheep?*, which became the most influential cyberpunk neo-noir thriller ever made, *Blade Runner*. Both are about Rick Deckard, a jaded bounty hunter killing off replicant human slave-workers on a poisoned Earth, and both are teeming with neuroses. The fears of the 1968 book (which features a lot of Basil Exposition dialogue such as Deckard's wife helpfully reminding him, 'You're a murderer hired by the cops') are around technology and 'World War Terminus'. By the time Ridley Scott's film is made, in 1982, we're dealing with corporate power, climate degeneration,

* It also spawned two (far less good) franchises, and a very good sketch in *The Simpsons* featuring a musical called *Stop the Planet of the Apes, I Want to Get Off!*

† *Under the Skin* languished in development hell for a decade – at one point it was going to be a big-budget science-fiction extravaganza starring Brad Pitt as a farmer, of all things.

genetic engineering and the rise of the global East. It's all rendered in stunning, smoke- and rain-filled noirish visuals by cinematographer Jordan Cronenweth – although I learned the film's distinctive gloomy look was also created out of necessity, to cover up the fact they were using existing sets because budgets were so tight.*

*Blade Runner*'s synthetic replicants, unlike the book's androids, move us, most famously through the monologue delivered by Rutger Hauer playing the dying Roy Batty (I still can't get over the fact that Dick gave his chief antagonist a name straight out of *Coronation Street*):

> I've seen things you people wouldn't believe. Attack ships on fire off the shoulder of Orion. I watched C-beams glitter in the dark near the Tannhäuser Gate. All those moments will be lost in time, like tears in rain... Time... to die.

Batty's words show us that, replicant or not, his memories are real to him. He has lived a life – and Harrison Ford's Deckard (replicant or not) has less humanity than those he kills.† But, as with *Children of Men*, does it matter when you have another

* Apparently, at first everyone forgot to tell Dick about the script, then he hated it, then he loved it and wrote, 'My life and creative work are justified and completed by *Blade Runner*.' It scared the bejesus out of William Gibson, though, who was halfway through writing *Neuromancer* when he saw the film: there, on screen, was the book in his head – clearly there was something in the ether.

† Hauer said of Ford, 'he thought he was playing the hero, but his character was just a guy who fucks a dishwasher and then falls in love with it.'

trench coat *and* another world-weary face chiselled by the gods?* Not to mention a Vangelis score and a flying car.

The final work of speculative fiction in my little cluster of impious adaptations is Virginia Woolf's *Orlando*. In some senses, it is just as 'high concept' as any of these, with a central conceit that's ripe for reinterpretation (no children being born! Earth taken over by apes! Time traveller changes sex!). Woolf's experimental 1928 novel, charting Orlando's journey from Elizabethan man to twentieth-century woman, was written for her one-time lover Vita Sackville-West to honour a life without boundaries. Jeanette Winterson has called it 'the first English-language trans novel'. By 1992, the time of Sally Potter's lavish, visually sumptuous film adaptation, Britain had recently passed Section 28,† so as a big queer thumb-nose she cast Quentin Crisp as Elizabeth I, Jimmy Somerville as an angel and treated the story 'as something in its own right, as if the book never existed'. She was, she said, cruel to the book in order to be kind to the film.‡

Potter's *Orlando* seems to me the perfect example of André Bazin's comment that 'The more important and decisive the

* 'This is the face of someone that painters would want to paint or poets would wax poetic about. A sculptor would sob openly while carving the scar on his chin. A face for the ages': Carrie Fisher describes Ford in *The Princess Diarist*.

† Part of a government Act forbidding 'the promotion of homosexuality' by public authorities.

‡ She also had an anti-imperialist agenda: 'By the late 1980s, there were already a lot of what I call "bonnet pictures" that were happily reinforcing the myth of heritage with no mention of where all the money came from to pay for the manicured lawns, great costumes and enormous houses – namely colonial rape and pillage. Inspired by Virginia Woolf's use of wit and irony, my film of *Orlando* was going to be a critique of all of the above. But lightly done.'

literary qualities of the work, the more the adaptation disturbs its equilibrium, the more it needs a creative talent to reconstruct it on a new equilibrium.' It's the old 'creation is destruction' mantra.

I suspect this is why the *Hunger Games* films, *The Road* and *High-Rise* (whose opening scene acts as a summa of J. G. Ballard's hooky first line: 'Later, as he sat on his balcony eating the dog, Dr Robert Laing reflected on the unusual events that had taken place within this huge apartment building during the previous three months'), felt slightly bloodless on screen. These gripping dystopian tales, lovingly recreated by brilliant filmmakers with relatively few changes, are all effective and stylish, but the divine spark is missing. As Irvine Welsh said, you want to 'smell the books' in adaptations; they should not be 'a digital photostat'.

Being too reverential towards a literary source can kill a film. As novelist and screenwriter William Boyd has noted, 'If you decide to adapt a classic or much-loved book, your working maxim should be, "How will it work best as a film?" However faithful it is to the original, if it's not interesting onscreen then you've failed.' When I asked screenwriter Rob Williams, who has worked on adaptations of everything from Philip K. Dick's *The Man in the High Castle* to *Killing Eve*, about the process, he agreed, saying that he identifies what drew him to a book in the first place, goes 'under the bonnet' to break it down and see what makes it tick (in the case of Dick it was freedom and fascism), but then gives himself the liberty to veer away completely. As a former illustrator, his mantra is make it visual, and make it your own – in fact, on one occasion he was specifically told not to read the book as the production company thought it would be a hindrance.

Can anything really be faithful anyway, and to what? No work of art is pure. It is fluid and ever evolving, both in how it is interpreted and how it is created. Every writer draws on the stories around them. I'm trying not to use the ugly academic word 'intertextuality' here, which just means that all texts refer to or rework (or rip off) other texts. Perhaps I should just quote *Alien* screenwriter Dan O'Bannon instead, who said, 'I didn't steal from anybody. I stole from *everybody*!'

# 8

# FROM SHORT TO MIGHTY: *DON'T LOOK NOW*

I like words so much I wrote a whole book about them.* I like them almost as much as the screenwriter Robert Pirosh, who wrote a fabulous job application letter to a Hollywood director in 1934 that starts: 'Dear Sir: I like words. I like fat buttery words, such as ooze, turpitude, glutinous, toady. I like solemn, angular, creaky words, such as straitlaced, cantankerous, pecunious, valedictory' and ends: 'I like the word screenwriter better than copywriter, so I decided to quit my job in a New York advertising agency … I still like words. May I have a few with you?'

But even those of us who love words (perhaps especially those of us who do) know that sometimes fewer of them are better. When concentrated into a small space like a poem or a short story, they can become turbocharged: a potent hit, like a shot of extremely strong coffee. And if, as most people seem to agree, a writer paints with words and a filmmaker paints

* *Blurb Your Enthusiasm*, available in paperback, priced £9.99!

with images,* I wonder if this means that the shorter a literary work, the easier it is for it to make the leap to screen; allowing the filmmaker more freedom to fill in the verbal lacuna with their visual imagination.

Short stories or novellas are behind many films now considered classics. *All About Eve*, *Rashomon*, *Apocalypse Now*, *The Queen of Spades*, *Rear Window*, *Night of the Demon* (adapted from M. R. James's 'Casting the Runes') and *The Man Who Would Be King* are all exemplary, as are more contemporary examples such as *Carol*, *Brokeback Mountain*, *The Shawshank Redemption*, *Lady Macbeth*, *Short Cuts* (inspired by the stories of Raymond Carver) and *Secretary*.† (I will also concede that there have been less successful films based on short tales, such as *Yentl*. One cannot help but admire Barbra Streisand's ambition in adapting Isaac Bashevis Singer's short tale about gender and religion into a full-blown auteur musical featuring a naked Mandy Patinkin, but it's a bit too long and there's only one truly excellent song in it.)

I was pleased to discover that the unnerving Ealing wartime film *Went the Day Well?*, in which a sleepy English village must defend itself against Nazi invaders – it features Thora Hird with a machine gun and a postmistress being bayoneted, among other jarring terrors – was based on a fourteen-page story by Graham Greene. The original seemed to me to be far more about class difference and the shame of killing, but the kernel

* 'A good film script should be able to do completely without dialogue,' said David Mamet.

† I enjoy Mary Gaitskill's stories of jaundiced individuals treating each other badly and admit that her criticism of the film *Secretary* for watering down the original is completely correct – but, still, James Spader...

of an idea was there, perfect for reinventing as a piece of civil defence propaganda.

As well as its elasticity, the nature of the short story itself makes it more akin to the experience of cinema: Hitchcock, that inveterate adapter (more on him later), noted that 'A short story is rarely put down in the middle, and in this sense it resembles a film.' Novelist and critic David Lodge described the form as 'end-oriented'. Short stories are an idea sustained and tautened; packed with suspense and mystery, pushing the action forward and often featuring a twist at the close of the tale, whether it is by Pushkin or Roald Dahl with his 'tales of the unexpected'. When I read a short work, I am more alert as a reader (it's the same when reading crime), looking out for clues and red herrings, braced for a burst of horror or a moment of intense emotion or bitter irony that tips me off balance – and, as William Goldman said, a screenplay is a series of surprises that we detonate as we go along.*

Philip Hensher's excellent description of the British short story as 'a ferocious ride with hidden traps and unpredictable bogs, explosions and patches of tranquillity or exhaustion' is also the perfect description of Daphne du Maurier's 1971 story *Don't Look Now*, which became a peerless film directed by Nicolas Roeg. It is fairly long by short-story standards, but still manages to compress an entire world of cosmic cruelty into forty-eight pages. It also contains one of the best opening (and closing) lines in fiction.

> 'Don't look now,' John said to his wife, 'but there are a couple of old girls two tables away who are trying to hypnotise me.'

* As Pedro Almodóvar said of the three Alice Munro stories that inspired his film *Julieta*, they contain 'terrible things within simple things'.

That's how it starts. John and Laura are in Venice, trying to come to terms with the sudden death of their five-year-old daughter Christine. There they meet two elderly twins, one of whom is a blind medium who says she can see Christine, and that she's warning her parents to leave the city. They also say John has second sight. But, due to a succession of fateful twists, John does not leave the city, and is murdered by a dwarf he has mistaken for a lost little girl. This is how he meets his end:

> He saw the vaporetto with Laura and the two sisters steaming down the Grand Canal, not today, not tomorrow, but the day after that, and he knew why they were together and for what sad purpose they had come … 'Oh God,' he thought, 'what a bloody silly way to die…'

Something he had seen earlier turned out to be a vision of his own funeral procession. Nothing is as it seemed, and everything is lost. There's also something very English about both this beginning and ending: social embarrassment and propriety with an undercurrent of strangeness.

Like many other 'female writers with a dark side' I admire – Patricia Highsmith, Muriel Spark, Shirley Jackson – Du Maurier's clean, compulsive writing was allied to a highly gothic imagination. As the novelist Sarah Dunant has said, she was 'the first genuinely brilliant popular psychological thriller writer'. Her novels such as *Rebecca* and *Frenchman's Creek*, both filmed, were huge bestsellers in her day and continue to be so.

But it is in Du Maurier's short stories that her blend of realism and festering horror is at its most potent. As the suitably outré blurb on the original volume containing *Don't Look Now* tells us, 'Here are no cosy tales for reading to a maiden aunt or an elderly cousin'.* In her stories the uncanny bursts through into ordinary, contemporary life in savage, predatory ways. In one a man is sacrificed to the god Dionysus by his wife on holiday; in another a woman wakes up after surgery to discover that everyone around her now has the head of an animal: the nurse a cow, her husband a vulture with a 'blood-soaked beak'.

Du Maurier once said of her husband, 'We are both doubles, so is everyone. Every one of us has his or her dark side.' She had affairs with men and women, and described her lesbian relationships as 'going to Venice'. *Don't Look Now* is a story of doubleness, twins, reflections, visions and a fatal mistaken identity. We are in the everyday world of a marriage, with its bickering and secret jokes, but also in the world of a gothic horror, with its decaying buildings, labyrinths, repressed feelings, darkness and monsters.

The story's Venice is one of twisting alleyways and dead ends, gloom and dread:

> The windows of the houses shuttered, the water dank, the scene appeared altogether different, neglected, poor, and the long narrow boats moored to the slippery steps of cellar entrances looked like coffins.

When John is murdered in a locked room, we not only discover the true identity of the serial killer that has been stalking Venice's streets, but have also been reminded of the utterly arbitrary nature of life and death.

* Originally published as *Not After Midnight: Five Long Stories* in 1971, the title was changed to *Don't Look Now and Other Stories* the year the film came out.

The critic John Mullan said of Du Maurier that 'her fiction makes for terrific films because she had the gift of tapping into our peculiar fears'. Her writing is cinematic too, with atmospheric scene-setting, even a sense of sound ('the quick patter of feet' behind them). There was always a chance *Don't Look Now* could make a good film, but in the hands of director Nicolas Roeg, it becomes a mysterious masterpiece. It's my favourite film.

When I first saw it, many years ago, I found it thrilling, strange and sexy. I still do, but I also find it increasingly sad. John and especially Laura's grief becomes the beating heart of the film, and I watch it, knowing what has happened and will happen, with a lump in my throat. As screenwriter Allan Scott, who adapted the story, said, 'It is entirely about grief.'*

With great technical skill, the film expands on Du Maurier's story and visualises its subconscious world. Two motifs throughout are water and the colour red. Little Christine, the couple's daughter, dies not from meningitis as in the original, but drowns in a pond while wearing a red coat – the same later worn by the diminutive murderer – in an astonishing opening sequence that cuts rapidly between scenes (a hundred shots in just seven minutes) to create a montage of foreboding.

This technique also features in the film's 'Notorious Sex Scene'™, where John and Laura making love (a vigorous, hairy *Joy of Sex* intertwining set to some nifty jazz flute) is interspersed with glimpses of them getting dressed afterwards before they go to dinner; John zipping up his flies and having a nip of whisky.

* An eight-year-old Scott was sent back to boarding school two days after his father had died and acknowledged that grief was an unconscious theme throughout his work.

The scene has been praised for showing a married couple having great sex, possibly for the first time since their loss.* I find it unbearable because they don't know this is going to be the last time too.

I realise this makes the film sound very dour, but it isn't at all, partly due to the warmth of its leads: a vulnerable, lovable Julie Christie, and Donald Sutherland, wolfish in a bubble perm wig. It is many-layered, as the film critic Peter Bradshaw calls it, 'a dense palimpsest of ideas and feelings ... the superimposition of the erotic and uncanny, the poignant and tragic'.

The film also suggests that John's death is not only foretold, but preordained. As Laura says, in a line I only noticed recently, 'You let her go near that pond ... You said you'd give your life in exchange for hers.' He hurtles towards his doom like part of some grim bargain, and his murderer smiles at him and shakes her head, as if to say, no, you fool, of course it was leading to this moment. Death laughs at us all. As John's life ebbs away, scenes from past, present and future collapse into each other in a cascade of images. *Don't Look Now* makes it impossible for us to look away.

Daphne du Maurier's reaction to the film was wholly positive; it was her favourite of the many adaptations of her works over the years. In a letter to the director, she tells a tantalising story of her work's genesis:

> Dear Mr Roeg, I saw your film of my story and your John and Laura reminded me so much of a young couple I saw in

* There were also lots of silly rumours at the time that the actors were 'actually doing it', which were of course not true, and as screenwriter Allan Scott said, 'It's not in Equity's contract!'

> Torcello having lunch together. They looked so handsome and beautiful and yet they seemed to have a terrible problem and I watched them with sadness. The young man tried to cheer his wife up but to no avail and it struck me perhaps that their child had died

Perhaps the film, by visualising the emotional core of the writing, made it even sharper, and more painful. And that is what a truly great adaptation can do.

It would be remiss of me not to mention Alfred Hitchcock here, the other great interpreter of Du Maurier's works – unsuccessfully, to his frustration, in the case of *Jamaica Inn*, and highly successfully in the case of *Rebecca* and later *The Birds*. By the time of the latter, 1963, he was free and easy with his source material, saying, 'What I do is to read a story only once, and if I like the basic idea, I just forget all about the book and start to create cinema.'

The original short story, set in Cornwall as Britain comes under attack from flocks of sinister birds, has an apocalyptic feel. Hitchcock changed the location to a sun-bleached California, and made the story one of mother–son obsession as well as fear. The written work was a creative prompt, and nothing more, offering the opportunity to channel something dark – to spray his fetishes around and torture another blonde leading lady, in this case Tippi Hedren, with whom he was infatuated.* As critic David Thomson implies, this might not have been entirely under his control.

* It also provided the world with the much-copied motif of sinister birds on telegraph wires. My favourite is the spoof sketch from the comedy show *Big Train*, 'Alfred Hitchcock's *The Working Class* (1963)', where a Hedren lookalike is terrorised by men in flat caps.

> By 1964 Hitchcock had revealed so much about himself ... the inability to shake off some motifs: suspense, voyeurism, guilt, fear ... I suggest that Hitchcock himself became distressed by them. He did not float in air alongside his films. They were business entertainments, but his mind emerged from them.

Stories are slippery things. We steal them, but we add something of ourselves to them too. As Roeg put it, 'The ideas are all around us; life, stories, plots are all here. The beginning is birth, the ending is death and all the rest is just anecdote.'

# Coda

## BIG BECOMES BIGGER WITH THE 1980s MINISERIES

This feels like the right place to pay homage to the opposite of small becomes great and visit a time of big stories, big budgets, big casts, big hair and, above all, big emotions. Welcome to the world of the 1980s miniseries, a unique and, I feel, undervalued cultural moment that urgently needs honouring. Bliss it was in that decade to be alive!

These series were also based on big books (in every sense) such as *Shogun* and *Scruples*; the kind for which phrases like 'an epic saga of passion, revenge, power, money and forbidden desire spanning two continents and three generations' and 'from the boardroom to the bedroom' were invented. None of them are under 500 pages. Their sales figures are whopping. And the viewing figures for their TV incarnations were even bigger: hundreds of millions, rather than the tens of millions who tuned into *Game of Thrones*.

It was true event television, before the all-powerful US networks got killed off by cable, then streaming, and we ended up with too much choice. When the original twelve-hour NBC *Shogun* was broadcast in the US in 1980, cinemas and restaurants reported a downturn because *everyone* was watching it. Based on James Clavell's 1,000-page novel about an English sailor stranded in seventeenth-century Japan (whose original blurb describes it as 'a glorious saga of the Orient'), *Shogun* also featured two essentials of the genre: a high-profile acting legend – in this case narrator Orson Welles – and he of the unfeasible bone structure, Richard Chamberlain, King of the Miniseries.

Chamberlain's reign was at its height with his steamy turn as Father Ralph de Bricassart, tortured by illicit love for Meggie Cleary on an Australian sheep farm, in the classic cassock-ripper *The Thorn Birds*, shown in the US in 1983 and the UK in 1984 (we always got these things a bit later). Their red-hot affair was such a sensation it allegedly caused the second largest electricity surge in British history, as everyone made a cup of tea afterwards.* The cast also boasted greats such as Jean Simmons, Christopher Plummer and Barbara Stanwyck, in full ball-breaking mode as the matriarch with unholy thoughts (sample dialogue: Chamberlain: 'I am, after all, a priest.' Stanwyck, her eyes flashing with lust: 'You are a *man*, Ralph de Bricassart!').

I adored it, despite my teenage embarrassment at having to watch sex scenes *in the same room as my parents*, but critics did not. Nancy Banks-Smith described it as 'Dallas with kangaroos', while Colleen McCullough, the droll, chain-smoking author of the 1977 novel, said it was 'Instant vomit! Rachel Ward couldn't act her way out of a paper bag and Chamberlain wandered about all wet and wide-eyed ... everyone sounded American except Bryan Brown, whose Oz accent stuck out like a dingo's bits'. (To set things right, McCullough wrote a musical adaptation of

* The 1990 England–West Germany World Cup semi-final was first.

her novel, which premiered in 2009 in Wales but unfortunately was deemed 'a tragic disaster in Swansea' by *Broadway World*.)

Wandering accents aside, *The Thorn Birds* did have wonderful, sweeping theme music (in this case by Henry Mancini), another miniseries must – no moment of heightened emotion was permitted without a full orchestra in the background. My favourite was the swoony piano score for *The Winds of War*, the (rather brilliant, actually) fourteen-part 1983 miniseries based on Herman Wouk's dreadnought of a novel. It also featured the regulation ageing Hollywood star who was too old for the role – in this case Robert Mitchum playing American naval attaché Victor 'Pug' Henry, described as moving 'like an imposing battleship' by the *New York Times*, and as 'the acting suit', rather unfairly, by others.*

This brings us to the grandest acting dame of them all, Angela Lansbury, in the greatest miniseries of all, 1984's scandalicious 'Which one of you bitches is my mother?' saga *Lace*, based on Shirley Conran's landmark novel of female friendship and unbridled ambition. Lansbury plays Aunt Hortense Boutin, who says things like 'Ah rememberrr Piaff' in an outrageuse French accent. As well as ticking off the essential miniseries components of Hollywood elders (Herbert Lom!), souped-up music and high-stakes storytelling, *Lace* takes us headlong into the full-on glossy glamour of the bonkbuster era. Here, killer one-liners are accompanied by killer heels, satin sheets, champagne on ice, bitch fights and theatrical overacting, as well as ladies in pillbox hats with little lacy veils, who remove enormous clip-on earrings when they answer the telephone.

* Possibly by Terry Wogan. True, Mitchum does have a way of strolling through scenes, but he's just so damn cool he doesn't have to make the effort.

These were stories of making it big in a man's world – see also *Scruples*, *Hollywood Wives*, *Mistral's Daughter* and *A Woman of Substance*, the 1984 British-American series based on Barbara Taylor Bradford's stonking (800-plus pages, naturally) rags-to-riches tale of a wronged housemaid who becomes a business tycoon. Its veteran star is Deborah Kerr in this case, and it is still, over forty years later, Channel 4's most watched drama of *all time*. News of a planned reboot has caused squeals of excitement – as have the most recent remakes of *Shogun* and, of course, Jilly Cooper's unrivalled *Rivals*. I wonder if, in a post-*Sopranos* age where we're all 'oversubscribed and underwhelmed'* and every bloody never-ending series has a dark anti-hero, some might be longing for the days of broad brushstrokes and clearly defined moral universes once more. Or maybe they just want to have some fun?

* From Peter Biskind's *Pandora's Box: The Greed, Lust and Lies that Broke Television*.

# 9

# THE BOOK WAS NOT BETTER: *THE GODFATHER, JAWS, THE EXORCIST*

We have reached the point in my book where I admit that its title probably breaks the Trade Descriptions Act. M'Lud, I confess: the book is not always better. I don't think this is because, as Anthony Burgess said, 'the brilliant adaptations are nearly always of fiction of the second or third class'. Poppycock. I wonder if it's because sometimes only film, with its unique ability to mimic real life – but make it bigger, better, more intense, more interesting – is the only medium that can scratch the itch for an instant visceral hit of emotion, a dose of Reality+.

*The Graduate*, *Vertigo*, *Psycho*, *The Silence of the Lambs*, *The Wicker Man*, *Kind Hearts and Coronets*, *Whistle Down the Wind*, *Deliverance*, *The Martian*, Ken Russell's *The Devils*, *The Bourne Identity*, *Master and Commander*, that arthouse-film-disguised-as-a-swashbuckler and, yes, *The Devil Wears Prada* (because Meryl plays it straight): these are just some of the films I like best, which are based on books I like less. None of them are terrible books – actually, *Ritual*, upon which *The Wicker Man* is based, is pretty bad – and some are truly great books. I just happen to treasure the films more.

My most treasured triumvirate of 'masterpieces that transcend their written sources' comprises *The Godfather*, *The Exorcist* and *Jaws*. All three turned insanely popular but highly flawed books into insanely popular and flawless films. All were part of the 'New Hollywood' wave of the 1970s, a time when the US, disillusioned and scarred by Watergate and Vietnam, rejected the dream factory for something edgier and more naturalistic; an era of method actors and rebel auteurs – for that read macho arseholes – as documented in Peter Biskind's *Easy Riders, Raging Bulls*.* And all involved shoots so hilariously hellish they have passed into cinematic folklore.

Each of their directors took a blockbuster book, and through it was able to retune the tone of a 'low' cinematic genre – the mob movie, the horror flick, the creature feature – to a level of genius. The result is films that are now so famous, perhaps even ubiquitous, that people can quote lines and hum the music even if they've never seen them. They've also been written about a *lot* already. But not so much the books that inspired them, each of which, as we'll see, is the perfect product of its time, and provides its own particular flavour of pulpy pleasure.

### *The Godfather*, 1972

'Ooh, are you guys watching *The God Father*?'
'*The Godfather*.'
'I've never seen it!'

* This book is acknowledged as a gossipy triumph, and it is, but I also found it slightly stinky with the misogyny of the age. Dennis Hopper beat up his wife, we're told, but she 'was by no stretch of the imagination a supportive person. She had a sharp tongue'.

> 'Oh my god, you've never seen *The Godfather*? This movie is a rich blend of Coppola's aesthetic genius and the triumph of Robert Evans and the architecture of the '70s studio system.'
> 'Can you start the movie over and just talk through the whole thing?'
>
> FROM THE FILM *BARBIE*

This scene in Greta Gerwig's film, where the Barbies trick the Kens into mansplaining to them as part of a covert operation to get Barbieland back, sums up why I didn't watch (or read) *The Godfather* until I was in my fifties. My main fears were (a) the film would be very brown, like the decade from whence it came; (b) it is revered by the sort of people who call themselves 'film buffs', like Comic Book Guy in *The Simpsons*, as above; and (c) it would take itself extremely seriously, in the manner of many lauded 1970s films, such as *The Conversation* and *All the President's Men*, which involve men talking and women being ignored.

All these things are true, but I discovered that I didn't care, because *The Godfather* was so deliciously entertaining. As my husband said before I girded my loins and went in – don't worry, it's basically like a soap opera or a miniseries. Thank goodness I married such a perceptive man. The story, of crime boss Vito Corleone, his four children and the struggles of his youngest son Michael to become *capo di tutti*, is a gripping melodrama of intrigue, revenge, power battles and family rivalries. It's *Dallas* with hit men and cannoli. It's *The Real Housewives of Long Beach*, beautifully shot and acted. It's magnificent.*

* A lot of people get high-minded about the film. Pauline Kael compared

The book, I discovered, is just a far more macho version of the sex and shopping sagas I devoured in my teenage years, such as Jackie Collins's *Lucky*. You'd call it sex and shooting, I suppose. In fact, there was so much sex in it I feared I might be pregnant by the end. Sonny Corleone, one of the key characters, is introduced by way of his penis size:

> He was built as powerfully as a bull, and it was common knowledge that he was so generously endowed by nature that his martyred wife feared the marriage bed as unbelievers once feared the rack ... even the most hardened and fearless *putain*, after an awed inspection of his massive organ, demanded a double price.*

The novel's dirty bits are outrageous and sometimes pretty tasteless, as was often the way with bonkbusters, and we shall draw a polite veil over Lucy Mancini and her massive fanny, a bizarre storyline that, thankfully, was excised for the film.

In all fairness, the novelist Mario Puzo said he was writing 'a bit of a potboiler'. He was in debt, he needed a bestseller, and everyone loves gangsters. According to the hot-shot producer Robert Evans's batshit memoir *The Kid Stays in the Picture* (which contains brilliant insults such as 'Eat *those* bananas, motherfuckers' and 'Fuck him and the horse he rode in on', as well as a story

---

it to Dickens, Coppola said he wanted to make *King Lear*, and David Mamet says in his wonderfully sour *Bambi vs Godzilla*, 'it is our American House of Atreus'. But these were all hugely populist art forms too.

* Luckily Sonny's manhood didn't make it into the film, although there's an amusing visual gag at the wedding where we see his wife making an 'it was this big' sign with her hands at the dinner table.

about meeting Nabokov while on amphetamines), Puzo came to him with some pages in an envelope, 'a twelve-inch cigar and a stomach to match', and said he was going to write a novel called *Mafia*. Evans immediately optioned it for $12,000 – 'I looked at it as a gift, a chit. One gambler helping another out of a heavy muscle jam' – and the rest is history.*

So Puzo was writing not just to make money – 'Fuck art, Mario. Start typing,' says his wife in the TV series about making the film, *The Offer* – but explicitly writing *for cinema*.

It is often said that certain kinds of writing are 'cinematic', but here you can actually see the writer conjuring up scenes precisely because he knows they'll work on screen: the wedding opener, with its contrast between outdoor revelry and the Don's inner chambers; the restaurant revenge shooting; and, *naturalmente*, the horse's head in the bed. There's even a Hollywood storyline: washed-up singer Johnny Fontane, denied a part by a vindictive producer, goes to the Don for help, who makes the producer 'an offer he can't refuse' (said head). The line 'Just a month ago he bought the movie rights to the biggest novel of the year. A bestseller' is an irresistible blurring of art and life.

Puzo's novel was indeed a bestselling sensation. It was therefore a 'pre-sold property' (I love this brutal Hollywood description of a book), a project with such recognition that it's guaranteed to be a hit. But nobody would film it because apparently gangsters were passé. Fortunately, Francis Ford Coppola was in even worse debt than Puzo, owing 'more money around town than Nathan Detroit in *Guys and Dolls*' (Robert Evans again).

* Puzo denied the meeting ever took place, and many other players at the time throw doubt on the veracity of Evans's memories. But they are entertaining all the same.

He worried that the book was 'a hunk of trash', but agreed to take the helm, provided he got to film it as a family chronicle, and a metaphor for American capitalism: as Michael assimilates the firm into US society, he becomes ever more corrupted.*

As soon as he'd got the job, Coppola set sail on a boat, and turned the ship's bar into his office, where he literally tore the novel up and plastered sections of it over the windows. But he never lost his respect for the book – he made a point of calling the film 'Mario Puzo's *The Godfather*', as he later did with his hamathon *Bram Stoker's Dracula*.

*The Godfather* shoot is famous for everything that could go wrong going wrong, everyone falling out, Coppola thinking he was going to get fired every day, and the Italian-American Civil Rights League getting involved and insisting the word 'mafia', which appears in the book, was 'disappeared' from the movie.†

Somehow, though, Coppola fulfilled his destiny: the film was a critical and commercial smash, winning Oscars and breaking records. He even got a Mercedes out of it, as part of a bet. He called it 'an educational film', and here's what it taught me: that there is something very pure about simple, unflashy directing, setting up a beautifully lit, painterly tableau and then shooting it with subtle intelligence.‡ That the language of gangsters – what

* According to Clive James's excellent book *Fame in the 20th Century*, 'Brando as the all-seeing, all-wise head mobster was a fantasy that the worldwide audience wished was real: an American president who knew what was going on and did not screw up.'

† The casting was tortuous too. Nobody except Coppola wanted Pacino for the lead; Evans called him 'that little dwarf'.

‡ *The Godfather*'s cinematographer Gordon Willis famously became known as the 'Prince of Darkness' for his love of chiaroscuro.

a 'button man' is, and a *consigliere*, and *omertà*, the criminals' law of silence – is fun. That everyone falls for the reserved, honourable Don, dispensing benediction to those who genuflect. That, as I'd anticipated, the women mostly get doors or fists slammed in their faces. I also learned from *The Godfather II* that, despite his velvety eyes and sad face straight out of a Byzantine mosaic, Al Pacino perhaps isn't as good an actor as Robert De Niro. (Sorry.)

Most of all, however, I learned that you should face your cinematic fears, and that some films really are classics for a reason.

### *The Exorcist,* 1973

'He set off a gun right next to my head. I said, "You nearly killed me!" He said, "It's okay, we've got Jack Nicholson waiting in the wings."'

ACTOR JASON MILLER ON WORKING WITH *EXORCIST* DIRECTOR WILLIAM FRIEDKIN

Now we take up our crucifix and vial of blessed water to face the demon Pazuzu, and the unholiest – and best – book in this sacred trinity: *The Exorcist*.

William Peter Blatty's novel of demonic possession was published in 1971, a time when Satan was definitely 'a thing'. As the dream of peace and love died at the end of the 1960s – 'They're selling hippie wigs in Woolworths, man,' says Danny the dealer in *Withnail and I* – the counterculture's fascination with spirituality turned away from *Steppenwolf* and Ravi Shankar towards more sinister gurus. A love affair with dark magic had begun.* The sinister occult leader Aleister Crowley (dubbed 'the wickedest man in the world') was the new obsession of rock bands like Black Sabbath, and writers such as Dennis Wheatley – author of, most famously, the books-that-became-films *The Devil Rides Out* and *To the Devil a Daughter* – became fashionable once more.

Where the counterculture goes, the mainstream publisher follows, and as Matthew Sweet notes, 'the railway bookstands of Britain were black with paperbacks', with imprints like Pan and Arrow feeding the appetites of the 'blood-randy middle classes'.† My aunty's bookshelves were a tantalising satanic buffet featuring titles such as *The Devil and All His Works* and *Man, Myth and Magic*, and when my sister and I snuck a look inside, there were black sabbaths, pentacles, robes, goblets, goat skulls and naked bottoms. Ouija boards were the hot topic of the playground; maybe they still are. I remember once being solemnly told that you should never, ever put one of Crowley's books by your bedside, because the evil within would cast a hex upon you.

In America, the dawning of this new dark age was presaged by the slaughter in Vietnam, the assassination of Martin Luther King and the ritualistic horror of the Manson murders. In short, the world was more than prepared for the devil. He'd already made an appearance in *Rosemary's Baby* and my favourite satanic-body-soul-transfer-tale, *The Mephisto Waltz* (both books and then films), but *The Exorcist* was something new. No longer was Evil, or Evillll, confined to the doings of cosmopolitan

* This is alluded to in Blatty's novel, with a subplot involving satanic gangs: 'They've got an awful lot of hippie joints down around M Street and Wisconsin. Pot-heads. Occultists. The police call them "hellhounds".'

† From the BBC radio documentary *Black Aquarius*.

degenerates. It had made its way into an ordinary American family home, and the body of a twelve-year-old girl, Regan.

The first thing to say about the novel is that it is a work of absolute moral seriousness. According to Stephen King, 'Within the frame of most horror tales we find a moral code so strong it would make a Puritan smile', and this is no exception. Blatty was a devout Catholic, taught by Jesuit priests, who offered him a path out of the poverty he'd grown up in. He'd wanted to write about an exorcism ever since hearing about a real-life case when he was fourteen. For him, it offered 'tangible evidence of transcendence ... If there were demons, there were angels.' In other words, it proved the existence of God. Initially wanting to produce a non-fiction account, he decided instead to tell the fictional story of Chris MacNeil, an actress living in Georgetown, Washington DC, the horrific possession of her daughter Regan, and Regan's eventual exorcism by priests Father Karras and Father Merrin, both of whom die in the process.

The book's weighty epigraph consists of a quote from the New Testament about the devil, an excerpt from an FBI wiretap recounting a gruesome Cosa Nostra murder, a graphic description of wartime torture in Vietnam and then three words: 'Dachau. Auschwitz. Buchenwald.' We readers are already pilgrims in an unholy land, about to do battle with 'the awesome power of evil in God's world', to quote Blatty's teacher Father Tom Bermingham, one of two real-life priests cast in the eventual movie adaptation.

The second thing to note is that, despite its grave purpose, the book is also – just like *The Godfather* – practically *begging* to be filmed. There's a Hollywood storyline, with Chris shooting a film at the start of the novel, whose director, Burke Dennings, is later murdered by Regan. Hot priest Father Karras, with his 'rock-muscled chest', is compared to Brando by movie-obsessed

Detective Kinderman as he investigates the crime ('I get passes for the best shows … I love to talk film').

The descriptions are overripe, to say the least: 'She watched as a beer truck lumbered by with a clink of quivering warm, wet promises', but the dialogue and the scene-setting are brilliant. In fact, it's remarkable how many scenes are transplanted almost identically to the film, from the prologue in Iraq, complete with mad dogs in the blazing sun, to the movie-poster arrival of exorcist Father Merrin (played by Max von Sydow) at Chris's Georgetown house: 'the tall old man hadn't moved, but was standing under street-light glow, in mist, like a melancholy traveler frozen in time'. To my delight, much of the 'cunting daughter' dialogue was exactly the same, word for word.

The reason for this, I discovered, is that once Blatty's book had become a bestseller and he'd sold the film rights, he wrote a script.* But when director William Friedkin saw Blatty's script, involving several flashbacks (which aren't in the novel) and a host of sub-plots (which are), he threw it out and instead grabbed a copy of the book and started marking up the parts he thought he could film. Blatty's resulting second script won the Oscar for Best Adapted Screenplay.

Like the Antichrist himself, the salacious stories surrounding the film are legion. Friedkin was, in the words of his star and friend Ellen Burstyn, 'a maniac'.† Among many deranged

* Blatty always wanted Friedkin to direct because, having seen *The French Connection*, he knew he would bring a sense of documentary realism to the project.

† My favourite Friedkin story, however, and the only line from *Easy Riders, Raging Bulls* that made me laugh out loud, is this, from before he got the gig: 'He was depressed, afraid he would never work again. He almost took a job as an editor at Random House'!

screaming-diva highlights, he fired guns on set to make his cast jumpy, nearly broke Burstyn's back with a stunt and, surely a mortal sin, slapped a priest round the face to get him into character. I assume they had good lightning conductors on set to avoid them being hit by that heavenly bolt. There was, in true Hollywood style, a curse, with several real-life deaths associated with the production. The one saving grace is that Linda Blair, the remarkably well-adjusted child actor who played Regan, seems to have been shielded from the worst of what she was being asked to do. 'It wasn't real to me,' she later said.

The tales of the film's success are even more juicy, and include nuns sprinkling holy water on people queuing to see it, audiences screaming, vomiting and even having heart attacks, and the TV preacher Billy Graham claiming that evil forces were embedded in the actual celluloid – although, conversely, many Catholics praised it, such as Father Bermingham, who was adamant that 'It has been a force for good.' The book caused no such moral panic, but once its grotesque images had come out of people's heads and on to the screen, they became dangerous.

In *The Fear of God*, the 1998 documentary made by *Exorcist* maven Mark Kermode, you can see the mutual respect and creative tension between writer and director. Blatty (calm in a cream pully) comes across as thoughtful and slightly anxious. Friedkin, in his regulation 'ageing nightmare auteur' outfit of large aviator specs, black polo neck and black leather jacket, is still clearly a demanding so-and-so. Blatty evidently hasn't quite got over what he saw as several key scenes being excised from the final cut, including the coda, where Detective Kinderman and Father Dyer walk off together, linking arms and quoting *Casablanca*'s 'the beginning of a beautiful friendship'. For him, this showed the audience that the devil had lost and 'all is right in God's heaven'.* Without it, audiences weren't sure who had won. But Friedkin is adamant: 'I don't want to direct how people feel.' He gave the story mystery, which is at the heart of faith, and of art.

Rewatching *The Exorcist* now, as I often do, I notice how long the build-up to the horror actually is, and how much I enjoy the outdoor scenes in leafy autumnal Georgetown, a setting described by Friedkin as 'cinematic as hell'. They make the contrast with the stifling inferno of what happens next even greater.

On the day the film was released, Blatty inscribed Friedkin's annotated copy of his novel with the generous words, 'To Billy – the first and only director who ever made a far better film than the book.'

## *Jaws*, 1975

> 'I stayed up at night fantasizing about how I could get myself off this picture short of dying'
>
> Steven Spielberg

Finally, the big fish. There are films that feel like homework, and films that feel like coming home. *Jaws* is, and always will be, my comfort film.

I can't be the only person who, with the masterpieces of

* To Blatty's delight, the missing scenes, including the coda and the notorious 'spider walk', were reinstated, thanks to Kermode, in a 2000 release, *The Exorcist: The Version You've Never Seen*: 'After all this time I finally feel like the movie does what I wanted it to do – and what I always thought the book did too. To excite the audience, but also to inspire in them a sense of the reality of transcendence.'

World Cinema at their fingertips on MUBI, sees a beloved favourite is on ITV3 and knows instantly that, despite the crap adverts, and despite another chance of cinematic betterment slipping away forever, we'll be watching it that evening. Given the choice, I will always want to see Brody battling a shark, or Ripley battling an alien, or lovely Sam Neill in *The Hunt for Red October* saying 'I vud liike to have seen Montaaana' in a Russian accent before executing a perfect 'head-roll-to-the-side death'. I'm baffled by people who don't have these films they turn to repeatedly. How can they be so hardy?*

I realise this doesn't make me very original. *Jaws* obsesses people. One fan described touching the remains of the *Orca* before it was stripped by souvenir-hunters as like holding 'the true cross'; one had Quint's speech (more on that later) read out at her wedding. 'We're gonna need a bigger boat' after the chum shot; the unforgettable, dizzying dolly zoom of Brody on the beach; John Williams's du-duh score: these things are totemic, as is the notion that *Jaws* invented the summer blockbuster – and, according to some misery guts types, cheapened the film industry with an ever-insatiable need for those summer dollars. Peter Biskind is one of these who saw it as the beginning of the end, and he puts the film's staggering success down to the fact that it 'transcended the political and demographic divisions between the *Easy Rider* counterculture audience and Nixon's *Towering Inferno* middle-Americans'. It seems unfair, however, to blame the pioneer for the lesser imitators that followed.

For any lunatics who haven't seen it, Steven Spielberg's 1975

* I'm torn between *Jaws* and *Alien* as my top comfort film, although, as a friend told me, they are both shark films, with the predator at an evolutionary advantage, but *Alien* is a haunted house horror too.

film, based on Peter Benchley's 1974 novel, is the story of a New England seaside resort that becomes terrorised by a great white shark. Police chief Martin Brody, played by Roy Scheider,* orders the beaches to be closed, but the mayor insists they stay open – until more people are attacked, and Brody takes to the sea with ichthyologist Matt Hooper (a wisecracking Richard Dreyfuss) and grizzled shark hunter Quint (a relentless Robert Shaw) to slay the beast.

It's the classic killing the monster story. As the film critic Antonia Quirke notes, it feels discovered rather than created: 'the definitive articulation of a myth'. You can't get much more primal than the fear that we humans, now top evolutionary dog but once the prey of sabre-toothed tigers and such, might get *eaten alive* by a creature that's been around since the dinosaurs.† The original movie trailer says it's 'as if God created the Devil and gave him… Jaws'. It also boasts the terrific tagline 'See it before you go swimming'.

Even before I was allowed to see the film, I remember older relatives talking about jumping out of their seats at 'that scene': a decapitated head popping out of a hole in a boat's hull. When I did see it, it was on a tiny black-and-white TV *on an actual*

* There was pressure on Spielberg to cast 'a name' like Charlton Heston, but he didn't want to, saying, 'I remember going to a party one night, and Roy Scheider came and sat down next to me and said, "You look awfully depressed." I told him, "Oh no, I'm not depressed. I'm just having trouble casting my movie." He asked what the film was … At the end of it, Roy said, "Wow, that's a great story! What about me?"'

† As Will Storr notes, humans' former status as prey animal is 'there in our fear of the dark. It's there in our universal preference to sleep with our beds against a back wall, in a position in which we can see the door … It's there in our automatic fear response: freezing is a classic strategy of prey animals'.

*boat* – admittedly a narrow boat on a canal, but those three feet of muddy water suddenly felt very scary.

I have loved it ever since, just as I do Spielberg, the director who has given me the most joy, especially with his populist favourites *E.T.*, *Poltergeist** and *Jurassic Park*, before he became weighed down by the need to be serious. The actress Margot Kidder described him as 'innocent of spirit', and at his best, Peter Pan Spielberg makes us recapture our sense of childlike wonder by sharing in his. It's why the sentimentality charge so often levelled at him annoys me: sentimentality is narcissistic, whereas he is a crowd pleaser, in the best sense.

But *Jaws* is not just Spielberg's best film, it is *the* best film. It is pure storytelling, flawless and perfectly balanced – between land and sea, calm and terror, man and beast, civilisation and the silence of the deep. It is fleet and fast, a cinematic machine, and just like a shark, it keeps moving, because if it doesn't it will die. I mean this literally too, as the film nearly did die: the shoot, described by Spielberg as 'a living nightmare', ran three times over budget and over schedule, the mechanical shark wouldn't work, the boat sank, the crew all cried in the 'show me the way to go home' scene because they were so desperate to leave, and he genuinely thought it had ended his career.†

By articulating a myth, the film created its own mythos. And like much great art – whether it's Dostoyevsky desperately writing in order to pay off his gambling debts, or Dickens meeting

* Tobe Hooper was the official *Poltergeist* director but Spielberg co-directed on the quiet while making *E.T.*

† My favourite *Jaws* fact is that Spielberg was so traumatised by the shoot he put celery in his pillow every night to calm himself, because the smell reminded him of his childhood.

the constant demands of serialisation – it was the result of a commercial imperative, and of terrible constraints.

It was only when I read the novel *Jaws*, however, that I fully realised what a work of genius the adaptation is – and that perhaps the adage that 'It's easier to make a good film from a bad book than a good film from a great book' is occasionally correct.* The story behind the book behind the film is every author's dream come true. Journalist Peter Benchley, who had been obsessed with sharks since he was a boy, received a modest advance after pitching a novel about a killer great white. Then word got round it was going to be a hit, and a feeding frenzy began. Before the hardback was even published, Benchley had been offered half a million dollars for the paperback rights – the equivalent of over $5 million today.

In the sort of book trivia I enjoy, the title was allegedly agreed on just before it went to print – some real duds had been mooted (*Dark White*, *Leviathan Rising*, *Jaws of Death*) before Benchley and his editor agreed on *Jaws*. In true publishing 'shit we're out of time let's have a stab in the dark' style, everyone thought it was weird but agreed it would at least fit on the jacket. And what a killer cover it was, in the mould of so many 1970s 'nudie lady' designs (*M*A*S*H* was a variation on the theme). It featured said lady swimming at the top of the water while a megalodon-sized phallic shark looms up beneath her, an image that has stayed more or less the same through every new reissue.†

The film rights were also sold before publication, and

---

* This line is from a fantastic play about the making of *Jaws* called *The Shark is Broken*, co-written by and starring Ian Shaw, Robert's son.

† Pleasingly, Basil Fawlty reads the book with the original jacket in an episode of *Fawlty Towers* while Sybil has an 'Oh I *know*' conversation on the phone in bed next to him.

Spielberg was desperate for the gig because, after swiping a proof from a Universal producer's desk, he said he knew exactly how to make the film: 'I know what to cut out. I know what to keep. That sea hunt for that shark is extraordinary!' He eventually got it because another guy in the running kept calling the shark a white whale.

It didn't take long for bad blood to begin between writer and director, though. Spielberg rejected Benchley's drafts for the scripts because he said the characters were so unlikeable they had him rooting for the shark. Benchley later had a cameo as a reporter in the film, but always thought his work had been butchered. Robert Shaw, in turn, called the novel 'a piece of shit', which is a little unfair. The shark writing is effective and atmospheric, as in the novel's nocturnal skinny dip opener:

> The fish sensed a change in the sea's rhythm. It did not see the woman, nor yet did it smell her … The vibrations were stronger now, and the fish recognized prey. The sweeps of its tail quickened, thrusting the giant body forward with a speed that agitated the tiny phosphorescent animals in the water and caused them to glow.

You can see why this scene was kept for the start of the film. It's when the humans get involved that the writing falls short. The novel's Brody is a local, filled with self-loathing, and resentful of the rich 'summer people' who visit Amity. His wife Ellen is unhappy she gave up her life of luxury as one of those summer people to marry a cop, and has a brief fling in a motel with Hooper to make herself feel better. Their marriage is filled with regret:

> Sometimes during the summer, Brody would catch himself gazing with idle lust at one of the young, long-legged girls who pranced around town – their untethered breasts bouncing beneath the thinnest of cotton jerseys. But he never enjoyed the sensation, for it always made him wonder whether Ellen felt the same stirring when she looked at the tanned, slim young men.

This is, incidentally, one of many 'boobing breastily' moments in the book, like so many of its benighted era, with Ellen looking at her reflection thus: 'She stood straight and admired the contours of her breasts', and even the shark's poor first victim reduced to a mammary gland: 'the woman's remaining breast looked as flat as a flower pressed in a memory book'.*

Spielberg knew he had to give us people to root for and, yes, to like. It's the new consensus that anyone who thinks characters must be likeable for us to relate to them is somewhat basic. Of course relatable characters can be unlikeable – Richard E. Grant's lying, cowardly leading man in *Withnail & I* is one of the best examples of this – but they should be interesting. And Benchley's midlife-crisis bores aren't. So Spielberg ditched the grubby affair and scrapped the novel's post-Watergate concerns with money and Mayor Vaughan's corruption.† Brody and his wife are both incomers from New York. Hooper turns from a spoilt rich kid to a loveable, sarky nerd, albeit still a rich one. Crucially, Spielberg splits the story perfectly in two, with the

* For more of this dubious pleasure, just search '#menwritingwomen' on X or anywhere on the internet.

† I adore the fact that Vaughan dresses 'with elegant simplicity, in timeless British jackets' in the book, but in the film he sports a jaunty blazer covered in anchors.

first half on land, and the second half a three-hander on a boat – in the book the sea hunt begins very late, and they go back home for their tea every night. Unthinkable!

Unlike the novel, Spielberg is *funny*. As Antonia Quirke says, 'Spielberg was the only one of the movie brats with a sense of humour, and above all, silent humour.' Two of my favourite scenes in the film mirror each other: Brody, at the end of a terrible day, sits at the dinner table, and his youngest son copies him as he links his hands and, to his delight, pulls a monster face. On the boat, Quint peacocks by crushing his beer can, and Hooper squares up to him by squashing his little plastic coffee cup. Later they compare scars, giggle and sing drunkenly. These scenes feel more real to me than any kind of 'dark complexity' we're often told is realistic. In real life people *are* funny, all the time.

The drunken night also boasts the film's crowning glory: Quint's monologue describing the real-life sinking of the USS *Indianapolis* in the Second World War, where hundreds of survivors waited for days in the water to be rescued, many of them picked off by sharks. It was created for the film, and worked on by two scriptwriters before Robert Shaw rewrote it and then delivered it in an unidentifiable Irish/American/Cornish accent – perhaps we should just call it 'seadog':

> Sometimes the shark would go away. Sometimes he wouldn't go away. Sometimes, the shark he looks right into you. Right into your eyes. You know the thing about a shark, he's got lifeless eyes, black eyes like a doll's eyes. When he comes at ya, doesn't seem to be livin'. Until he bites ya and those black eyes roll over white. And then, ah then you hear that terrible high-pitched screamin' and the ocean turns red.

Phwoar, what a speech. It's *electrifying*, and it's the emotional climax of the film. We realise that if Quint can't kill this memory by killing the shark, then we're on his suicide mission, hurtling towards his final bloody embrace in the creature's maw.*

Against this, you really notice the paucity of the book's dialogue (Quint just calls the shark things like a cocksucker, surely physically impossible). When Shaw and Dreyfuss weren't winding each other up, the cast ended up improvising most of their lines every night at dinner, and last-minute script troubleshooter Carl Gottlieb wrote it down – as Roy Scheider said, 'we became a little repertory company'. Quint's salty speak was based on a local fisherman, and on notorious hellraiser Shaw's own repository of dirty rhymes, such as 'This is the story of Mary McGee, lived to the age of a hundred and three. For fifteen years she kept her virginity, not a bad record for this vicinity', for which Spielberg was desperate to secure the rights, until Shaw told him not to worry; it was from a tombstone in Ireland.

I don't want to sound too down on the book. The film would not exist without Benchley's inspiration and, after shark attacks increased following its monster success, he dedicated his life to the species' conservation. The novel also kept the film alive: according to producer Richard D. Zanuck, 'Had the book not been a huge success, they would have shut down the operation', and the world would have been deprived of a cinematic masterpiece.

* The speech also inspired a whole novel, Robert Lautner's superb work of literary ventriloquism, Quint. His description of the sharks sashaying up from the ocean floor, 'coming up like they were on a spiral staircase. Hundreds of 'em beneath my boots', will stay with me for a long time.

I share Benchley's reservations about the ending of the film, though, where the shark is blown to pieces by Brody shooting a gas tank in its mouth. It's always worried me. Hasn't Brody just created more bait for more sharks to come and eat him and Hooper? Even the final scene of them reaching the beach doesn't quite quell my anxiety. And won't the lack of a shark corpse throw the whole venture into doubt – will Mayor Vaughan, or anyone else, even believe them?

Spielberg insisted, however, because he said the result would be 'pure elation'. It is. And that, after all, is what going to the movies is all about.

# 10

## DREAMS ON SCREEN: *THE COMPANY OF WOLVES* AND OTHER FAIRY TALES

A stepmother decapitates, dismembers and cooks her stepson for dinner. A father is consumed by lust for his own daughter. A girl slices off her own heel to make a shoe fit. Children are left to starve in the woods. A little man is so angry he tears himself in half.

Welcome to fairy land.

'Once upon a time fairy tales weren't meant just for children,' begins the blurb on *Angela Carter's Book of Fairy Tales*. I think most people know by now that fairy stories don't usually contain fairies, and were often pretty dark and violent – in an early version of *Sleeping Beauty* Aurora is raped and bears twins, and in several *Cinderellas* the ugly sisters have their eyes plucked out by birds – more akin to horror stories, before they had (some of) their savage excesses purged for the middle-class nursery, then their monstrous parents and wily girls subdued by Disney. Part of the reason we know all this is because of Angela Carter, through her anthologising, translating and, above all, her wild and kinky retellings of traditional tales.

I once read that there are now more dissertations written about Angela Carter than about the entire eighteenth century, which made me worry that writing about her some more might be 'a lot', as they say in America. But then I remembered how much I adore *The Company of Wolves*, Neil Jordan's 1984 film adaptation of her retelling of *Little Red Riding Hood* in *The Bloody Chamber*, and I decided to venture into the woods anyway.

Let me introduce *The Bloody Chamber* to you by way of the blurb on the back of my old Penguin edition. It says:

> From the lairs of the fantastical and fabular and from the domains of the unconscious…
>
> Lie the brides in the Bloody Chamber – Hunts unwillingly the Queen of the Vampires – Slips Red Riding Hood into the arms of the Wolf – Pimps our Puss-in-Boots for his lustful master …

This eccentric (and eccentrically punctuated) piece of blurbing gets the tone of Carter's filthy fabulism right. The stories in this collection take fairy tales back to their earthy, oral roots, and they are also a Freudian feast of sado-eroticism, tapping into what Carter called the tales' 'latent content', pulling them apart and centring female desire. Here the women turn the tables: a horse-riding mother rescues her daughter from Bluebeard's castle; a girl tames a carnivorous Beast and is transformed into something animal herself ('his tongue ripped off skin after successive skin … and left behind a nascent patina of shining hairs'); when the wolf says all the better to eat you with, 'The girl burst out laughing; she knew she was nobody's meat' – before going to bed with him.* They were published in 1979; as podcaster John Mitchinson noted, they're like a

* And who can blame her? 'His genitals, huge. Ah! huge.'

punk cover album of fairy tales. Even now, Carter's brand of Liebestod has the power to disturb.*

I admit that I don't *love* Carter's novels, which I accept is because of my limitations as a reader who has trouble digesting opulent, lavish writing, rather than her limitations as an author. She was without boundaries. *The Bloody Chamber* not only brought her huge success but constrained what she laughingly referred to as her 'self-indulgent purple prose' within the tight form of the short tale.

Its influence has been immense. As the author Anne Enright noted, 'I look at those Disney films like *Frozen* and I think, who's given Angela Carter's estate ten per cent? She invented the princess who turns things on their head.' From witchlit to romantasy, and from lesser imitations such as the Leonardo DiCaprio-produced *Red Riding Hood* (one of *Time*'s ten worst movies of that year) and 2025's *Snow White* ('exhaustingly awful' Peter Bradshaw), to delightful riffs on the tropes such as *Enchanted* and Stephen Sondheim's *Into the Woods*, her legacy is everywhere.† Even the ending of Robert Eggers's *The Witch*, where said witch laughs as she flies up into the air, liberated by selling her soul to sexy Satan, seems Carteresque.‡

* Many feminists were highly critical of her attitude towards sex and violence, and Carter's 1978 provocation of a book *The Sadeian Woman*, reappraising de Sade as a 'moral pornographer', was damned by Andrea Dworkin.

† Her literary disciples include Salman Rushdie and Jeanette Winterson. I also found Barbara Comyns's 1959 novel *The Vet's Daughter* a spookily similar precursor of Carter's disturbing fabulism.

‡ For your reading pleasure: a terrifying musical instrument called an 'Apprehension Engine' was invented just for *The Witch*. It sounds exactly like a portal to Hell.

Wolves have always meant lust, as Duran Duran acknowledged, and Max Factor divined when it produced a lipstick called 'Riding Hood Red' in 1953, 'a ripe young red … to bring the wolves out'. Carter knew this too, and brought werewolf lore into 'The Company of Wolves', to turn it into a fruity story about the adolescent awakening of a young girl, Rosaleen, with lycanthrope as libido magnet. 'The worst wolves are hairy on the inside', we learn in both book and film. But we also learn there's nothing to be afraid of.

Carter called the film treatment a 'menstrual movie' about crossing the threshold into womanhood, and with the Irish filmmaker Neil Jordan, then relatively unknown before he went on to make hits like *The Crying Game* and *Interview with the Vampire*, she found her perfect adapter. Jordan said he was attracted to the 'devilish intelligence' of her tales, and they wrote the script together, based on her (fabulous) 1980 radio adaptation, meeting every day to compare notes and then going home at the end to dream up even more fantastic scenarios.

'No form of art goes beyond ordinary consciousness as film … deep into the twilight room of the soul,' said Ingmar Bergman, and cinema, according to Fellini, uses the language of dreams – all those montages, slow-mo scenes and rapid cuts from our unconscious night-time brains recreated on screen. Carter described fairy tales as 'dreams dreamed in public', a collective storehouse of our darkest fears and deepest desires. So it's fitting that the entire film of *The Company of Wolves* is told as our heroine Rosaleen's dream.

Everything looks as heightened and strange as a dream too. The sets, based on eighteenth-century landscape paintings, are as lush as Carter's velvety prose (although in reality the budget was ludicrously tight and they only had about a dozen trees, moved around on rotation). There are impressively grisly man-turning-into-wolf animatronics. There is Angela Lansbury as Granny, who warns Rosaleen of the dangers of wolves/men, before her head gets smashed like a china doll. There is Terence Stamp playing the Devil in a white Rolls-Royce (of course).* There are phallic toadstools and phallic trees, and bloody flowers, and eggs which hatch tiny porcelain babies that cry. Fecund doesn't really do it justice. For anyone with even the remotest turn of gothic imagination, it's a joy. In a sense, the style *is* the substance.

I cherish this film because it feels completely and utterly of itself and its own imaginative world, but it is also a 1980s dark fantasy (an outré genre that also includes *Labyrinth*, featuring David Bowie in a fright wig; *Legend*, featuring Tom Cruise and unicorns; *The Dark Crystal*, featuring terrifying puppets; *Ladyhawke*, featuring Rutger Hauer as wolf and Michelle Pfeiffer as hawk; and *The Neverending Story*, featuring nobody famous but a cracking song). It's a classic portmanteau horror film too, where Granny, and then Rosaleen, tell four wolf-related stories within the story itself, all of which have their origins in Carter's book.

Apparently, Jordan wanted to end the film with Rosaleen diving through the floor of her bedroom and back to dreamland, but they couldn't make it work, so in the end the wolves crash through the windows and into the real world of the film – as the toys of Rosaleen's childhood smash to the floor. As the credits roll, a voiceover reads the rhyming moral from Charles

* It was originally going to be Andy Warhol, but he insisted on filming in New York, which would have blown the budget. Imagine *that* parallel universe.

Perrault's 1697 version of the tale, *Le Petit Chaperon Rouge*:

> Little girls, this seems to say, Never stop upon your way,
> Never trust a stranger-friend; No one knows how it will end.
> As you're pretty so be wise; wolves may lurk in every guise.
> Handsome they may be, and kind, Gay and charming – nevermind!
> Now, as then, 'tis simple truth – Sweetest tongue has sharpest tooth!

This pert little sing-song rhyme is a great nod and wink to the literary source.* It also reminds me what a spooky experience fairy tales are, and not just because of their deeply weird nature. According to eminent folklorist Jack Zipes, as soon as humans could use language we started inventing stories of gods, magic, demons, warriors and beasts to explain the world and map our violent reality. We can trace any 'classical' fairy tale back to 'tales of antiquity, perhaps even prehistory, that concern rape, sibling rivalry and mating'. Crikey. Fairy tales, because of their origins in oral storytelling, give us that sense of communing with something extremely ancient: 'Another world, another time, in the age of wonder.'†

* Carter added a more tart, down-to-earth moral at the end of her prose translation of Perrault's original: 'Now, there are real wolves, with hairy pelts and enormous teeth; but also wolves who seem perfectly charming, sweet-natured and obliging, who pursue young girls in the street and pay them the most flattering attentions. Unfortunately, these smooth-tongued, smooth-pelted wolves are the most dangerous beasts of all.'

† From the opening of the sword and sorcery movie *Conan the Barbarian*, which Clive James described as for 'people who read dumb books about old swords'.

I think this is what makes every 'tale as old as time' (our old favourite, Angela Lansbury) cinematic catnip. Icelandic sagas, as seen in the bonkers-brilliant *The Northman*, Arthurian legends (A24's *The Green Knight* is a stunning reimagining), *One Thousand and One Nights*: it seems audiences can't get enough of them – I know I can't. As I write there are two new *Odyssey* films in the ether. Perhaps it's because cinema is the closest thing we've invented to time travel (everyone wants to go to Ancient Greece or Rome, right?), allowing us to visualise what's unreachable. Perhaps it's because our imaginations turn to the mythic in uncertain times – although when haven't humans lived in uncertain times? – with these mysterious, untameable stories acting as a barometer for each generation's political and social concerns. Perhaps it's because 'anon.' is such a powerful word, and their uncertain authorship allows total freedom to those who adapt them.

Because myths and traditional tales can be found in every culture, they seem to tap into some timeless truth; the genetic make-up of all stories. Many male critics or philosophers (such as Jung, Propp and Levi-Strauss) saw folk tales as embodying these universal archetypes, with their tasks, magical allies, quests and disguises. The women seem to say it's a little more complicated. For Carter, similar plots became seeded around the world, from Persia to China to the Caribbean, not because they were universal, but 'because stories are portable, part of the invisible luggage people take with them when they leave home … the perennially refreshed entertainment of the poor'.* For critic Marina Warner, they were rooted in material reality – tales of

* The earliest known version of the Cinderella story featuring a lost slipper is from AD 850–60 in China.

the underdog, of cunning and common sense; lessons in surviving a harsh world where there wouldn't be enough to eat, and where many women died in childbirth to be replaced by a stepmother.

Fairy tales are special because they were mostly the province of women: the 'old wives' tales endlessly spun for millennia until they reached the ears of collectors, most notably Perrault at the end of the seventeenth century and the Grimm brothers in 1812 – Perrault, the crafty old marketer, even used the female guise of Mother Goose for his *contes de fées* to give them that authentic feel of homespun wisdom. They live on through retelling. Carter compared them to soap operas, with their reversals of fortune and glamorous rich folk. Marina Warner compares them to standup comedians, who 'must sense the aspirations and prejudices, the fears and hunger of its audience … its oral origin makes the fairy tale long to please'.*

The fairy tale has staying power because it is impure and unfixed, every teller adding their own touch. One traditional closing formula says, 'This is my story, I've told it, and in your hands I leave it.' It made sense that with the advent of cinema, the stories jumped happily from the voice and the page into the hands of filmmakers.

Cinema plundered fairy tales from its earliest days, with Georges Méliès (of *A Trip to the Moon* fame) adapting Perrault's *Cinderella* in 1899, followed by *Bluebeard* and *Little Red Riding Hood*. Hans Christian Andersen's strange, sad stories – the result

* For psychoanalyst author of *The Uses of Enchantment*, Bruno Bettelheim, they were therapy, fitting a child for the harsh realities of life, with figures such as the evil stepmother acting as a conduit for ambivalent feelings towards a parent.

of his extraordinary imagination and folk tales he remembered from childhood – have inspired everyone from Powell and Pressburger's *The Red Shoes* to Japanese anime. But looming over it all is Walt Disney, he of the world's most famous signature, the entrepreneur who 'makes God seem a little slow and old-fashioned'.* Disney's films drew on established sources from global myths to British novels, but he saw that fairy tales were the most lucrative ur-stories of all. His films are now the way most children consume fairy tales, implanted in young minds like a meme. Even his first feature-length animation, *Snow White* (1937), is still one of the highest-grossing movies ever.

Undoubtedly 'Uncle Walt' sanitised the tales, giving them happy endings, banishing the eroticism and making the princesses drips – although Disney has moved slowly with the times, as in *Beauty and the Beast*, where pumped-up muscle boy Gaston is the villain and Belle tames a partner who respects her mind, and *The Princess and the Frog*, which saw the first Black princess. Many early Disney films are still highly weird today, however – I defy anyone to watch the 1940 *Pinocchio* with a young child and not need a stiff drink afterwards.†

The Disney empire now encompasses Marvel, Star Wars, Pixar, Avatar, Hulu, the Muppets and more, at the time of writing. US cultural imperialism? Probably. But its films have been magical childhood viewing for millions, even if they are the

* David Thomson, *The Big Screen*.

† Disney's other problematic aspects are well documented: he was a virulent anti-trade unionist, who brought in armed guards when his cartoonists tried to start a union, and the company has an uncomfortable history when it comes to racism, from *Dumbo* to an ill-fated antebellum plantation attraction called 'Dixie Landings'.

result of rapacious commercial interests. In its earliest form, cinema showed street scenes, the milieu of ordinary people; 'a genuine folk-art', according to film theorist George Bluestone. Disney embraced, and monetised, folk tales because they are populist. Maybe, as David Mamet cattily said, individually the audience are idiots, collectively they're geniuses. But it shows that you can't keep a good tale down.

And if we are entering, as some fear, a kind of post-literate age, where communication is primarily oral (think MAGA soundbites and TikTok videos), then I would wager that – more than any of the other types of literature I've written about – fairy tales, built to last, retold by the illiterate, captured on the page and then freed by animation, will be just fine. Should I...? Oh, go on. I predict they'll live happily ever after.

# 11

# HAPPY LIKE MURDERERS: THE RIPLEY NOVELS

If there is a greater pleasure to be had than watching John Malkovich play the aesthete and murderer Tom Ripley in the 2002 film *Ripley's Game*, I need a hit now. It is one of the most hypnotic performances I've seen; a series of odd yet hysterically funny *tableaux vivants*. Look! Here is John/Tom embroidering a silk sampler in bed with his beautiful wife. Here he is proudly taking a soufflé from the oven. Here he calls a florist to ensure the Chinese peonies will be delivered for said wife's harpsichord recital, while a car containing his enemies burns in the background.* Sometimes he strikes a pose in a jaunty beret, which Peter Bradshaw described as 'a cross between Frank Spencer and Ben Stiller's creation Derek Zoolander'. And then there's that *voice*: flutey, languid and yet hesitant, as if he's trying on words to see how they fit. The enjoyment is only increased by the actor's own eccentricity. Journalists often describe interviewing Malkovich as 'unnerving' and mention incidents like

* It's an especially amusing scene to those who remember his finickity alter-ego obsessing over mail-order towels in the film *Being John Malkovich*.

the time he stalked his own stalker with a hunting knife. How very Patricia Highsmith.

Like many, I am obsessed with Patricia Highsmith and her creation Tom Ripley, and for me no other actor could play him better than John Malkovich. I also adore *Ripley's Game* because it is the perfect Three-Star Film. The modest pleasures of these films are underestimated. Their scores generally hovering around the sixes on IMDb, they are concerned more with solid storytelling than action, with workmanlike filming rather than flashy direction or stunning cinematography. They are quietly soulful, sometimes slow. Funnily enough, like *Ripley's Game* and another favourite, *Enigma*, they often star Dougray Scott. If I see five stars, it makes me nervous that a film is going to be too long, too bombastic, too hungry for Oscars, too pleased with itself. A Three-Star Film just gets on with the job.

But back to Tom Ripley. If you haven't read them (please read them), he is the hero – or anti-hero if you prefer – of five novels written over the course of Patricia Highsmith's career, sometimes known as the Ripliad. In the first, *The Talented Mr Ripley*, Tom Ripley is sent on a mission by a US shipping tycoon to bring his errant son Dickie Greenleaf back from Italy. Instead, Tom falls in love with Dickie's luxurious lifestyle, murders him, assumes his identity and takes his fortune. Later Ripley novels show Tom married to an heiress in a beautiful French chateau called Belle Ombre, tending his garden, dealing in art forgeries and calmly killing anybody who threatens his secluded life.

Ripley is unmoved by his crimes, and he gets away with it, every time, with the reader's full approval. Identifying with a villain is not new. He's in a tradition of anti-heroes going back to *Paradise Lost*'s Satan (who gets the best lines), and his off-spring are today's superstar serial killers, whether they are the vigilante Dexter, Villanelle in *Killing Eve* or Hannibal Lecter in *The Silence of the Lambs* – or in an even greater masterpiece, the 1980s neon-fest *Manhunter*.* But, and I think this is crucial, Ripley is not really a psychopath. He is an amoral creature, outside of society's rules. He kills not out of any dark impulses, but purely because of necessity. Highsmith makes this seem reasonable. When David Edgar was writing a play about Albert Speer, he said the audience reaction he wanted was not 'yes please' or 'no thanks', but 'you too?' or 'there but for the grace of God'. Highsmith leads us all to wonder what we might do if we knew we'd get away with it.

We all like to think we are different and special, and Ripley appeals to those of us who think we are that way because we sometimes loathe humanity. The ones who, if we brave the cinema with all its noisy eaters, choose a seat to the side – why would we want to sit in the middle with everyone else? Who get that sinking feeling in the park when confronted by those frantic fun seekers, with their frisbees and enthusiasm. The ones who just want to be left alone. The writer and cartoonist Alison Bechdel really warms to this theme, confessing that 'I really feel capable of murder when I'm reading a Ripley book. I feel like I could throttle someone with my bare hands, dig a hole in my backyard and bury them in it. It's a terrifying feeling, but also strangely empowering.'

Highsmith is a writer readers give themselves to. Graham Greene famously called her 'the poet of apprehension'. You could not read her, he said, without constantly checking over

* In *Manhunter*, Brian Cox plays Lecter with chilling blankness. In *The Silence of the Lambs*, Anthony Hopkins camps it up gloriously, inspired, he said, by a combination of Hal in *2001* and Katharine Hepburn.

your shoulder – she wrote a novel called *People Who Knock on the Door*, for heaven's sake. She described her own writing style as plain and uses its unadorned flatness to take us to some very dark, clammy places. Everything is described in the same tone, whether it's drinking a cup of coffee or bludgeoning somebody with an oar. Never has the word 'deadpan' been more apt. The critic Susannah Clapp describes her sentences as stalking us; 'that very even, measured tread, one after the other, is actually like hearing footfalls at night behind you'. The drip-drip repetition of 'Tom said', 'Tom saw', 'Tom thought' means we see everything through his solipsistic eyes. We are voyeurs inside his head.

Many novelists believe that their fictional characters exist independently of them – Tolstoy maintained that Anna Karenina decided she would throw herself under the train – but Highsmith took it to another level. It was Ripley, she said, who wrote the novel; she was merely taking dictation. Sometimes she would sign herself off as 'Tom (Pat)'.

I know the rule that you shouldn't read too much of a writer's real life into their characters, but there's good reason to break it with Pat/Tom. There's the 'little Hell' of her gothic childhood, beginning even before her birth when her mother tried to abort her by drinking turps, later saying to her, 'It's funny you adore the smell of Turpentine.' She once set fire to her own hair at a party because she was bored. She carried her beloved pet snails in her handbag (several of which she also smuggled into France under her breasts to avoid quarantine laws). She was also a sometime stalker, following the woman who inspired the heroine of *The Price of Salt* (later *Carol*) to her home on more than one occasion.

Highsmith saw herself as an outsider. She grew up having to hide her identity as a gay woman, undergoing six months in psychoanalysis in her twenties to 'cure' herself. We all perform a version of ourselves to the world to a certain extent, and Highsmith's writing revels in this, with its shadow-play, stalking and dark reflections.

This psychological ambiguity, along with suspenseful plots and surface sheen, is why her novels have inspired so many film adaptations, 'the most richly weird of all authorial screen legacies'.* They range from Alfred Hitchcock's famous version of her first novel, the perfect-double-murder-story *Strangers on a Train*, to Paddy Considine's fine turn in her mutual stalking novel *The Cry of the Owl*. Adapters project what they like on to her splintered, shifting characters – but none more so than the chameleon-like Ripley, who tries on personalities for size: 'If you wanted to be cheerful, or melancholic ... you simply had to act those things with every gesture.' He is the most frequently mined ore, because, in the words of director Anthony Minghella, he is 'one of the most interesting characters of world literature'.

Ripley has been interpreted by many actors. Highsmith's least favourite was a Stetson-wearing Dennis Hopper in *Ripley's Game*, because she said, with Hyacinth Bucket-like disdain, he made her hero 'a little more common'. Her favourite was the suave British actor Jonathan Kent who, in a truly Ripley-esque turn of events, was hired to follow Highsmith for a 1982 *South Bank Show* documentary. When she spotted her stalker, she slammed him up against the wall, before the director explained everything. 'You're God damn fucking lucky – he's perfect,' she said.

Ripley's first fictional outing, 1955's *The Talented Mr Ripley*, with its shadowy inverted rags-to-riches story, has proved the

* Nigel Andrews, *Financial Times*, 'The Talented Miss Highsmith'.

most irresistible of the Ripliad. Most recently, this was adapted as 2024's *Ripley* on Netflix, which I really wanted to like, but couldn't. Not because Andrew Scott was too old (although he was), but because it was too faithful. Steven Zaillian's adaptation took the deliberate flatness of Highsmith's prose literally, translating it into a kind of deadening torpor on screen, making the darkness manifest. He's really sinister! each frame screamed. Isn't this noirish and uncomfortable!

I much prefer Réne Clément's 1960 *Plein Soleil*, where Ripley is played by Alain Delon's cheekbones. The audience are voyeurs, ogling Ripley and his cheekbones as they forge Dickie's signature, try on his clothes, cash his cheques, sail on his boat, murder him.* Anthony Minghella's liberty-taking 1999 version, which I adore, recreates many of these scenes, and both films are obsessed with Mediterranean sunlight, beautiful places and beautiful people. His Ripley is played by a fresh-faced Matt Damon, whose bland good looks are perfect for our man's 'thoroughly forgettable face'.

Minghella deliberately fast-forwarded the setting of his story by a few years to the time of *La Dolce Vita* and the clothes, settings and ridiculously attractive cast reflect this gorgeous opulence. He introduces music to the story via Dickie's love of jazz (it's painting in the novel), and Ripley's love of opera, captured in a fabulous scene where he weeps at *Eugene Onegin*.† Jude

* He also seduces Dickie's girlfriend Marge and, eventually, the law catches up with him, a change Highsmith despised.

† The 'person cries while watching opera from a box' scene is one of my favourite cinematic tropes, whether it's in *Moonstruck*, *The Untouchables* or *Pretty Woman*'s 'so good I almost peed my pants' Vivian. 'She said she liked it better than *Pirates of Penzance*,' explains Edward to a confused old lady.

Law's Dickie is a golden embodiment of the vast carelessness of wealth, attracting us all into his orbit. In one of the excellent lines from Minghella's script, Marge, his fiancée (played by Gwyneth Paltrow), says, 'It's like the sun shines on you, and it's glorious. And then he forgets you and it's very, very cold.' Marge is far savvier here, the only character to cotton on to Tom, and there's a new character, Meredith Logue, played by Cate Blanchett; another Hitchcock blonde to mirror Marge, and a trigger for some clever plot trickery that (strike me down) actually improves on the book's slower second half.

The best addition by far is an exquisite Philip Seymour Hoffman playing trust fund kid Freddie Miles as a drawling, semi-deranged monster, whose murder we cheer – especially when he insults Ripley's taste in home furnishings as '*so* bourgeois'. The class resentment is deliberately dialled up. Why shouldn't Tom have nice things? we think. Why shouldn't any of us who weren't born into wealth? (As *Lace* author Shirley Conran brilliantly pointed out, 'Don't let anyone tell you that money isn't important. It is if you haven't got any.') When Ripley smashes Dickie's head in after he's told him 'You can be quite *boring*', it's revenge for all awkward nerds and poor relations. Crucially, this film gives Ripley a motive too – Dickie provokes him.

Tom is humanised further when he's allowed a brief moment of love and recognition as a gay man with Peter Smith-Kingsley (a minor character in the novel), before he ruins it all by murdering him too, and is left shattered in a hell of his own making.* Minghella called his film a 'cautionary tale'. He couldn't quite

* Things are never that overt in the Ripley novels, which Olivia Laing called 'the greatest novels about the closet that have ever existed'.

bring himself to follow Highsmith to the end. I wonder, too, does Minghella also turn Ripley into a 'tragic gay' stereotype? And is a clear-cut sexual identity too narrow for him anyway? Maybe he is even more suited to today's age of fluidity and ambiguity.

There's no moralising with our friend Mr Malkovich, who 'gets' Ripley the most, as does the director of *Ripley's Game*, Liliana Cavani – her notorious film *The Night Porter* depicted a sadomasochistic relationship between a concentration camp guard and an inmate; no comfortable certainties there. When Cavani and Malkovich were asked why Ripley fascinates us, their answers were illuminating:

> *Liliana Cavani*: Everyone who is free, by that I mean people who are free to do what they want, are fascinated by Ripley. He too is a free man whose paramount aim in life is to satisfy his own well-being.

> *John Malkovich*: People like him because he does things many of them would love to do. He thinks and acts in a conscious way and always self-servingly. And most people would like to silence their conscience and do the same.

Their Ripley, who cons a dying man into carrying out a hit job for him, has reached his coolly amoral apotheosis in a godless world beyond good and evil. 'I don't worry about being caught,' he says at one point, 'because I don't believe anyone is watching.' His prime motivation is getting back to his dahlias when the messy business of killing is over.

Today, Patricia Highsmith has become hip. Her books never sold as well in the States as in Europe (when an agent told her it was because none of the characters were likeable, she replied,

'Perhaps it is because I don't like anyone'), but now we are ready for her world – partly because she made us ready. 'I think Pat was born a little too early,' said one friend. Morally complex killers who get away with it are everywhere; in fact, to read a psychological thriller where a neighbour or a nanny or a best friend wasn't a murdering sociopath would be most refreshing.

Highsmith, who said she wrote not with a moral purpose but for amusement, is having the last laugh. She adored the bleak writings of Dostoyevsky, Nietzsche, Sartre and Camus, and regarded the criminal as the perfect existentialist hero, 'an average man living more clearly than the world permits him'. Ripley also reminds me of Camus's killer Meursault because he glories in the physical, sensual world; in sunlight, water, surfaces and *things*. Ripley likes the finer things because 'Possessions reminded him that he existed, and made him enjoy his existence. It was as simple as that.' *This* is what makes him a figure for our times. Yes, he is an expression of darker impulses, but also our material desires and our need to be accepted. As Anthony Minghella put it, 'His actions are an extreme response to emotions all of us recognise: the sense that there is a better life being lived by somebody else, somewhere else.'

Just look at the very modern Ripley-like figures of Anna Sorokin, the 'fake heiress' who swindled her way through New York high society, or the strange case of crime writer Dan Mallory, who conned the publishing world with fabulist tales (such as pretending to have brain cancer) and once started a PhD on Highsmith and lied about having completed it – a colleague even said, 'There's this guy in the office who has a *Talented Mr Ripley* thing going on.' *Saltburn* would not exist without Tom Ripley, although to many that would be no bad thing.

Tom Ripley isn't the first impostor in fiction, but none speak to us quite in the way Ripley does today, when we can create a perfect, phoney life every day on screen. 'I always thought it would be better to be a fake somebody than a real nobody,' he says in Minghella's film. His anonymity is his talent, and his curse. He is whoever he wants to be, because the alternative is being inconsequential or, even worse, invisible.

# 12

# STORIES ABOUT STORIES ABOUT STORIES: *AMERICAN FICTION*

Me, I love it when a book lies. As a rule, I don't want to be reminded that the characters and scenarios I'm reading about have been invented by a writer and aren't real. I want to sink into my lovely bath of made-upness without someone pulling the plug out. If verisimilitude is what you're offering, I'm your woman.

Metafiction, i.e. fiction about fiction, not only pulls the plug out, but pokes you constantly like an annoying (admittedly highly intelligent) toddler shouting haha I'm not real! I'm an artificial construct! Look at how I'm drawing attention to my own status as a work of fiction by highlighting the process of writing! Do you get it, do you? Tom Wolfe was not a fan, wailing, 'Another story about a writer writing a story! Another *regressus ad infinitum*! Who doesn't prefer art that at least overtly imitates something other than its own processes?' Sometimes I agree. I find reading metafictions a bit tiring – although in the most capable hands they can also be funny and moving, such as Graeme Macrae Burnet's recent novel *Case Study*, where a writer called 'GMB' follows a trail of documents concerning a monstrous psychiatrist.

Metafiction can wrongfoot publishers too. There was once a move at Penguin to free the classics from scholarly introductions, so somebody decided it would be a good idea to reissue Nabokov's *Pale Fire* without its foreword or footnotes.* The only problem was that they were part of the novel's metafictional joke: the creation of an invented writer called Charles Kinbote, who we soon realise is a lunatic, believing himself to be king of a country called Zembla. The mistake was caught before the book went to press – but not the misspelling 'Nabkov' on the spine. Ouch. (Almost as bad as the misprint I failed to spot in a quote saying the book was 'the biggest favour I've ever done for my brian'.)

By showing us the gap between art and real life that realism seeks to conceal, metafictions flatter readers and make us feel we're in on the joke. For this reason, they offer an intellectual challenge to serious filmmakers. What could be more alluring than adapting a work that is already saying it's unfixed, that plays with narrative and winks to its audience? For all their verbal high jinks, metafictions are practically flaunting themselves for reinterpretation on screen, the little teases.

The cinematic results have been mixed, to say the least. John Fowles's 1969 novel *The French Lieutenant's Woman* combines the pleasures of a juicy Victorian melodrama with modern knowledge of the era's sexuality and pert authorial asides like 'This story I am telling is all imagination … I live in the age of Alain Robbe-Grillet and Roland Barthes'. It has two different endings – one about three-quarters of the way through, where

* Unlike many of Nabokov's other novels, there has never been an adaptation of *Pale Fire*, although in his BFI Film Classics book about *Lolita*, Richard Corliss begins with a 99-line poem called *Pale Film*.

the hero Charles Smithson marries his fiancée and propriety is upheld, and one where he abandons it all for an affair with the titular heroine.

Successive screenwriters had tried to adapt it, unsuccessfully, until Harold Pinter came along, with the idea of turning it into a film about making a film (sort of like *Singin' in the Rain*, but with far fewer laughs).* There's a clapper board at the start, and the action moves between the fictional affair to a real one between the lead actors. It's a great conceit, but the execution is po-faced, and some of the acting surprisingly bad. Jeremy Irons as Charles, who is a bit of a shit in both stories – how could anyone cheat on the fragrant Penelope Wilton? – does the 'lean-and-hungry-sexual obsessive' thing he would later take to insane levels in *Damage*, while Meryl Streep, in her one-and-only dud performance, speaks with a declamatory 'I'm an actorrr daahling' English accent that makes it sound as if she's throwing her voice. The novel works because, in the words of writer Sam Jordison, 'it comes from the heart as much as the head'. The film doesn't quite engage either of these. As film critic Philip French said, it is 'an elegant white elephant'.

If this is one of the worst metafictional adaptations, some of the more successful include Tom Ford's pitiless thriller *Nocturnal Animals*, adapted from Austin Wright's novel of marital revenge *Tony and Susan*, where a woman reads her ex's novel and it becomes a brutal film within the film. There's also Spike Jonze's *Adaptation*, written by Charlie Kaufman about a

* Let us not forget that, despite his genius as a playwright, Pinter is also responsible for some of the most ham-fisted poetry ever committed to paper, as regularly parodied by Craig Brown. Just read 'American Football' and you'll see what I mean.

screenwriter called Charlie Kaufman trying to adapt a (real) 'unfilmable' novel *The Orchid Thief* without resorting to the tropes of the three-act structure, a love story, voiceovers and car chases, while, of course, all these things happen.* And, delightfully, there is *The Princess Bride*, William Goldman's self-aware, tall fairy tale, which purports to be an abridgement of a long, boring book read to the author by his father. He adapted it himself for Rob Reiner's perfect film, using the framing device of a little boy being read to by his grandfather (aka Columbo!).

Another goodie is Michael Winterbottom's *A Cock and Bull Story*, an extremely loose, knowing adaptation of Laurence Sterne's 1759 novel *The Life and Opinions of Tristram Shandy, Gentleman*. With its digressions and bookish fun and games, Sterne's bawdy shaggy dog story is pretty much acknowledged to be, in David Lodge's words, 'the grandaddy of all metafictions'. The blurb I wrote for the Penguin Classics says: 'A joyful celebration of the endless possibilities of the art of fiction, *Tristram Shandy* is also a wry demonstration of its limitations.' Wasn't I pleased with myself? In the film, Stephen Fry sums up the book's point far better: 'That life is chaotic … we can't make it fit any shape. Life is too full, too rich to be captured by art.'

So the book becomes a film about trying to make a film adaptation, and trying to order chaos, along the lines of Godard's dictum that a film should have a beginning, a middle and an end, though not necessarily in that order. I laughed at how everyone

* Susan Orlean, author of *The Orchid Thief*, said, 'It took a while for me to get over the idea that I had been insane to agree to it, but I love the movie now. What I admire the most is that it's very true to the book's themes of life and obsession, and there are also insights into things which are much more subtle in the book about longing, and about disappointment.'

has their favourite bit of the novel they want included, and by the final rushes nobody is happy. It toys with truth and fiction: Steve Coogan and Rob Brydon play exaggerated versions of themselves playing Tristram and Uncle Toby (a forerunner of their successful double act in Michael Winterbottom's later TV series *The Trip*).

Its many joys include an immaculate Roger Moore impression by Brydon, Coogan naked in a giant womb and an ongoing subplot about which one of them gets to wear the highest heels ('I should dominate!'). There are so many good jokes in Frank Cottrell-Boyce's inspired screenplay, including this scene between Manchester music impresario Tony Wilson, playing himself interviewing Coogan:

> *Coogan*: It's a postmodern classic, written before there was any modernism to be post about ... it's way ahead of its time. In fact, it was listed as No.8 in the *Observer*'s Top 100 Books of All Time.
>
> *Wilson*: That was a chronological list.
>
> *Coogan*: Right...

The joke's even better because in Winterbottom's previous film *24 Hour Party People*, about Factory Records, Coogan was cast as Wilson; in the words of New Order's Peter Hook, 'the biggest twat in Manchester being played by the second biggest twat in Manchester'. *A Cock and Bull Story*'s major flaw is that by using comedians in many roles, it just highlights how good the 'proper' actors – notably Keeley Hawes, Roger Allam and Ian Hart – are in comparison. They make me want to believe. That's the problem with 'levels of reality': as Clive James wrote, there's always one that is really real, and sometimes 'the other comes off worse'.

One of the most successful film-within-a-film-of-a-book-within-a-book of recent years is *American Fiction*, writer-director Cord Jefferson's award-garlanded 2023 adaptation of Percival Everett's sly, many-layered novel *Erasure*. It's the story of an upper-middle-class Black writer, Thelonious 'Monk' Ellison, who is constantly told that his work is not 'black enough'. He writes dense, difficult novels that nobody buys. At a party an agent tells him 'that I could sell many books if I'd forget about writing retellings of Euripides and parodies of French post-structuralists and settle down to write the true, gritty real stories of black life. I told him that I was living a black life.' In one telling scene, apparently based on a real-life event, he can't find his novels in a bookshop, until he discovers they've been put in the 'African American Studies' section.

Monk despises bestsellers such as the fictional *We's Lives In Da Ghetto*, which, he feels, pigeonhole and package Black trauma. But his mother is ill and alone following his father's suicide and he needs money for her care. So he writes a pastiche of the genre he reviles: *My Pafology*, under the pseudonym Stagg R. Leigh. And guess what, he's offered a fortune for it. What could possibly go wrong?

*My Pafology* is reproduced in full in the novel, alongside Monk's academic paper on Barthes (complete with footnotes on the hermeneutic code), ideas for stories, historical dialogues and musings on woodwork, all scattered throughout. It's definitely what you would call 'experimental', and, maybe because of this, or because I saw it first, I like the film more – but mostly because it's a beautifully acted family drama in the mould of late 1970s/early 1980s Oscar winners *Ordinary People*, *Kramer vs. Kramer* and *On Golden Pond*, the likes of which we rarely see these days.

The meta-elements are still there, with dramatised scenes from *My Pafology* intruding into the film's real world and a fantastic 'hey it's just a movie' breaking-the-fourth-wall ending to rival that of *Blazing Saddles*, but the real lives are at the heart of it. The performances are stellar – as Jefferson said, 'This is what happens when you offer black actors real roles instead of giving them a couple of lines so the white lead can save the day.' Jeffrey Wright is perfect as the fussy, pretentious Monk. Tracee Ellis Ross is utterly winning as Monk's sister, their playful banter a joy to watch. The standout for me, however, was Sterling K. Brown as his brother Bill, who is given more nuance than the 'newly liberated gay' cliché of the book. A scabrously embarrassing wedding scene becomes an exuberant affair in the film. In fact, all the moments between the Ellison clan members are joyful and tender.

Perhaps it is 'a sweetened version of his polemic', as the *Los Angeles Times* said, but I think it improves on the satire in places. Monk now meets the author of *We's Lives In Da Ghetto*, Sintara Golden, on a literary prize panel, which doesn't happen in the book. *My Pafology*, which nobody knows Monk has written, is up for the award, but although neither of them thinks it's much cop, they're ignored ('I just think we should really be listening to black voices right now,' says a white jury member). Yet Golden also challenges Monk's snobbery, his devaluing of other perspectives and his notion of 'black potential'. As she says, 'Potential is a word people use when they think what they see in front of them is not good enough.'

Hollywood may have congratulated itself for being more 'inclusive' following the #OscarsSoWhite protest, but, oh irony of ironies, the statues went to the white men in 2024, for *Oppenheimer*, which left me a bit cold. *American Fiction* was nominated for five, but only won for Best Adapted Screenplay. Percival Everett was optimistic when praising the film, though, saying that 'in the last four or five years as this generation of young black artists are popping up, the people interested in making and adapting work has changed. It used to be 60-year-old white guys looking to option something. And now it's these young people who are interested in art.'

Kurt Vonnegut, a master of metafictions (*Slaughterhouse Five* includes the line 'I've finished my war book now. The next one I write is going to be fun'), wrote a lot about art's inability to contain the painful messiness of real life: 'Artists use frauds to make human beings seem more wonderful than they really are ... Films and books and plays show us people talking much more entertainingly than people really talk, make paltry human enterprises seem important ... Actually, practically nothing is going on.'

I like the fraud. I prefer to be moved rather than dazzled, or ideally both. I thought *American Fiction* should have won the awards because, like the best metafictional novels, it appealed to both head and heart. And something *was* going on, the thing that goes on for all of us: life, death, old age, family, relationships, in all their chaos.

# 13

## MISERY: WRITERS GO TO HOLLYWOOD

'Having your book turned into a movie is like seeing your oxen turned into bouillon cubes'

John le Carré

One of the perks of working in publishing – it's not the wages – is the opportunity to go to the annual sales conference. In the past these used to be lavish affairs in exotic locations such as Spain and Birmingham, when everyone would hop on a coach for a jolly, in the manner of Boggs' lavatory factory staff on their works outing in *Carry on at Your Convenience*. There was drunkenness, dancing, snogging and once somebody got squashed by a wayward theatre prop. The bacchanals of yore have passed now, but every so often we still get to go and see some of our authors on stage – usually looking slightly terrified (apart from the historian Simon Schama, who I remember bounded in shouting 'Hello, campers!').

A recent highlight was Helen Fielding being extremely funny about her Bridget Jones novels being turned into films. Her greatest fear, she said, was 'Being a nightmare, in enormous sunglasses and a leopard-skin turban saying

"You murdered my baby!"' She aimed instead to be more like a parent to a teenager, where the best thing you could hope for was keeping them off the weed.* Adam Mars-Jones wrote something similar when his confrontational novel *Box Hill* was turned, with 'drastic divergences', into the joyous 'rom dom com' about a BDSM relationship, *Pillion*: 'If you've given up a child for adoption it's bad manners to hang around the school gates – even worse if you sold the child in question.'

It made me wonder, how do writers cope when they make a cinematic pact with the devil? Not all authors are as intensely relaxed about handing over their offspring. Those in the 'you murdered my baby!' camp include P. L. Travers, who famously cried when she saw the premiere of *Mary Poppins*: 'I said, "Oh, God, what have they done?"' James Ellroy hated the adaptation of *LA Confidential* (I can only assume he was immune to Russell Crowe's boviform charms). Stanislaw Lem thought Tarkovsky's *Solaris* had misunderstood his work, as did Bret Easton Ellis, who found the film of *American Psycho* simplistic. As far as I'm concerned, those authors don't know they're born. These films are great!

Far less stressful to be in the pragmatists' camp, just taking the money and running – as Hemingway said, it's like meeting halfway across a bridge: they throw you a bag of cash, you put it in the car, and drive off. Nabokov was even more brutal, saying, 'All I want from the cinema is compensation in hard currency.' These writers seem to know their place in the Hollywood pecking order: as a necessary evil, whose work is vampirised, the body left for dead.

* She also made a great joke about the size of Hugh Grant's part.

I assumed this was more usual in the bad old days of Hollywood, as documented by the high-flying (and mostly high) producer Julia Phillips in her outrageous, offensive memoir *You'll Never Eat Lunch in This Town Again*. It's notable mostly for the number of drugs she ingests ('I had been partaking from a panoply of mood enhancers, stimulants, and depressants all day. Every once in a while, I would strike upon the perfect chemical combination: for Oscar night it's been a diet pill, a small amount of coke, two joints, six halves of Valium, which makes three, and a glass-and-a-half of wine. So far.'). She's also brutally honest about the role of novelists in the industry. Here she writes about a lunchtime discussion of the 1967 film of Charles Webb's *The Graduate*:

> I'm a little confused about why anyone got screenplay credit. It's pretty clear to me they just passed out copies of the book on the set. The decibel level rises as the discussion moves to the subject of just how much Charles Webb was paid. I have heard twenty grand and he's working in a shoe store in the East Village. Everyone else involved with the movie will make millions ... I make a vow in my mind that I will not fuck the writer if I ever get into a position of power. It is my first glimmer of the prevailing showbiz attitude towards writers: at once on a pedestal and under the thumb.

I'm not sure that much has changed, though. In *American Fiction*, a literary agent notes that 'Nobody in Hollywood reads, they get their assistants to read. The whole town runs on book reports.' I once went to a preview of a film of the novel *Perfume* (top celebrity spots included the lovely late Alan Rickman, and Helena Bonham Carter with then-husband Tim Burton, both looking exceedingly confused, as if they'd just been woken up), and overheard the top brass there saying things like 'Have you read the book?' 'Oh no.'

When the sumptuous and soapy *Conclave*, all swishing cassocks and scheming cardinals, won Best Adapted Screenplay at the 2025 BAFTAs, there was a brief flurry of outrage on X because viewers thought that Robert Harris, who wrote the novel and could just about be spied hovering at the back of the stage, wasn't thanked.* It turned out he had been, but it was cut, which seems about right given the status of novelists in the film industry. He wasn't even invited to the Oscars. Harris, however, seems to be admirably level-headed about the page-to-screen process, saying that 'if you sell your house, you can't go back 18 months later and complain if they've put a new kitchen in or knocked through downstairs. If you didn't want that to happen, you shouldn't have sold it.'

Sometimes, however, authors don't just cut and run, but get involved in the screenwriting process too. Graham Greene was one of the most successful novelist contributors to cinema. He loved films, wrote about them as a critic, sometimes sold his books outright, but also wrote over forty screenplays based on his work.† Even that moody miracle *The Third Man*, made on the hoof and out of necessity in the rubble of war, was based on an idea he'd scribbled down twenty years before,

* When I saw Robert Harris at a Penguin sales conference, he announced himself on stage with the words 'God, this is like a Nuremberg rally'.

† One of Greene's less successful film reviews was an article about a Humphrey Bogart movie in which the Bogart character was alleged to say that the graft and crime in the great city where he was a cop was 'feudal', when in fact what Bogart said was 'futile'.

then later scripted, and then published as a novella based on the treatment.

The novelist William Faulkner, who wrote or collaborated on at least fifty screenplays, came to Hollywood in 1932 to make some cash. He said studio work was 'like chopping cotton or picking potato bugs off plants; you know damn well it's not painting the Sistine Chapel or winning the Kentucky Derby. But a man likes the feel of some money in his pocket.' In a brilliantly resigned article called 'The Novelist and Films', Eric Ambler, whose spy thrillers have been adapted many times, claimed to have heard a Hollywood producer say, 'Thank God that's over', when the writer delivered his script. 'Now we can get down to film-making.' He describes what he calls 'the legend':

> The hero's script is mangled beyond recognition in order to provide a part for a nymphomaniac film star. The producer turns out to be a pimping monster. The novel – 'this sensitive study of adolescence' as one critic called it – becomes a roaring musical about campus life in the Middle West. The novelist returns sadder, wiser and sick at heart to the battered old desk in his mother's attic.

But what about writers who appreciate cinema's ability to do what novels can't? Zadie Smith is one of these, saying very open-handedly that 'In a novel, one scrabbles in the dirt for motivation or stretches for decorative language to hide the lack of it. In film, no such disguise will be tolerated by the viewer. It cannot be fudged.' Hilary Mantel similarly praises the sunny clarity of film, noticing how 'in ten seconds, the screen can show nuances of character or plot developments that in a novel, or on stage, would be impossible to depict'. She also said, brilliantly, that an adapter must 'put down the text, and dream it'.

Kazuo Ishiguro is another admirer of film's power. A movie obsessive, he has also dipped his toe into screenwriting, with *Living*, his quietly wrenching adaptation of Akira Kurosawa's 1952 classic *Ikiru*, relocated to London and starring Bill Nighy. When it comes to his own novels being adapted, as they have, magnificently, with *The Remains of the Day* and less successfully perhaps with *Never Let Me Go*, he is adamant that he'll never do it himself and that filmmakers must never approach his books reverentially. He is very honest about the reason, saying:

> It might sound like modesty when I encourage film adaptations to 'move on' the story. But actually it's a form of egomania. I have aspirations for my stories to be like those of, say, Homer. Or to become like certain fairytales and myths, moving through the centuries and varying cultures, adapting and growing to speak to different audiences. My novels are themselves made up of materials I've inherited, imbibed and remoulded. When something goes from book to film it's a campfire opportunity: it's when the story should grow and evolve.

It's the perfect description of adaptation.

Ishiguro credited cinema with being as much of an influence on his writing as literature, and I'm not the first to note that film changed the way writers write. James Joyce – who opened Ireland's first cinema – saw that the medium would transform everything. Montages, flashbacks, dissolves, cuts; they're all there in *Ulysses*. The influence got increasingly overt. It can be seen in Evelyn Waugh's fluid cutting between scenes; in Greene's preference for exciting plots derived from spy thrillers, gangster movies and westerns; in Christopher Isherwood's *Goodbye to Berlin*, where he writes, 'I am a camera, with its shutter open, quite passive, recording, not thinking' (Isherwood also became a screenwriter).

Naturally there were also more mercenary reasons for the change. In 1967, André Bazin wrote a bit snootily that 'a great number of American crime novels are clearly written with a double purpose in view, namely with an eye on a Hollywood adaptation'. There are now few commercial writers who don't have at least one eye on a movie deal – including Michael Crichton, who, as Martin Amis observed, writes prose as directions. Amis describes *The Lost World* as 'a creative-input memo to Steven Spielberg … Reading these passages, why, you can almost hear the cinematographer unscrewing his lens cap'. The novelist Rebecca Makkai recently noted in her article 'You're Writing a Book. So Stop Writing a Movie' how her creative writing students subconsciously imbibe the techniques of film; for example, always describing a character's eyes because they are so used to seeing close-ups, whereas in real life, 'is eye colour honestly the first thing you notice about someone?'

In the twentieth and twenty-first centuries, it's nigh impossible to disentangle novelists from film. Which brings me to Stephen King. He's had more books adapted than any other living author – over three hundred at the last count, if you include remakes. The most recent at the time of writing include a TV series of *The Institute*, of which one critic said 'this is how you butcher a Stephen King novel', and a new, acclaimed dystopian film, *The Long Walk*. He has spawned such a screen mythos that there was a miniseries called *Castle Rock* featuring characters from the 'Stephen King universe'.

I don't think, however, that this is because, Crichton-like, King deliberately writes novels-as-screenplays. I think he's the

Dickens of our age, and not just because of his prolificacy, popularity or gift for gripping the reader, but because the vividness of his novels comes from his own imagination; he can't help but write that way. One filmmaker said, 'Give him an orange and he'll write a novel about it.' Christopher Walken (who starred in an early adaptation of *The Dead Zone*) called him 'the dreamer of America'. It's almost like he can't quite believe what he's come up with. His first novel, *Carrie*, was put in the bin and nearly destroyed until his wife rescued it. *Pet Sematary* lay in a drawer for a year as he was too scared to go near it.* It's a kind of pathological creativity; the pen as divining rod.

When it comes to adaptations of his work, King is in the free-range rather than helicopter-parenting camp, saying, 'I want a dollar, and I want approvals over the screenwriter, the director and the principal cast … I want to be part of the solution, not part of the problem … if they want to make changes, if they want to be a little bit out on the edge, I'm all for it. I like it.'†

Stanley Kubrick's 1980 movie of *The Shining*, King's novel about writer Jack Torrance who goes mad while caretaking the Overlook Hotel and tries to murder his wife and psychic son Danny, is, famously, the exception. King described it as 'a big, beautiful Cadillac with no engine inside it'. His main objections were that (a) Torrance had no character arc because, played by Jack Nicholson, he's clearly nutso to start with, and (b) the rational, calculating Kubrick could not conceive of the

* The *New York Times* review said, 'If Mr. King's aim in writing *Pet Sematary* was not entirely serious … then why, somebody please tell me, was I holding on to his book so hard that my knuckles had begun to turn white?'

† Even he balked at the *sixth* spinoff of the *Children of the Corn* stories, though.

supernatural, so he had to make the character evil instead of the hotel.*

King said that Kubrick 'used to make transatlantic calls to me from England at odd hours of the day and night, and I remember once he rang up at seven in the morning and asked, "Do you believe in God?" I wiped the shaving cream away from my mouth, thought a minute and said, "Yeah I think so." Kubrick replied, "No, I don't think there is a God," and hung up.'

It was the fatal combination of a novelist who writes about, and with, feelings, meeting a director who didn't really seem to have any. Read about Kubrick, who once insisted on eighty-five takes of a scene, and words like 'genius' come up, but so too do words like 'monster' and 'control freak'. Apparently (and, I hope, apocryphally), during the filming of *2001*, stuntman Bill Weston nearly suffocated to death because Kubrick insisted on no air holes in his space helmet – he had to contort his body into the shape of a crucifix so that the filmmaker would notice. During the filming of *The Shining*, Shelley Duvall got so stressed her hair started falling out, although she always took care to be gracious and kind about the director in interviews afterwards.†

I still find Kubrick's *The Shining* terrifying every time: not just because of its operatic visual style and queasy ground-level shots of little Danny riding his tricycle (for which the Steadicam

* King stated, 'I'd like to remake *The Shining* someday, maybe even direct it myself if anybody will give me enough rope to hang myself with.' He got the rope – in fact, the budget was bigger than Kubrick's. I want to be kind, but *Stephen King's The Shining* is not great, even though it does have a hose with teeth and monsters made out of topiary.

† Another of King's objections was that he found the film's portrayal of Jack's wife Wendy misogynistic; I agree.

was perfected), but also because it now seems to me a film about domestic violence and the danger that can come from within the family. It's also the ultimate film about writer's block (other contenders include *Wonder Boys* and *The Wife*). Some of King's best writing is about writing, not just his guide *On Writing*, but in the fictional writers he creates.* His 1987 novel *Misery*, however, takes it to a whole other level. It's like William Strunk's *The Elements of Style* meets *The Texas Chainsaw Massacre*.

Reading *Misery* while you're in the middle of trying to write a book, as I have just done, is an unsettling experience. The story goes like this: novelist Paul Sheldon has killed off the central character of his bestselling historical romances, Misery Chastain, and just completed the edgy, autobiographical novel he really wanted to write. But his car crashes in a snowstorm and he's rescued by his 'number one fan'. She's also insane. She burns Sheldon's manuscript, keeps him prisoner and forces him to write a new *Misery* sequel resurrecting the titular heroine. Now *that's* a deadline.

It all came, in true King style, from an actual dream. His description in *On Writing* is worth reproducing in full:

> My wife and I went to London on a combined business/pleasure trip. I fell asleep on the plane and had a dream about a popular writer (it may or may not have been me, but it sure to God wasn't James Caan) who fell into the clutches of a psychotic fan living on a farm somewhere out in the back of beyond. The fan was a woman isolated by her growing paranoia. She kept some

* Some of his best adaptations feature writers too, such as *Salem's Lot* and *Stand By Me* – I do not include the execrable *The Secret Window*, starring the over-egging, overrated Johnny Depp, in this list.

> livestock in the barn, including her pet pig, Misery. The pig was named after the continuing main character in the writer's best-selling bodice-rippers. My clearest memory of this dream upon waking was something the woman said to the writer, who had a broken leg and was being kept prisoner in the back bedroom. I wrote it on an American Airlines cocktail napkin.

The woman becomes Annie Wilkes, one of his greatest creations, and one of fiction's most disturbing psychopaths; a woman who won't swear – instead she uses a horrible array of folksy insults like 'dirty bird', 'cockadoodie', 'oogie' and 'Mister Man!' – but has no qualms about crippling Paul to stop him running away. An actual psychiatrist analysed the character and diagnosed her with psychopathy, bipolar personality disorder with sadomasochistic tendencies, delusions of grandeur and a false sense of morality, which seems about right.

What's really fascinating, though, is the way Paul's story plays out. At first he forces himself to write under duress; soon, he loves it. Soon, in fact, he's more productive than he's ever been, turning out twelve pages a day. He's writing for his life, but it's also what really makes him feel alive, and he wants to live to see how the story turns out. In a very funny twist, Annie also makes Paul a better writer ('I've got Lizzie Borden for an editor,' he says), throwing out unconvincing plots and making him start again.

Like many of King's books, it's about addiction (he said he was 'sick with drugs and alcohol' when he wrote it). Paul becomes addicted to the painkillers Annie gives him. Annie is an addicted fan, something even more pertinent in the age of Stan culture. And she's addicted to reading one more page to see what happens next, to 'The power of the gotta. I turned out to be a pretty passable Scheherazade after all.'

For Paul, writing is misery, but it's a gotta too, in every sense. I think anyone who's ever written anything, whether it's homework at school or an entire book, feels what Hemingway allegedly said: 'There is nothing to writing. All you do is sit down at a typewriter and bleed.' I didn't notice most of this stuff when I first read the novel; this time around I couldn't see anything else.

The dearly missed Rob Reiner's 1990 film of *Misery* remains my favourite King adaptation, and a lot of that is because of the intense, intelligent performances. Kathy Bates said, 'I became Annie. There was no going back. Rob Reiner told me not to take Annie home with me at night, but that wasn't possible. I was in it', and you can tell. There's an enjoyable irony in the fact that James Caan, who described himself as 'Hollywood's most hyperactive actor', was cast (after William Hurt was deemed too cerebral, Warren Beatty too pretty, although he helped with the script) as a man who is bed-bound. Apparently, it drove him crazy, and you can feel the tension. He also refused to read the original novel, so chapeau to that really.

*Misery* was King's favourite novel at the time of filming, so the rights were still available because he hadn't found the ideal adapter. When he heard Reiner was interested he agreed, on condition that Reiner direct, because he'd loved his warm, funny, empathetic interpretation of *Stand By Me*.* 'Heart' is a word King uses a lot. He described *The Shining* as having 'no heart', whereas he loved *The Shawshank Redemption*, Frank Darabont's now (not at the time) smash adaptation of his short story because 'the story had heart; the movie has more'.

* Reiner's production company Castle Rock was named after King's make-believe town in Maine; even now I get a thrill seeing their lighthouse logo at the start of a 1980s/'90s film.

Rob Reiner watched all of Hitchcock's oeuvre as preparation, and joined up again with famed screenwriter William Goldman after their success on *The Princess Bride* (the best fantasy rom-com ever made) to turn the novel into what he called a psychological chess game. Reiner was funny too; he'd also directed *This Is Spinal Tap* (the greatest rock com ever made) and *When Harry Met Sally* (the greatest rom-com ever made), and the film I quote more than any other – if you know why, you just know, the way you know about a good melon.* He managed to get the pitch of *Misery*'s gallows humour exactly right.†

All the changes from book to film are good ones. Reiner tones down the gore, cutting a scene of slaughter by lawnmower because he thought it would be jumping the shark. Instead of Annie chopping Paul's foot off with an axe, she 'hobbles' him with a sledgehammer ('God, I love you,' she says, orgasmically, as Paul screams). This reminds me that in *The Shining* film Jack attacks his family with an axe rather than the croquet mallet from the novel – do King's weapons ever get used as he originally wished?

The film opens out the novel's world, with some adorable verbal sparring between the elderly sheriff Buster and his wife Virginia. We get the thrill of Lauren Bacall as Paul's agent, who apparently Reiner was so delighted to cast that he let her choose her own Armani wardrobe. We also see Paul complete his new novel at the start. There's a great description of him in the screenplay's opening:

* Easter egg: the book Billy Crystal reads in said film is *Misery*.

† Goldman also co-wrote a far less successful Broadway play of *Misery*, starring Bruce Willis, of which one critic wrote, 'You're more likely to experience chills sitting in a tepid bath'.

> He's the hero of what follows. Forty-two, he's got a good face, one with a certain mileage to it. We are not, in other words, looking at a virgin. He's been a novelist for eighteen years and for half that time, the most recent half, a remarkably successful one.

Which actor would not want to play this part? Goldman wrote this: 'Stars, you have to understand, play gods. They have to be perfect. They can't have a flaw unless they can wink at the audience and say, "I'm really wonderful."'

But my favourite film addition is the Liberace montage. A brief whisper in the novel of Annie's love for the grinning, bejewelled maestro of kitsch candelabras is turned into a delicious montage where we see Paul bashing out his *Misery* novel, the manuscript growing, Annie reading, the sheriff working things out, and Paul lifting up the typewriter to strengthen his upper arms and do battle, all set to Tchaikovsky's Piano Concerto No. 1. I wish more films had a Liberace montage.

It's right after this that Annie gets the blues, and comes out with one of the film's best lines: 'I know you don't love me – don't say you do – you're a beautiful, brilliant, famous man of the world; and I'm… not a movie star type … You'll never know the fear of losing someone like you if you're someone like me.' *The Shining* gives us horror and humour. *Misery* does this too, but it also adds pity.

# 14

# PERFECT BOOK, PERFECT FILM: *THE NAME OF THE ROSE, A ROOM WITH A VIEW, THE TURN OF THE SCREW*

As the search for perfection is a fool's errand, I would never claim the following books and films are practically perfect in every way, like Mary Poppins. To quote Henry James, excellence does not require perfection. Or to misquote Grace Jones, they're not perfect, but they're perfect for me. I admire both equally and I don't think I could choose between media.

Together, these books and films enhance and support each other. If they were a married couple, they would be Tom Hanks and Rita Wilson rather than Burton and Taylor – bringing out the best in each other, rather than getting drunk, buying diamonds and scratching each other's eyes out.

I was quite torn about this indecision – other strong contenders for 'perfect book to perfect film' were *Trainspotting*, *The Night of the Hunter*, *The Prime of Miss Jean Brodie*, *The Go-Between*, *The Handmaiden* (based on *Fingersmith*), all versions of *Little Women*, *Picnic at Hanging Rock*, *The Leopard*, *Room*, *Small Things Like These* and that other flawless adaptation of a Claire Keegan novella, *The Quiet Girl*, based on *Foster* (my husband would also say *The Spy Who Came in from the Cold* should be here). In the end, however, I decided that my blessed trinity would be *The Name of the Rose*, *A Room with a View* and *The Innocents*, adapted from *The Turn of the Screw*. They're all historical, by complete accident. They are also, in their own way, mystery stories, whether that mystery be a book, a heart or a haunting. And solving that mystery is where the pleasure, and the pain, of each work lies.

### *The Name of the Rose*

'What's Umberto Eco? Translate that now! What is it? He's a person? What does he do? He's a semiologist? What's a semiologist? What is it?!'

Alan Partridge

I know a number of people who have similar feelings of panic and fear around Umberto Eco, specifically his 538-page 1980 novel *The Name of the Rose*. Recently a friend told me she'd pretended to have read it while in a publishing meeting about historical fiction. For many years I was one of these people too, the doorstopper I'd inherited from my great-aunt sitting unread on my shelf, like a reproach, for many years after I'd seen the film. It might have been one of the bestselling books of all time, but it also had a reputation for being dense, difficult – and long.

I don't think that, to my knowledge, a novel (or for that matter a film) has ever been described as 'mercifully long'. There's something in all of us that grits our teeth when tackling a lengthy work of art and thanks the Lord when the end is in sight. To quote Geoff Dyer: 'There is invariably a sense of relief when it becomes clear that the band, despite our collective imploring, are *not* coming back, that the house lights have flicked on … Land! We're almost there, we've made it, can practically taste the scurvy-healing lager being poured in a bar afterwards.'*

I did grit away, in the end, and then of course felt like a fool for putting it off for so long, because *The Name of the Rose* is great in every sense. It has become part of my triad of perfection because it is one of the most bookish books I've read, but managed to become, due to some inspired filleting, an incredibly filmic film. The reason is that, for all its metafictional games, it is a great story, with a great central character – and, as Ray Bradbury put it, 'Plot is no more than footprints left in the snow after your characters have run by on their way to incredible destinations.'

The *New York Times* quote on my Picador film tie-in edition sums up the novel perfectly:

> Imagine a medieval castle run by the Benedictines, with cellarists, herbalists, gardeners, young novices. One after the other half a dozen monks are found murdered in the most bizarre of ways. A learned Franciscan who is sent to solve the mystery finds himself involved in the frightening events … a sleuth's pursuit of the truth behind the mystery also involves the pursuit of meaning – in words, symbols, ideas, every conceivable sign the visible universe contains.

The learned Franciscan-turned-detective in question is Brother William of Baskerville, a man devoted to reason and rational

* From his excellent book about endings, *The Last Days of Roger Federer*.

enquiry in an age of superstition.* His story is the spine of a meaty, dense novel, stuffed with allusions, asides and leisurely descriptions. The pacing is languid because, as Eco said, 'If somebody wanted to enter the abbey and live there for seven days, he had to accept the abbey's own pace.' There's a six-page description of a door. There are many digressions on herbs and holy relics. There is a very long, elaborate dream, a sort of holy feast-cum-orgy-cum-medieval snuff movie, which also gives Brother William an invaluable clue. But then it's a medieval chronicle, written down by William's young assistant Brother Adso when he's an old man; what would we expect?

The book is a literary shaggy dog story. At the start a man called Umberto Eco tells us he was given a mysterious book 'by a certain Abbé Vallet' that was a reproduction of Adso's lost manuscript, just like a 'found footage' horror film, or *Don Quixote*, which Cervantes tells us is translated from several texts. It's a book about books too, its mystery centring around a forbidden library, which contains a book that kills.† There are literary allusions to everything from Conan Doyle (at one point Baskerville says, 'It seems elementary' and I punched the air) to Borges's 'The Library of Babel'. We are told, in one of many book-related quotes that could happily grace a Waterstones tote bag, that 'The good of a book lies in its being read.' We are also told that 'A book is made up of signs

* He follows a line of rational-religious detectives in literature, including Cadfael and Father Brown (you could also include Simenon's Maigret here, who is often compared to a priest or confessor).

† Spoiler: it is a copy of Aristotle's second book of *Poetics* dedicated to comedy, which is deemed so dangerous to read that the elderly monk Jorge of Burgos poisons its pages.

that speak of other signs, which in their turn speak of things. Without an eye to read them, a book contains signs that produce no concepts; therefore it is dumb' – not only a good argument against censorship, but a good summation of semiotics, the study of the meaning of signs and symbols, and Eco's profession.

The whole book is a search for meaning, which we try to grasp and feel slipping away from us. At the end I felt an enormous sense of loss. It reminded me that all stories are echoes of lives lost to time; as Hilary Mantel said of history, 'It's what's left in the sieve when the centuries have run through it – a few stones, scraps of writing, scraps of cloth.' And, as when finishing Mantel's *Wolf Hall* trilogy, not only was I bereft, but I started seeing its world layered over mine, with ghosts around every corner. What would Brother William think of cars and planes and trains? What would Thomas Cromwell make of the Tower of London now surrounded by tourists? How would the minds of centuries ago cope with it all?

So how do you film a deeply bookish book? Casting an incredibly famous Scottish actor (who used the same accent in every role) as a medieval English monk might not seem like an obvious choice. It certainly put the frighteners on Columbia Pictures, which withdrew its funding because Sean Connery was considered past his best after the Bond retread *Never Say Never Again*. But for me he is perfect as William of Baskerville (I should say Bashkerville really, shouldn't I?), giving a performance of such twinkly intelligence that it could be nobody else. Unlike the experience of many who hate having their imaginations invaded by a film's actor, I was delighted to have Connery's mellifluous brogue in my head when reading the book.* The casting against type of ladykiller as monk adds to the pleasure. In a scene where William and Adso (played by a youthful Christian Slater) discuss the latter's deflowering by a village wench and ponder the perils of women, Connery says, regretfully, 'Of course I don't have the benefit of your experience.' James Bond, a virgin! Inconceivable.

Rewatching the film post-book, I was struck by how similar the spines are. Wisely, the filmmakers ditch the theology and stick with the golden thread of the murder. They knew that the maverick detective battling against the odds is the fictional character audiences love to identify with the most – our avatar, as screenwriter John Yorke puts it – and that solving the mystery is storytelling in its purest form, 'literature's heroin'.†

What we lose in scholarly musings we gain in atmosphere, with a miraculous rendering of the novel's medieval world. We're in full-on mucky, smelly Middle Ages territory, where, as with *Monty Python and the Holy Grail*, the only way you can spot a king is because he hasn't got shit all over him. There is mud. There are tubs of blood. There are grotesques straight from Pasolini, with knobbly faces, pustules, sores and odd tufts

* Philip Hensher was brilliantly grumpy on this with regards to Andrew Davies's *Bleak House* TV adaptation: 'I don't want forever to have to think of Gillian Anderson as Lady Dedlock, and certainly not of Johnny Vegas as Krook. How many novels have been subtly corrupted in the imagination like this?'

† As Aaron Sorkin said, 'I write about people who are smarter than I am.' Hence my favourite screen trope, people doing their job really well, whether it's Don Draper acing a pitch or Atticus Finch saving a life in court.

of hair (as the *Washington Post* waggishly noted, 'the monks all look vaguely like Marty Feldman'). There are smoky pyres and filthy hovels. Life really isn't pleasant for a peasant. There is 1980s synth music. Think *Highlander* or *Robin of Sherwood* meets Hieronymus Bosch, the ultimate sales pitch.*

This is not only deeply enjoyable, but a neat way of visualising the religious schism at the heart of the novel: whether or not the Church should follow Christ's teachings on poverty, shown in the contrast between the enormous, wealthy abbey looming on the hilltop and the greasy villagers below. When the abbey catches fire, it is as if we are in hell itself.†

Yes, there are broad brushstrokes to illuminate our world, and neat shortcuts. The inquisitor Bernardo Gui, who slopes off quietly in the book, becomes a Moriarty-like evil adversary, accusing William of being the murderer but handily getting pushed over the cliff by an angry mob (has there ever been any other kind of cinematic mob?). Less realistic, but dramatic and satisfying. Similarly, the fate of Adso's peasant girl, accused of witchcraft and hauled off to be burned in the novel, is a happier one thanks to a last-minute intervention. He still sees her face years later. A line about the inadequacy of language from the novel, 'This was the only earthly love of my life, and I could not, then or ever after, call that love by name', is paraphrased as the last line of the film. Stamping its own

* Jean-Jacques Annaud's attention to detail involved four years' casting and preparation, building the biggest set since *Cleopatra* on a hill outside Rome, specially woven habits and removing fillings from actors' mouths.

† I wonder if it's telling that years later Annaud made a fictional film about a more recent church conflagration, in Paris of 2021, *Notre-Dame on Fire* – he described fire as 'the perfect charismatic villain'.

meaning on a novel about meaning, the film makes clear that the girl is the rose.*

My favourite filmic addition is a touching scene where William escapes the library fire and drops the pile of books he's saved in order to hug Adso. Is the film saying some things are more important than books? Or is it an attempt to impose an 'arc' on a character who does not really change in the novel? Probably. 'Story is an ancient cultural form remade by the movies, as profound and misleading as the cult of happiness, everything working out for the best', says David Thomson. I'm glad the film of *The Name of the Rose* wants to make us happy, though. After all, in Eco's words, a novel is 'a machine for generating interpretations'.

His initial reaction to the movie was famously ambivalent: 'A book like this is a club sandwich, with turkey, salami, tomato, cheese, lettuce. And the movie is obliged to choose only the lettuce or the cheese, eliminating everything else – the theological side, the political side. It's a nice movie', although apparently he softened towards it over time. I think there's some meat here, though. To use another food metaphor (one beloved of book reviewers), if the novel is a rich, deeply satisfying stew, then perhaps the film is a delicious chateaubriand with bearnaise sauce. Or something. We are left with an intellectual murder mystery centring on books, one with just enough erudition to make us feel clever as we watch it – just like a host of French movies released around the same time, such as *Betty Blue*, *Manon des Sources*, *Subway* and *Jean de Florette*, which were adored by arty audiences. (The *Betty Blue* poster also decorated the bedroom

* Eco doesn't make it this easy for us, however, saying he chose the rose for his title because it's a symbol so familiar it has lost all meaning.

of every male heterosexual student in Britain between approximately 1986 and 1996.)

As a bat-call to clever types, the film calls itself 'A palimpsest of Umberto Eco's *The Name of the Rose*' in its opening credits.* It's adding another meaning, not making a copy.† Everyone puts their own stamp on a work. That is the beauty of this book; and indeed of any book. I leave the last word to Thomas à Kempis, via Umberto Eco: '*In omnibus requiem qaesivi, et nusquam inveni nisi in angulo cum libro*.' ('In all things I have sought peace, and nowhere have I found it except in a corner with a book.')

### *A Room with a View*

'E. M. Forster never gets any further than warming the teapot. He's a rare fine hand at that. Feel this teapot. Is it not beautifully warm? Yes, but there ain't going to be no tea.'

KATHERINE MANSFIELD

Let's get the haters out of the way first. In their corner, we have Mansfield's famous burn above, along with F. R. Leavis disparaging (a bit homophobically, I assume) Forster's 'spinsterly

* A palimpsest is a manuscript or parchment that has had the original writing scraped off so that it can be reused, but still bears traces of the original underneath the new writing.

† Subsequent adaptations include an eight-part 2019 TV miniseries, a passion project produced by and starring John Turturro, which I found well meaning but overstuffed (one reviewer compared it to 'monk soup'). There is also a two-act 'grand opera' version, which I feel Eco, with his description of the book's 'long recitatives and elaborate arias', might have loved.

touch' and Julian Barnes landing the final punch with 'fusty, musty, dusty'.* There is a prevailing view of Forster as tweedy and snobbish, a 'vicar in the drawing room' kind of novelist, like Jane Austen with a failure of nerve.

I'm not entirely unsympathetic to the criticisms; I feel bad for never having warmed to *A Passage to India* or *Howards End*. But all those who think Forster is a snob should read his short story 'The Other Boat' to see how much he despises the class system, straight society and imperialism.† And I will duke it out with anyone over his 1908 novel *A Room with a View*. Perhaps this is because, according to Zadie Smith, a famous Forster fan, it is a young person's book, and I am very immature. But it is also because it is one of the funniest, warmest, most joyful novels I have read. Yes, even 'the nicest', as Forster later said.‡ It is as far from fusty as you could be. It is like being bathed in sunshine, and even though it was written over a hundred years ago, it's as fresh and perfect as a new spring leaf – as is the film adaptation.

When I'm writing a blurb for a classic novel, I generally try to avoid saying things like 'it's as relevant today as it ever was', because (a) it's subjective and (b) it's a cliché. But I'll say it anyway. *A Room with a View*, the story of unformed teenager Lucy Honeychurch, who has her passions awakened by

* Although Barnes wrote generously about his change of heart towards Forster in *Changing My Mind*.

† From the collection *The Life to Come*, published after Forster's death because most of its stories were about love between men.

‡ In his 1958 essay 'A View Without a Room', imagining the subsequent fates of his characters. I was pleased Freddy Honeychurch wasn't killed in the First World War – I'd always imagined that as a young officer he would be one of the first to go.

free-thinking George Emerson on a trip to Italy, then represses them before finally understanding her own heart, is as Relevant Today as it Ever Was. The reasons? Firstly, it is really, really funny. It's comedy in its purest, most classical Shakespearean sense: a chaos of misunderstandings (the word 'muddle' is used again and again in the novel) that are finally resolved as lovers unite in a happy conclusion; magically suspended mid-air in brilliant symmetry and youthful perfection. Everyone and everything is bedevilled by opposites and coincidences, there's a marriage at the end and even an Italian setting.

Unlike Shakespearean comedies, however, it is properly funny too (I'm not the first to notice that no one ever *really* laughs at them unless it's to show they get the joke). The humour comes from Forster's skewering of types we all recognise. Any of us who have been charmed by a rustic village abroad for being 'so real' or enraptured by *cucina povera* will wince at bohemian novelist Eleanor Lavish exclaiming, 'Look at that adorable wine-cart! How the driver stares at us, dear, simple soul!' or 'One doesn't come to Italy for niceness ... one comes for life.' (She also hates English tourists, as we all do, unless it's us.) Anyone who, like me, has martyrish tendencies will squirm at Lucy's cousin and chaperone, the magnificent Charlotte Bartlett, a living embodiment of passive-aggression before the term was even invented. On a picnic: 'The ground will do for me. Really I have not had rheumatism for years. If I do feel it coming on I shall stand.' Frequently: 'What a nuisance I am!'

Forster said in a letter that his characters, inspired by the people he encountered in genteel boarding houses on a post-graduation trip to Italy with his mother, 'feel more real to me than any others I have created'.* We see these people, as Lucy encounters them in Florence's Pension Bertolini; we know people like them.

The main reason Forster matters today, however, is his belief that, in order to be truly happy in the world, we must know ourselves. I suppose these days we would call it 'doing the work'. His novel is gossamer-light, yet gracefully woven into it are more symbols and contrasts than you could shake an undergraduate essay at. The greatest is between rooms, which represent stifling oppression, and views, which mean letting in the light: the examined life. When Lucy encounters the elderly Mr Emerson in Santa Croce, he tells her:

> You are inclined to get muddled, if I may judge from last night. Let yourself go. Pull out from the depths those thoughts that you do not understand, and spread them out in the sunlight and know the meaning of them.

'To this extraordinary speech', we are told, 'Lucy found no answer.' Forster's plea for honesty, not just with others but with ourselves, speaks to us just as much now as it did in an age of absurd social rules. When Lucy is kissed by George in a field of violets (it's corn and poppies in the film), she can't even put a name to her emotions, so she buries them and, on returning to England, becomes engaged to the pretentious Cecil Vyse, an intellectual, aesthete and snob – or, as Zadie Smith says one of her students put it, a proto hipster. Lucy always thinks of

* By all accounts the trip was a bit of a disaster as Forster was a calamitous traveller, beset by lost possessions, a sprained ankle, a broken arm and an attack of flea bites.

Cecil in a room, she says, not outdoors. He tries to kiss her in the woods, and it's a disaster. To marry him will mean spiritual and sexual death.

George Emerson returns on the scene, luckily, but Lucy still can't admit her feelings for him, despite having bad dreams: 'her body behaved so ridiculously'. She nearly muddles her life away, and we all know it. In one of many moments where Forster talks to us from on high, as he manipulates his cast, he tells us:

> It is obvious enough for the reader to conclude, 'She loves young Emerson.' A reader in Lucy's place would not find it obvious. Life is easy to chronicle, but bewildering to practise, and we welcome 'nerves' or any other shibboleth that will cloak our personal desire. She loved Cecil; George made her nervous; will the reader explain to her that the phrases should have been reversed?

Forster is talking about sex, of course, and warning against its denial. At the end of the novel, when George and Lucy are on honeymoon, back at the Pension Bertolini, the reader is allowed into their bedroom, a daring move twenty years before *Lady Chatterley*. As they sink to their knees by the open window, 'it was the great joy that they had expected'. We always hoped George and Lucy would have good sex, and it's nice to have it confirmed.

It doesn't feel like a conjecture too far to surmise that Forster's warning against repressed desire comes from his own double life as a gay man, closeted to all but his closest friends, who came of age when Oscar Wilde was doing hard labour in Reading Gaol. George was called Meredith in earlier drafts of the novel, the name of Forster's lover at Cambridge.* According to the writer Benjamin Dreyer, Lucy isn't the only one who feels the pull of his strapping hero: 'I'm perpetually amused at how the immediate reaction of Freddy Honeychurch, the brother and surrogate id of our gradually supremely romantic heroine, Lucy Honeychurch, on first seeing stalwart young George Emerson is to try to get him naked.'

Dreyer is referring to the novel's nude bathing scene, when Freddy, George and the Reverend Beebe cool off with a bracing woodland dip. It's one of the novel's many set pieces (others include a bloody knife fight and the kiss in the Tuscan hills) that work perfectly on screen. In the film, we're treated to much clean-limbed splashing from beautiful, floppy-haired Julian Sands and Rupert Graves, nude wrestling straight out of Ken Russell's *Women in Love* and Simon Callow running around like a tubby little satyr.

Why do I think the 1985 film, directed by James Ivory and produced by Ismail Merchant, is as perfect as the novel? First, I must dismiss any silliness over Merchant Ivory as representing some kind of twee 'heritage cinema'. As the critic Kim Newman pointed out, they are as 'British' as films produced by an Indian, directed by an American and written by a Pole can be. It's easy to forget how fresh and arresting, even unusual, this film seemed when it first appeared, and still does.

It's also as sexy as hell. Unlike George and Lucy's chaste kiss in the novel, they chew each other's faces off on screen. There's full frontal male nudity, as discussed. The film is described as 'handsomely mounted' by the BFI, and for a generation of

* Hugh Owen Meredith, later the inspiration for the character Maurice. *A Room with a View* is dedicated to H.O.M.

young viewers who saw it, that was exactly what we wanted to happen to us – or at least to be snogged ardently on a Tuscan hillside. From the film's swoony opening titles, set to Puccini's aria *O mio babbino caro*, to the final, ravishing scene of the happy lovers overlooking the Arno, it's difficult not to be swept off your feet.

And oh, the cast, as perfect as a cast could be. Eighteen-year-old Helena Bonham Carter, making her debut, looks exactly as Forster describes her, with the right mix of awkwardness and grace. Sands is intense and otherworldly. But this is an ensemble piece, every role expertly filled by the cream of British thespian talent at a time when a generation who'd honed their craft in 1950s and 1960s rep theatre were now in their prime, and in abundance. So we have an adorable Denholm Elliott as George's father, Rosemary Leach as Lucy's mother (a performance I cherish because Mrs Honeychurch – jolly, loving, always in charge and saying things like 'How dare you be so serious' – reminds me so much of my own mother) and, of course, those grand dames Judi Dench and Maggie Smith, camping it up respectively as Eleanor Lavish and Charlotte Bartlett.

Best of all is Daniel Day-Lewis as Cecil Vyse. For my money, this is his greatest, funniest and most subtle performance, before he became a Serious Actor in Serious Films. On a physical level, it is astonishing: the scene of Cecil battling a wasp in the garden of Windy Corner should alone have won him a dozen Oscars.

Forster's characters may irritate the hell out of us, but we never hate them – his satire is too generous for that. He likes to pop into their heads and show us what they're thinking, enlarging our empathy. When Lucy breaks off her engagement to a 'painfully bewildered' Cecil in the novel, we're told that 'By a cruel irony she was drawing out all that was finest in his disposition'. The film does this without words, in a scene where Day-Lewis forlornly sits on the stairs and buttons up his boots, and somehow makes our hearts ache for Cecil in the process.

Ruth Prawer Jhabvala's sensitive, judicious screenplay is a masterclass in what to cut, what to keep, and what to add. So much of Forster's crackling dialogue is retained, wisely, as are his chapter titles, which frame the film's scenes (*Lying to George*; *Lying to Cecil*; *Lying to Mr. Beebe, Mrs. Honeychurch, Freddy, and the Servants*; *Lying to Mr. Emerson*) and add a touch of irony.

There are inspired additions, however. 'And did she really?' asks a scandalised Charlotte of Miss Lavish, as they gossip about an older Englishwoman marrying an Italian half her age – an Easter egg for fans of *Where Angels Fear to Tread*. One of Charlotte's many 'I shall never forgive myself's is given the tart retort, 'You always say that, Charlotte, but you always do forgive yourself.' And when Lucy finally realises she loves George, she simply says, in exasperation, 'Of course I do! What did you all think?'

Jhabvala not only gets that warm Forsterian teapot scorching hot, she manages to cut to the heart of the novel, while preserving it. In her words, 'Any adaptation you do it diagonally. You can take up the theme but you can never, never, never do it literally.' She shows us that, to use Cecil's words, 'The cause of Comedy and the cause of Truth are really the same'.

A final thing: the film's ending is slightly happier than the novel's, where the Honeychurch family won't speak to Lucy because they're so disgusted by her hypocrisy over George. She now has iron in her soul, whereas George is 'a baby'. Will the lovers stay happy? Or will they, as we fear at the ending of *The Graduate*, come to wonder what on earth they've done? The film's ending banishes such doubts, and for that, I am grateful.

As Shakespeare knew when ending his comedies, perhaps nobody needs reminding that the happiness is hard-won and precarious; that life is sweet but fleeting.

### *The Turn of the Screw*

'The oldest and strongest emotion of mankind is fear'

H. P. Lovecraft

Everyone enjoys being a bit scared, but as I am a very risk-averse person – in the same job for decades, phobic about flying, probably unable to leave the house altogether soon – I like to get my adrenaline rush from horror films rather than bungee jumping or white-water rafting. As horror director Wes Craven said, 'Horror movies don't create fear, they release fear.' Or, as a friend of mine said, they're a workout for the psyche.

My peak perfection scary book to scary film is *The Innocents*, adapted from Henry James's novella *The Turn of the Screw*, and I'm not alone. Pauline Kael described it as 'the best ghost movie I've ever seen', Truffaut as 'the best English film after Hitchcock goes to America', Martin Scorsese as one of the scariest movies of all time. According to Christopher Frayling, 'All films become ghost stories, after the actors have died. But *The Innocents* remains the finest ghost movie based on the finest ghost story ever written.' That's quite a claim, and I happen to agree. But I also think *The Innocents* deserves to be in my Holy Trinity for two other reasons. One: although Henry James wasn't very interested in the burgeoning art form of cinema, far preferring the theatre, in *The Turn of the Screw* he has inadvertently written the perfect horror movie script. Two: Jack Clayton's 1961 film also gives the lie to the claim that you somehow can't show 'the inner life', or consciousness, on screen.

Let's start with the story itself. Like so much great art, it all began in Croydon.* Henry James was staying in said borough at the Archbishop of Canterbury's residence, Addington Palace, in 1895, where he heard a half-remembered tale of devilry and wrote this in his notebook:

> Note here the ghost story told me at Addington … the mere vague, undetailed, faint sketch of it … the story of the young children left to the care of servants in an old country house, through the death, presumably, of parents. The servants, wicked and depraved, corrupt and deprave the children; the children are bad, full of evil, to a sinister degree. The servants die and their apparitions, figures, return to haunt the house and children, to whom they seem to beckon, whom they invite and solicit, from across dangerous places … so that the children may destroy themselves … there is a suggestion of strangely gruesome effect in it.

Two years later, the American periodical *Collier's Weekly* asked him for a story, and he remembered 'the vividest little note for sinister romance that I had ever jotted down'. The novella *The Turn of the Screw* was the result, adding a 'fireside tale' prologue in the traditional ghost story style, and making the narrator a nameless governess, who (in her mind) must protect her orphan

* In its defence, as well as Croydon's most famous daughter, Kate Moss, the south-east London borough was the birthplace of Peter Cushing, Dame Peggy Ashcroft and David Lean no less, who has a brilliant independent cinema named after him there.

charges, Miles and Flora, from the demonic undead servants Peter Quint and Miss Jessel, who want to relive their sexual relationship by possessing the children. The terror reaches such a pitch that, at the end of the story, Miles dies of fright.

James wanted to make the story as terrifying as possible for his new US audience, and even scared himself, telling his friend Edmund Gosse that when he'd finished correcting the proofs, 'I was so frightened that I was afraid to go upstairs to bed.' The only person who seemed to be unmoved was his doughty secretary William MacAlpine, to whom James, now unable to write for long periods, dictated the tale: 'this iron Scot betrayed not the slightest shade of feeling! I dictated to him sentences that I thought would make him leap from his chair; he short-handed them as though they had been geometry.'

Others reacted more violently than MacAlpine. *The Bookman* said, 'we have never read a more sickening, a more gratuitously melancholy tale'. In the US, *The Independent* magazine damned it as 'an outrage upon the holiest and sweetest fountain of human innocence'. That killjoy guardian of the canon F. R. Leavis called it 'a non-significant thriller' but, to paraphrase Mandy Rice-Davies, of course he would.*

James's attitude was ambiguous. He called his tale 'a shameless pot-boiler', but a few years later said that a pot-boiler could be 'in the lives of all artists, some of the most beautiful things ever done by them'. Then the Freudians came along and

* The other ghostly James, M. R. James, who entertained his Cambridge students with chilling tales every Christmas Eve, publishing them as *Ghost Stories of an Antiquary*, disapproved of the sexual element, calling it 'a fatal mistake ... sex is tiresome enough in the novels, in a ghost story ... I have no patience with it.'

interpreted it as all being in the sexually repressed governess's head, and ever since debate has raged, as much as literary criticism can rage, about whether the ghosts are real or a figment of her fevered imagination.*

I'm more interested in the novella as a blueprint for the perfect horror film. According to horror movie nut Mark Kermode, there are specific conventions that define the genre. *The Turn of the Screw*, it turns out, has them all. There is the 'journey to a new place', whether it's Janet Leigh driving to the Bates Motel, Jonathan Harker travelling to Dracula's castle or, in this case, the governess's coach ride to the remote country estate of Bly, after being ordered by the children's guardian that 'she should never trouble him – but never, never: neither appeal nor complain nor write'. We have the big house with secrets; what Stephen King called 'the bad places'. And we have monsters, in this case corrupted, perhaps even diabolic, children (see *The Exorcist* and *Rosemary's Baby*), which is the worst kind of horror, as Graham Greene brilliantly noted:

> We are all of us emigrants from a country we can remember little of: it haunts us and we try to reconstruct it, but all that is most important about it escapes us. We feel that we have never been so happy since we left it or so miserable, but we can't remember how happiness felt or the quality of the misery: we watch our children's eyes for hints ... horror happening to a child seems twice the horror because we don't know what he feels and can't help him: it is James's *Turn of the Screw.*

* As someone once said of academic feuding, it gets so vicious because the stakes are so low.

Ticking off more from Kermode's list, there is a chase. A final exorcism. Even a final girl, the trope of so much horror from *Halloween* to *Scream*. (Miles: 'Well – so we're alone!') There are jump scares:

> Three things. They were practically simultaneous, yet they had flashes of succession. My candle, under a bold flourish, went out, and I perceived, by the uncovered window, that the yielding dusk of earliest morning rendered it unnecessary. Without it, the next instant, I knew that there was a figure on the stair.

Virginia Woolf said that what you remember most in the novella is the silences, which become like sound directions: 'The sounds of evening dropped. The rooks stopped cawing in the golden sky.'

It all adds up to a novella that is highly stressful to read: claustrophobic, fraught, nervy. It traps us inside the overwrought, self-obsessed governess's mind. Henry James is a novelist of consciousness, his characters hyper self-aware, his sentences often like puzzles, where you operate on hunches about what's going on, but aren't quite sure. H. G. Wells described his prose as like an elephant trying to pick up a pea in the corner.

Despite all this, adapters can't get enough of him, possibly because he feels more modern than the Victorians before him, with his concerns about sex, status and the self (as the critic Susie Boyt put it, 'fine feelings and fine furniture'), or maybe for the practical reasons of sumptuous period locations and good parts for American actors. I also think filmmakers love the psychological ambiguity of James, because it allows for their own interpretation.

Naomi Alderman is one of many authors who have written eloquently on how films can sometimes 'flatten' the rich interiority of novels, because they 'cannot access that inner world in the same way'; what Hamlet calls 'that within which passeth show'.* Perhaps a movie can never quite replicate that sensation of being *inside* another person's head, of communing with their soul somehow, that occurs in novels such as *Jane Eyre* or *Wolf Hall*, but I think you can show the mind's life on screen.

In *A Theory of Adaptation*, Linda Hutcheon dismisses the notion that some books are 'untranslatable', or that film is a superficial medium because, as Brecht claimed, it demands 'external action and not introspective psychology'. In her view, 'External appearances are made to mirror inner truths, and in fact film has at its command many techniques that verbal texts do not', such as camera angles, *mise-en-scène*, lighting, sound design and the power of the close-up. I concur. We don't need to be told that 'in that moment, my heart was breaking', as we are in Ishiguro's novel *The Remains of the Day* – we see a whole universe of emotions pass across Anthony Hopkins's face on screen. In Lynne Ramsay's adaptation of *We Need to Talk About Kevin*, fractured chronology and jarring sound reflect the unreliable narrator's psychic state – at one point she stands next to some roadworks just to blot out her baby son's non-stop crying – while Charles Laughton's expressionist masterpiece *The Night of the Hunter* takes us into the woman-hating mind of serial

* However, some scientists, such as Nick Chater in *The Mind is Flat*, say there's no such thing as the inner life anyway. 'The inner world is a mirage ... we invent interpretations of ourselves and other people in a flow of experience ... There is nothing more to the mind than the fleeting contents of our stream of consciousness.'

killer 'Preacher', played by Robert Mitchum, through visual symbolism, such as the moment his flick-knife pierces his trouser pocket as he watches a stripper perform. Inner states are made manifest through sight and sound.

Jack Clayton's 1961 film adaptation of *The Turn of the Screw* uses many of these techniques from the moment its credits open. For nearly a minute we see nothing but a black screen, and hear an eerie folk song about a weeping willow (even eerier when I discovered it's sung by a woman pretending to be a little girl). Then the sound of a nightingale, then a woman sobbing, then gradually a pair of hands, clasped together as if in prayer. Then, at last, lead actress Deborah Kerr's anguished face, and her voice saying, 'All I want to do is save the children – not destroy them.'*

Destroy them ... what? Is she mad? Clayton was of the 'possibly' school. When Deborah Kerr asked him, 'Do you really think she sees these spooks or is it all in her mind and is she actually just going round the bend a little bit?' he said, 'You make up your mind.' So she keeps us guessing, just as Clayton does. Even the fact that she was twenty years too old for the part adds to the unease. Why is she behaving like a blushing teenager as she accepts the uncle's offer to go to Bly?† What's happened in her past? Her performance is magnificent, using

* We eventually learn that this beginning is in fact the end of the film; everything has come horribly full circle. The fantastically dramatic US ad campaign for the film forewarned audiences to 'see this picture from the very beginning to the mind-stunning end'.

† Michael Redgrave was cast as the amiable bachelor after Cary Grant got turned down because he wanted to reappear at the end. In Clayton's words, he was 'probably the only director who ever said "no" to Cary Grant!'

every part of her lovely, expressive face. When the ghosts of Quint and Miss Jessel appear, and boy do they, she sees them before we do: in the words of critic Penelope Gilliatt, 'her lips draw back like a horse that smells fire'.

We never learn, in novella or film, exactly what the children saw when Quint and Miss Jessel were lovers, but James's language – 'sickness', 'grossness', 'disgust' – drops more than enough hints that they have been morally, possibly even sexually, corrupted. The film's production design mirrors this by turning Bly into a decaying, *unheimlich* Eden, rotting and fetid. The roses are overblown. A beetle crawls out of a gross cupid statue's mouth. Lighting director Freddie Francis (who used so many high wattage bulbs Kerr wore sunglasses on set) even painted some of the trees so they would look unnaturally bright.* The offness is reinforced with the queasy 'Dutch' angles and sinister reflections that have been the mainstay of horror's visual language since *The Cabinet of Dr Caligari*, all of which capture perfectly what's going on inside the governess's head.

Sound, the *sine qua non* of horror, is ramped up and heightened, with insects, birds and whispers becoming something monstrous.† And the songs! They are terrifying. Not just Flora's 'Willow Waly', but the demonic little incantation that Miles recites near the end of the film, 'Enter! My Lord! Come from

* I only discovered the film was made at the National Trust's Sheffield Park and Garden in East Sussex after I'd visited, thank goodness. I never want to see Miss Jessel across that lake.

† Heightened sound is used to terrifying effect in films such as *The Babadook*, *The Witch* and, earlier, David Lynch's *Eraserhead*. He felt his sound mixer was so crucial to his film's success that he kept his ashes in a box in the floor under his mixing desk.

your prison!/Come from your grave!/For the moon is arisen!' This was one of the elements added by William Archibald in his 1950 Broadway play, which also gave the film its title, *The Innocents*. Archibald was contracted to write the first draft of the film's script too, but Clayton found it too stuffy. He enlisted John Mortimer to improve the dialogue, most notably with the housekeeper's description of 'Rooms used by daylight as though they were dark woods' by Quint and Miss Jessel, which is about as obscene as a Victorian allusion to sex gets.

But it was with the arrival of Truman Capote that the script really took off – Clayton maintained that the finished result was ninety per cent his work. He brought in suspense, tension and sadomasochism. From the sounds of this naughty note to Clayton, he clearly enjoyed himself:

> Dear Jack – or should I say Quint...
>
> Hope you will like this – and if not, don't worry, we will make everything right. Anyway, have been very busy with it.
>
> Onward.
>
> Your loving slave
>
> Mary Jessel

Capote put aside *In Cold Blood*, his non-fiction novel about two murderers awaiting the gallows, to work on the script (over lunch at Shepperton Studios he was heard rather tastelessly saying, 'They gotta swing before I can publish, God dammit!'). He added the scene where Miles tells Miss Giddens she is a 'damn dirty-minded hag' – toned down from 'damn dirty-minded bitch' at the censors' request. 20th Century Fox head Spyros Skouras also phoned Clayton every day for two weeks begging him to remove the film's shocking final scene, where

Miss Giddens kisses Miles on the mouth as he dies in her arms. Luckily they refused, and, ickily, it remains.

I'm genuinely unsure whether the ghosts are meant to be real or not by the end of the film, which is the point. But I still think the 'it's all in her head' interpretation is a get-out clause, or, as horror writer Jeremy Dyson says, 'an escape valve', just like Pam Ewing waking up in *Dallas* and realising it was all a dream. I also reckon it comes from a certain snobbishness towards the genre, with many critics saying *The Turn of the Screw* is brilliant *despite* being a ghost story.* But ghosts have been around in literature since its origins, and James was a believer, with a lifelong interest in the paranormal. He once wrote, 'I see ghosts everywhere', and I think they were more than metaphorical.

Isn't it more thrilling if both interpretations are true? Yes, the governess is going mad, but yes, at the same time, the ghosts are real and they're driving her insane? Now that's a scary thought.

* For example, Pauline Kael: 'a higher plane than the simple fears of most ghost stories'; academic Susie Boyt: 'ghosts that would be simple and uncouth in the hands of others can lend themselves to the deepest and most subtle investigations in the works of Henry James'.

# PART III

## What the Hell Were They Thinking?

# 15

# SILLY BOOK, SILLY FILM: *THE DA VINCI CODE, FIFTY SHADES OF GREY, THE FOUNTAINHEAD*

'For everything holy, there is something unholy.'

Thus speaks a wise monk in the superb film *The Omen* (which became a poor novelisation). For every perfect book to perfect film, there is a bad book that becomes a great film, or a great book that becomes a bad film, or, as we shall see, a deeply silly book that, in turn, becomes a deeply silly film.

*The Omen*'s diabolical trinity are the devil, the antichrist and the false prophet. For the purposes of this chapter, my 'silly book, silly film' threesome are Dan Brown's *The Da Vinci Code*, E. L. James's *Fifty Shades of Grey* and Ayn Rand's *The Fountainhead*. Each of these novels is extremely popular, and extremely long; none of them, I hope it's fair to say, is written by a renowned prose stylist. And all three film versions are a bit rubbish.

They also fall quite neatly into three categories, which I would define as 'fantastical adventure hokum', 'erotic shenanigans' and 'rot that takes itself seriously'. In the first of these I would place *Battlefield Earth*, John Travolta's doomed Scientology turkey based on L. Ron Hubbard's novel; most films inspired by the purple prose of Edgar Rice Burroughs, including *Greystoke: The*

*Legend of Tarzan*, where the Lord of the Apes has a French accent, and the flop *John Carter* (the leading man's name, appropriately, was kitsch); and the Christian apocalyptic thriller *Left Behind*, based on a deranged bestseller and starring Nicolas Cage looking like he is being held against his will.

In our erotic category (we would have called this 'the erection section' at school), we have humdingers like *The Lonely Lady*, a little-known 1983 film with the honour of a zero per cent approval rating on Rotten Tomatoes, based on the raunchy rags-to-riches saga by 'the Rembrandt of the trashy novel' Harold Robbins; *Indecent Proposal*, the tale of a man who sells his wife for the night for $1 million, so bad I had to watch it through my fingers; and *The Blue Lagoon*, the deeply exploitative 'sensual story of natural love' about two youngsters washed up on a desert island (for which Brooke Shields won the inaugural Golden Raspberry Award, aka the Razzie), an adaptation of a pioneering 1908 ick-lit novel.

Finally, bringing up the ignoble rear there are our misguided attempts at seriousness, such as *Forrest Gump*, the sentimental, heavy-handed, borderline offensive adaptation of a novel with all those qualities, and the creepy, saccharine piece of historically tin-eared mush *The Book Thief*, dubbed 'Harry Potter and the Holocaust'.

But without further ado, let the game of 'which is worse, book or film?' begin. Sometimes it's a very tough call.

### *The Da Vinci Code*

There are certain times when whole societies, even the entire world, seem to succumb to a kind of collective madness. One of these was the death of Princess Diana, which sent hordes of people who had never met her into paroxysms of grief. Another was in 2003, when millions of otherwise sane human beings became obsessed by Dan Brown's novel *The Da Vinci Code*, a nearly 600-page piece of blarney about secret societies, ancient conspiracies, homicidal monks and the bloodline of Jesus Christ. I should know, as I was one of them.

I remember my friend and I visiting Temple Church in our lunch hour (blessed were we that it was just up the road from the office) because it was in the book, and actually *measuring our own arms* to double-check whether Robert Langdon (the only Professor of Symbology ever, because it is a made-up discipline) was right about the divine proportion that is at the heart of all things in art and nature. It was gibberish, but we were mesmerised, gobbling it up like Special Stuff.*

Ian McKellen, who played Professor Leigh Teabing in the film adaptation, summed it up pretty well: 'While I was reading the book, I believed it entirely. Clever Dan Brown twisted my mind convincingly. But when I put it down, I thought, "What a load of codswallop".' *The Da Vinci Code* is the one-night stand of books: seems like a great idea at the time, leaves one feeling rather shamefaced afterwards. Or to quote the gleefully offensive but effective Pot Noodle TV ad from years past, which boasted the tagline 'The slag of all snacks' (I know): 'That felt so wrong and yet it felt so right.' It is also fun to join in a craze, like a Victorian going mad for penny farthings and sugar tongs. According to Derek Thompson in his book *Hit Makers*, 'Consumers are not just buying a product; what they're really buying is entry into a popular conversation. *Popularity is the product*.'†

---

* The mysterious meat sold by butcher Hilary Briss in the TV comedy *The League of Gentlemen*. You never find out what it is.

† It also gave snobs like me the chance to remind everyone that Leonardo

I even read *Angels and Demons*, the less-famous first Robert Langdon mystery (which I seem to remember having some kind of invisible car in it, although perhaps I had too much Night Nurse), and possibly *The Lost Symbol* too, but it's hazy. After reading about his latest, *The Secret of Secrets*, which bears the kind of title a small child or somebody entering a 'Dan Brown parody title' competition would give a story, and was reviewed by Sam Leith as 'weapons-grade bollocks from beginning to end', I'm almost tempted to stray from the path of righteous reading and go there again.

Dan Brown doesn't care what I think anyway. *The Da Vinci Code* has sold over 80 million copies and made him a fortune. I don't think he takes himself too seriously either. His author biography notes that *TIME* Magazine credited him with 'keeping the publishing industry afloat; renewed interest in Leonardo da Vinci and early Christian history; spiking tourism to Paris and Rome; a growing membership in secret societies; the ire of Cardinals in Rome; eight books denying the claims of the novel and seven guides to read along with it; a flood of historical thrillers; and a major motion picture franchise'.

I'm afraid the haters, including Stephen Fry ('botty-dribble … loose stool-water'), Salman Rushdie ('A novel so bad it gives bad novels a bad name') and the linguist Geoffrey K. Pullum (the 'worst prose stylist in the history of literature … staggeringly, clumsily, thoughtlessly, almost ingeniously bad') look a bit po-faced in comparison. They should just accept that some of us have very catholic reading tastes – though not in the Opus Dei sense, I should add, no cilices for me.

---

should never be known as Da Vinci, because that was where he was from, so *akchewerly*, it would be like calling Jesus 'of Nazareth'.

Yes, I'll admit that some of Brown's prose really does stretch our notions of a sentence being the right words in the right order, such as 'As he advanced, his dark eyes seemed to scorch the earth before him, radiating a dark clarity that forecast his reputation for unblinking severity in all matters'. Robert Langdon's sidekick, the slinky French cryptographer Sophie Neveu, is described as having 'a haunting certainty to her gait', and I'm not sure what that means. Brown also likes to wear his learning very heavily. Like an overenthusiastic tour guide, he dumps as much information as he possibly can at the most inopportune moment, such as: 'These were the gardens in which Claude Monet had experimented with form and colour, and literally inspired the birth of the impressionist movement. Tonight, however, this place held a strange aura of foreboding.' He also informs us that 'Jesus Christ was a historical figure of staggering influence, perhaps the most enigmatic and inspirational leader the world has ever seen.' Who needs Wikipedia?

It is a deeply silly book. But it is also, like those other pulpy novels such as *Jaws* and *The Godfather* that made masterly cinema, crying out to be filmed. Every short chapter – in fact nearly every page – ends on a cliffhanger. There is a MacGuffin* (the Holy Grail), there are chases, and there are striking images, such as a naked dead man in a pentacle in the Louvre. (It made me think of the film producer who read Charles Webb's *The Graduate*, and immediately got two pictures in his head: a boy in a scuba diving suit and a boy with a girl at the back of a bus, which became the film's most memorable scenes.) In the hands of a director with a light touch and visual flair, *The Da Vinci Code*

* Alfred Hitchcock's coinage for a device or object that drives a film's plot, but has little actual significance.

could have been the new *Raiders of the Lost Ark*. Unfortunately, Ron Howard, a director known for his solid, unflashy entertainments, decided to take it seriously.

Words like stodgy, stolid, dull, bloated and plodding were grimly trotted out to describe the resulting film adaptation, where Robert Langdon, played by a pained-looking Tom Hanks neutered of all his natural charm, and Sophie Neveu, a soporific Audrey Tatou, mostly walk around a lot explaining things. (Perhaps Hanks knows he's been miscast, as Langdon is described as 'Harrison Ford in tweed' in the book, one of the boldest 'buy my film rights' power moves in literary history.) Lines such as 'I need to get to a library!' were greeted with catcalls at Cannes, and the flashbacks to Biblical times are like the history videos we used to watch at school – and not nearly as fun as today's *Horrible Histories*.

Still, it was a critic-proof smash, the highest-grossing film of Hanks's career at that time, and highly controversial too, with protests from the Church on opening weekend (sadly no nuns spraying holy water on people in the queues like *The Exorcist*, though). It was banned in several countries, including the Faroe Islands of all places, and caused sixty-one-year-old Sister Mary Michael to spend twelve hours praying on her knees outside Lincoln Cathedral while filming took place inside – Westminster Abbey had said no but Lincoln, which received £100,000 to allow film crews in, clearly needed the money.

In a documentary about the making of the film (my husband and I accidentally stumbled upon the set while walking in London), Dan Brown seems to have had a smashing time, and describes it as a 'wonderful collaboration'. In fact, everyone involved is rather lovely, including an earnest Ron Howard, who was nominated for a Razzie for Worst Director but pipped to the post by M. Night Shyamalan. Perhaps if they'd had a 1970s style diva brat in charge it might have been a more exciting film. Or perhaps, as those of us who have read the book know, *everything* happens for a reason.

***Fifty Shades of Grey***

Fittingly, this 2015 film was described as 'the most intensely anticipated literary adaptation since *The Da Vinci Code*' by the *Guardian*. However, unlike that film, adapting E. L. James's erotic blockbuster does not sound like a wonderful collaboration.

Everyone involved seems to have had a terrible time. A rift grew between author/producer E. L. James, who said 'the most important thing' was to keep her fans happy, and director Sam Taylor-Johnson, for whom the most important thing was, presumably, to try to make a decent film. She remembered that 'Every scene was fought over. It was tough. It was like wading uphill through sticky tar.' Leading woman Dakota Johnson described the experience as 'crazy' and 'psychotic', and makes it sound as if they were almost shooting two different films in tandem:

> James had a lot of creative control, all day, every day, and she just demanded that certain things happen. There were parts of the books that just wouldn't work in a movie, like the inner monologue, which was at times incredibly cheesy. It wouldn't work to say out loud. It was always a battle. Always ... We'd do the takes of the movie that [James] wanted to make, and then we would do the takes of the movie that we wanted to make ... It was like mayhem all the time.*

* The constant battles over scripts and shooting meant that for the next

The movie was a smash, making $500 million at the box office and garnering some of the worst reviews put to paper ('about as stimulating as a cold shower', 'if anyone is punished by *Fifty Shades*, it is the audience'), so much so that poor Jamie Dornan, who plays kinky billionaire Christian Grey, said he and his wife 'shut themselves off from the world for a bit' in Sam Taylor-Johnson's country house to escape the 'ridicule'.

If you are one of the lucky few who is not familiar with the story of *Fifty Shades*, it is about Anastasia 'Ana' Steele, probably the only university student in history who is (a) a virgin, (b) has never got drunk and (c) never masturbated. *Chacun à son goût* and everything, but I would wager that, statistically, the likelihood of all three of these is slim. She goes to interview the billionaire Christian Grey in his phallic skyscraper and he, in the well-worn tradition, sees something different in this fresh-faced ingénue and seduces her, first with 'vanilla sex' and then some light spanking in his Red Room of Pain. It's absolutely no different from any other Mills & Boon Bluebeard nonsense about a poor, naïve virgin who is conquered by a domineering rich brute but ends up conquering *his* heart; its only point of difference is sadomasochism (a BDSM USP?).

Grey is a tiresome bossy-boots who is constantly barking things at Ana like 'Eat!', 'Sit down!' and 'Have you been drinking?' in the manner of an irate parent. The sex is tastefully filmed, with a lot of boob on display but nary a penis in sight (I thought James wanted to please the fans?). I wonder what this film would have looked like if Lars von Trier had got his

---

two, even worse, films in the trilogy Taylor-Johnson was replaced by James Foley, E. L. James was given 'unprecedented control', and screenwriter Kelly Marcel was replaced by James's husband Niall Leonard.

hands on it. It's more product porn than any other kind, with Grey playing a grand piano topless in an apartment the size of an aircraft hangar, fingering rows of designer shirts like Patrick Bateman, quaffing fine wines, driving a fleet of Audis (possibly a Batmobile too, at least that's what it looked like to me) and piloting a helicopter emblazoned with the word 'GREY'.*

It retains some of the worst lines from the book, such as 'If you were mine you wouldn't be able to sit down for a week!' and 'I don't make love. I fuck. Hard', and, as far as I could tell, adds some even worse ones, like 'I am mad. Ball-twitchingly mad.' But at least it ditches Ana's leaden internal monologue, which mainly consists of saying things like holy crap, holy shit, holy fuck and 'Holy Hell, he's hot', plus shouting 'Ah!' and 'Aargh!' at the climactic moments. (I never once thought, like Rob Reiner's mom in *When Harry Met Sally*, I'll have what she's having.) Dakota Johnson is the saving grace, giving a performance of humour and charm, whereas Dornan just looks as if he wants to escape – as his Ulster accent occasionally does.

I saw the film before I read the book, and I concur with the *Seattle Times* reviewer who wrote, '*Fifty Shades of Grey* the movie, for the record, is not quite as bad as *Fifty Shades of Grey* the book. But that's not saying much.' Like Dan Brown, E. L. James has a severe case of mentionitis, with everything explained in detail, often to great comic effect: 'It's called Spem in Alium, a forty-part motet by Thomas Tallis ... I've always wanted to fuck to it.' Ana flushes and bites her lip, Grey glowers and whispers darkly, but mostly there's a lame babyishness to the language

* Presumably spotting the similarity to his novel *American Psycho*, Bret Easton Ellis tweeted, 'I'm putting myself out there to write the movie adaptation of "Fifty Shades of Grey" ... and its two sequels.'

('He's my very own Christian Grey-flavored popsicle') that made me long for the ballsy drama of Shirley Conran's *Lace*, or the knockabout humour of Jilly Cooper's randy stable hands.

The bonkbuster queens, incidentally, were less than impressed with the book. Cooper called Grey a 'terrible, terrible silly man' and said, 'I don't think there is anything very liberating about being bashed around by him … I can't see how anyone would fancy him.' Barbara Taylor Bradford, author of sweeping sagas like *A Woman of Substance*, gamely read it for a piece in *The Lady*, and reported back: 'I can't help but think it's rather mediocre. Juvenile even … it is ultimately just Mills & Boon with a little added sex … A shopping list for couples looking to spice up their love lives.'

Apparently, it did just this, becoming not just one of the fastest-selling novels of all time, but also dubbed 'mummy porn' and credited with causing a spike in the sales of lingerie and sex toys (plus, I read, in injuries from misguided BDSM practices, yuck). Capturing a market eager to fill their Kindles with smut, and with a ready-made audience in place (it had originally been self-published as *Twilight* fan fiction), it also, in true 'publishing phenomenon' style, led to a panic-induced rash of copycat books. At least these were fun to publish, even if not to read – I remember a colleague deciding whether the poster they were working on for a Sylvia Day novel should have 'Come and get it' as the tagline, or the reverse… (the film also afforded similar opportunities, with 'Mr Grey will see you now' on the poster for the first film, and 'Don't miss the climax' for the last).

James flogged the hell out of her story, with sequels and three further novels repeating everything from Grey's point of view. Things have moved on since then, with the horny elves of romantasy riding high, perhaps as readers retreat further and further from grim reality. According to the latest Amazon 'Romance Glossary', the genre now encompasses everything from 'Dark Academia' to 'Daddy Dom', 'Boy meets ghoul' to 'Spicy Cinnamon Roll Hero' and 'Pool Boy'. Exhausting. But, rest assured, 'Vanilla Sex' is still there.

***The Fountainhead***

There are plenty of phallic skyscrapers in the novels of Ayn Rand, as well as domineering brutes. If you are not aware of the Russian-American philosopher and novelist, her credo is best summed up as 'won't somebody please think of the billionaires?' She espoused, in her words, 'the virtue of selfishness', and her most famous books, *The Fountainhead* (1943) and *Atlas Shrugged* (1957), portray thrusting, heroic captains of industry battling to make money while being held back by boring things like regulations, workers' rights and, you know, other human beings. It's the individualistic 'Greed is Good' mantra from the 1980s film *Wall Street*, but couched in hundreds of pages of unreadable prose.

Needless to say, Donald Trump loves her. He claimed that *The Fountainhead* is one of the few works of fiction he's read, because 'It relates to business, beauty, life and inner emotions. That book relates to ... everything.' The alt right, venture capitalists and 'move fast and break things' Silicon Valley types love her too, and Alan Greenspan, former Chairman of the Federal Reserve, was one of her most loyal acolytes. Her books have sold tens of millions – in one survey, Americans named *Atlas Shrugged* their favourite book after the Bible. And while her philosophy of 'Objectivism' is now pretty much discredited in academic circles, her popularity continues to rise.

As Gore Vidal wrote in 1961:

> Ayn Rand's 'philosophy' is nearly perfect in its immorality, which makes the size of her audience all the more ominous and symptomatic as we enter a curious new phase in our society. Moral values are in flux. The muddy depths are being stirred by new monsters and witches from the deep. Trolls walk the American night. Caesars are stirring in the Forum. There are storm warnings ahead.

Sound familiar?

Her veneration of the strong and her scorn for the altruistic or charitable feel perfect for today's performative nastiness. As Lisa Duggan, author of *Mean Girl: Ayn Rand and the Culture of Greed*, says, 'The contempt, the indifference, the assumption of superiority. Those are all very Randian … And that's the power of her vision, that there is such a wide swath of people with overlapping and sometimes conflicting political and policy views who can imagine themselves in her scenarios. And the end result of that is primarily this affective, cruel, greedy meanness.'

I fully understand Rand's allergy to collectivism – her family were brought to the brink of starvation by the Russian Revolution, her father's pharmacy seized by the Bolsheviks – but it seems a leap to turn this loathing into a fictional scenario where, notoriously, a trainload of people are accidentally poisoned with noxious fumes but so what, because one was a teacher who taught children to be team players, and one was married to a civil servant.

With *The Fountainhead* at over 700 pages and *Atlas Shrugged* over 1,000, Rand's novels bring to mind a quote by Ambrose Bierce, 'The covers of this book are too far apart.' They are haranguing, overwrought vehicles for ideology, filled with pages of speeches, such as the one at the end of *The Fountainhead*, where architect Howard Roark, who has been taken to court for blowing up a housing project, defends himself thus:

> Now observe the results of a society built on the principle of individualism. This, our country. The noblest country in the history of men. The country of greatest achievement, greatest prosperity, greatest freedom. This country was not based on selfless service, sacrifice, renunciation or any precept of altruism. It was based on a man's right to the pursuit of happiness. His own happiness. Not anyone else's. A private, personal, selfish motive.*

This is nothing, however, compared to the sixty-page monologue by John Galt in *Atlas Shrugged*, the noble plutocrat who leads a strike of victimised millionaires, which took Rand two years to write. Undeterred by her novels being unwieldy slabs, Rand was determined to see them filmed. In fact, the movies were the reason she left the USSR for America. Hollywood formed her fantasies of the New World, and she went there as soon as she could, marrying an actor and becoming a script doctor and screenwriter.

When *The Fountainhead*, despite lousy reviews, became a word-of-mouth hit, she happily sold the film rights to Warner Bros. and was signed up to write the screenplay. The resulting 1949 movie was panned – 'a towering achievement in trash', in the words of David Thomson. Rand was clearly a ruddy

* I was not surprised to learn that there is a hedge fund named after him, Roark Capital Group. I was even less surprised to learn that the former Tory Chancellor Sajid Javid said he reread this court scene twice every year, including to his wife, until she made him stop.

nightmare on set, not allowing a word of deviation from her precious script. Director King Vidor wanted Bogart for the part of Roark, but she insisted he hire her matinee idol, that laconic, all-American western hero Gary Cooper. Perhaps it was a good choice. As Thomson notes, 'Bogart was smart enough to sneer at the film's hysteria. Cooper never noticed it', and, watching his performance, I definitely got the impression that, whether he's discussing the properties of alabaster or reciting lines like 'A building must have integrity', Cooper doesn't quite grasp what he's saying.

But then this is not a cerebral film. It's mostly a phallic film, with the trailer showing a massive skyscraper and the words 'Towering to new dramatic heights comes Warner Bros.' proud presentation of ... *The Fountainhead*'. Roark's love interest Dominique, played by Patricia Neal (with whom Cooper began an on-set affair) lustfully watches him drilling a piece of rock with all the earth-moving symbolism that implies – it reminded me of the comic scene in *Shirley Valentine* where Pauline Collins has sex with Tom Conti to a montage of waves crashing on the shore, a ship's mast rocking and trains whizzing through tunnels. As Nora Ephron said of *The Fountainhead*, it is 'a very silly book', and this is a silly film.*

It is like *Citizen Kane*, however, compared to the three, yes, three-part movie of *Atlas Shrugged*, which began its fateful journey to screens in 2011. This genuine turd of a film (it 'sits there flapping on screen like a bludgeoned seal', declared *Rolling Stone*) is shoddily made and horribly filmed in 'restaurants and

* The Marxist Slavoj Žižek named it as one of his top five films, saying it's 'ultracapitalist propaganda but it's so ridiculous that I cannot but love it'. He also called cinema 'the ultimate pervert art'; I concur.

bedrooms that look borrowed from a hotel no doubt known as the Robber Baron Arms', to quote Roger Ebert. The dialogue is even worse, consisting mainly of conversations about steel prices and lines like 'They are not getting my metal!' and 'That train will run if I have to drive the damn thing myself' (in an impressive refusal to acknowledge the twenty-first century, trains still seem to be the future here, with TV news reports telling us about new railway tracks in tones of breathless awe).

Each part of the trilogy had a new director and a new cast, so that everyone has to explain who they are at the start of each one. In the first film John Galt is played by someone who cannot move his face very much, in the second by a human ball of rage (up close, he's almost purple), and in the third, crowd-funded barely-there effort, he seems to be ten years younger with different coloured hair. It's execrable, incoherent tosh. It's so gross in its ultra-capitalist worship of wealth that it makes *Dynasty* look like some kind of Soviet-era play about a day on the collective farm – and *Dynasty* had far, far better production values. This is literally a train wreck.

As the *Guardian* said, 'The story behind the *Atlas Shrugged* movies is one of such towering hubris and misfired ambition that it probably stands as history's most perfect counterpoint to anything Ayn Rand ever wrote.' For me, it's the perfect summa of her philosophy. Nobody wanted to watch it, and it lost money. The free market worked.

# 16

# THE UNFILMABLES: *GATSBY* AND OTHER CONUNDRUMS

'If it can be written, or thought, it can be filmed'

Stanley Kubrick

When it comes to adaptation, I am on team Kubrick.* In theory, no book is unfilmable. Saying it's impossible to represent a book on screen is like saying it's impossible to represent it with an image on the cover, or in an illustration (although, as I discovered in an article by Professor Julia Thomas, some nineteenth-century critics feared the illustrations in Dickens's novels would damage readers' imaginations by influencing their mental pictures of the characters). It is just a case of translating the verbal into the visual, although, as David Cronenberg put it, 'there is no dictionary for that translation. You really have to

* In the opposite camp is director Jonathan Miller, who said, 'Most novels are irreversibly damaged by being dramatized as they were written without any sort of performance in mind at all', although he still managed to produce one of the greatest adaptations of all time, *Whistle and I'll Come to You*, based on the M. R. James story.

reinvent the novel for the screen; and that often means being extremely brutal.'

Some novels are literally unfilmable, however, because their authors, presumably unable to face the necessary brutality, won't allow it. After getting burned with the disastrously dull adaptation ('A botch job for the ages' *Rolling Stone*) of her Pulitzer Prize-winning novel *The Goldfinch*, author Donna Tartt disowned the film, fired her agent of thirty years and refused to sell the rights to any of her books – including her bestseller *The Secret History*, which languished in development hell for several years and now belongs to her again.* Carlos Ruiz Zafón never faced this problem with his smash hit *The Shadow of the Wind* because he refused to sell in the first place, believing that the story was meant to be experienced through reading alone. It was the same for the notoriously particular J. D. Salinger who, after the critical failure of the only ever adaptation of his work, *My Foolish Heart*, based on his short story 'Uncle Wiggily in Connecticut', said he would never allow *The Catcher in the Rye* to be filmed while he was alive and that Holden Caulfield was 'essentially unactable' – although Marlon Brando, Jack Nicholson, Tobey Maguire and Leonardo DiCaprio wanted to try. Salinger refused them all. However, in a 1957 letter released on his death, he said that he was considering 'leaving the unsold rights to my wife and daughter as a kind of insurance policy'.†

* As the *Guardian* noted, '"unfilmable" is often just code for "we tried and it didn't happen", an excuse for all the films trapped in development hell, such as *John Milton's Paradise Lost* (Bradley Cooper was once lined up to play a hunky Lucifer).' Now that I would like to see.

† To date, the rights are retained by the Salinger Trust and no adaptation is forthcoming – although in 2020 a documentary revealed that Walt Disney

Refuseniks aside, there has generally been a consensus that certain novels lend themselves to adaptation less readily than others. The film journalist Thomas H. Sheriff calls it 'the Dune Problem and the Ulysses Problem': in other words, books that are too long, complicated and fantastical to condense, and those that are concerned with the inner world and therefore hard to represent visually. As he acknowledges, this is hooey. The technology has now caught up with the first problem, as Denis Villeneuve's Oscar-winning interpretation of Frank Herbert's science-fiction epic showed (I still have a soft spot for David Lynch's barmy, far less successful *Dune*). *Ulysses* has been filmed too, fairly successfully, by Joseph Strick, who remembered thinking 'It's written like a movie' when he first read the book, and turned it into an extremely 1960s piece of moody avant-garde mixed with kitchen sink drama.*

*Catch 22*, *The Lord of the Rings*, *His Dark Materials*, *Cloud Atlas*, Thomas Pynchon's twisty metafictions, Henry James's novels of consciousness: so many unfilmables have been proved no such thing. Even *Don Quixote* made it to screen courtesy of Terry Gilliam, first with the 2002 documentary *Lost in La Mancha*, which chronicled how his doomed attempt to (yes, quixotically) film Miguel de Cervantes's 1,000-page-plus doorstopper was beset by calamities including his leading actor suffering a herniated disc, NATO jets ruining the sound and unexpected floods in the Spanish desert. Gilliam finally made his film, *The Man*

---

wanted to make an animated film titled *Dufus*, with German Shepherd dogs!

* It became notorious for its use of the word 'fuck', and, amazingly, I discovered, was banned in Ireland until 2000. Ireland's film censor at the time, Sheamus Smith, said, 'The ban is being lifted now because nobody thought to bring it back before.'

*Who Killed Don Quixote* in 2018, with Jonathan Pryce and Adam Driver in the leading roles, showing both relentless determination and a shocking disregard for the perfect image of life imitating art.

If a director has the vision to pull it off (and manages to avoid biblical plagues on set), every book is adaptable. I would like to throw one spanner in the works, though. You could call it the Psmith problem. It's when a writer's words are so enjoyable on the page, with their own special 'word music', as Douglas Adams said of P. G. Wodehouse, that it seems hard to replicate that particular pleasure on screen. This could be because the joke is in the reading, such as Wodehouse's recurring character Rupert Psmith, who has added the P to his surname to distinguish himself from other Smiths, but always notes that the P is silent, like in pshrimp. (There's a similar joke in Waugh's *Decline and Fall*, with the 'correct' pronunciation of the made-up surname Beste-Chetwynde being 'Beast-Cheating', lampooning the ruling classes' love of excluding the proles with all their Beauchamps, Cholmondeleys and Featherstonehaughs.)

Sometimes the pleasure, especially in Waugh, simply comes from 'the order in which the words, and the information they carry, are arranged', as David Lodge notes. Lodge points out the passage in *Decline and Fall* where Paul Pennyfeather has been debagged by the drunken toffs of Oxford's Bollinger Club: '"God damn and blast them all to hell," said Paul Pennyfeather meekly to himself as he drove to the station, and then he felt rather ashamed, because he rarely swore.' It's the placing of 'meekly' that hits home. There are similarly subtle joys to be found in the pages of Barbara Pym's novels about doughty church spinsters. Lines like 'I am not at all like Jane Eyre, who must have given hope to so many plain women who tell their stories in the first person', and 'people like us had to rely on the tea-urn' from *Excellent Women* made me laugh out loud, but I wasn't sure I could ever imagine Pym on screen.*

Perhaps one answer to the Psmith problem is 'make it a musical'. Damon Runyon, whose tales of Broadway hustlers became the evergreen *Guys and Dolls*, had such a distinctive, slangy style that it became known as Runyonese. Adam Gopnik calls it 'street ornate ... the pages stop turning while we admire the sentences'. Typical sentences include:

> One evening along about seven o'clock I am sitting in Mindy's restaurant putting on the gefilte fish, which is a dish I am very fond of, when in come three parties from Brooklyn wearing caps as follows: Harry the Horse, Little Isadore and Spanish John.

It's irresistible on the page, and somehow the screenwriter Abe Burrows, a Latin scholar, managed to make it sing on stage too. According to one of the show's producers, 'Abe understood the problem and fiddled with the tenses and contractions and adapted the dialogue so cleverly that you were fooled into thinking that you were hearing Runyon.'† In the same way, Anita

* Then lo, I read that a UK production company had acquired the rights to this novel, with the producer saying, 'I look forward to creating a "Pymverse" and bringing this iconic author's uniquely British tales of comic observation and unrequited love ... to a wider TV audience.' I live in hope.

† *Guys and Dolls* is not only the Great American Musical, it is also a textbook example of what musical numbers should do: the 'plan song' ('Luck Be a Lady'), the 'I AM song' ('Guys and Dolls'), the 'allies song' ('Sit Down, You're Rockin' the Boat'). It's pleasingly perfect.

Loos's *Gentlemen Prefer Blondes*, the divinely misspelt diary of girl-about-town Lorelei Lee ('the Eyeful Tower' is 'devine') was turned into frothy song-and-dance numbers; her observation that 'kissing your hand may make you feel very, very good but a diamond-and-safire bracelet lasts for ever' becoming one of the most iconic scenes in movie history.

The acknowledged master of American slang in recent decades (whose novels I can't imagine being made into musicals, but never say never) is the crime thriller writer Elmore Leonard. With his pared-back style ('leave out the parts that readers tend to skip', he quipped) and his focus on dialogue and action, he's often described as one of the most cinematic authors in the English language. To date, more than twenty of his novels and stories have been adapted for film and TV – but what's surprising is how few of them are actually any good.

The successful ones include the early westerns *3:10 to Yuma* and *Hombre*, Steven Soderbergh's *Out of Sight*, with George Clooney and Jennifer Lopez, and Quentin Tarantino's *Jackie Brown*, based on *Rum Punch*, starring a transcendent Pam Grier as the gun-smuggling air steward and Robert Forster as the soulful bail bondsman who falls for her. (I think these last two work because they acknowledge that Leonard doesn't just write about cool, funny criminals, but about jaded people with a lot of baggage who still get the hots for each other.) The mediocre ones are numerous, much to Leonard's disappointment. He said the 1969 adaptation of his crime novel *The Big Bounce* was 'the second-worst movie ever made', and it wasn't until he saw the 2004 remake that he knew what the worst was.*

* Another lowlight was *Be Cool*, featuring the horror of Vince Vaughn as a jive-talking gangster, which is something nobody should ever have to witness.

I think the reason there are so many Leonard flops is that some adapters forget his style is laid-back as well as pared-back. Look at one of his many excellent first lines, in this case from *Freaky Deaky*: 'Chris Mankowski's last day on the job, two in the afternoon, two hours to go, he got a call to dispose of a bomb.' All those sub-clauses slow you down as you read, with their own special swinging rhythm, 'as American as jazz ... a kind of marijuana tense, creamy, wandering' (Martin Amis). This fancy talk needs subtly reworking for the screen. It can't be taken lightly. According to journalist Noah Taylor, 'screenwriters come along thinking Leonard has already done their job for them, resulting in half-assed retellings'.

For the greatest example of pleasure on the page not necessarily equating to pleasure on screen, we come to that Great Unfilmable, *The Great Gatsby*. To quote the *New York Times*, it's 'practically conventional wisdom that Fitzgerald's novel is unfilmable, because its real power comes not from the plot but the prose'. There's something about his style, at once burnished (Sarah Churchwell calls it 'art deco opera') and elliptical, that successive filmmakers have found difficult to translate into film language.

I can see why they try, though. *The Great Gatsby* is huge. Although considered a failure in Fitzgerald's lifetime, the novel became a hit when copies were given to US servicemen in the Second World War, and its popularity has grown ever since. Now, a hundred years after publication, it's acknowledged as one of the Great American Novels, a mainstay of school reading lists, with millions of copies sold globally every year and therefore an eager audience for any new adaptation (or musical, such as the one that recently finished its run in London).

It also, with a kind of spooky poetic symmetry, feels uncomfortably spot on for our age of mindless ambition, vast fortunes and rich, unaccountable bullies. When Donald Trump hosted, yes, a *Great Gatsby*-themed party at Mar-a-Lago, this was Jon Stewart's response:

> The slogan of the party, as people were losing their food benefits was, I shit you not, 'a little party never killed nobody.' Did you even read *The Great Gatsby*?! Spoiler alert, the party killed somebody! Two-bodies! How do you not know that? I knew that, and I've only read the Cliff notes.

It's no wonder that everyone started sharing the novel's famous quotation on social media: 'They were careless people ... they smashed up things and creatures and then retreated back into their money or their vast carelessness, or whatever it was that kept them together, and let other people clean up the mess they had made.' I should say that the careless people in *The Great Gatsby* are the old-money couple Tom and Daisy Buchanan. Gatsby, born a poor farm boy, was once Daisy's lover and has amassed an illegal fortune in order to reinvent himself and win her back. When they rekindle their affair, Daisy accidentally kills someone in a hit-and-run, after which the Buchanans flee, leaving Gatsby to death and ruin. This tawdry tale is seen through the eyes of the narrator, Nick Carraway, as he is at first intrigued, then dazzled, then revolted by Gatsby.

*The Great Gatsby* is like a death wish for America, showing the hollowness of the myth of the self-made man, and the great crimes beneath great fortunes – a theme that's been played out in its culture ever since, from *The Godfather* to *Mad Men*. Fitzgerald was adamant that he was making a study of how money corrupts, saying, 'I have never been able to forgive the rich for being rich, and it has colored my entire life and works.'

As Sarah Churchwell notes, 'For people who think it's about parties, read it again.' (There are only three parties in the novel, and one of them is a seedy little gathering where Tom breaks his mistress's nose.)

The reason filmmakers turn to it, however, *is* the parties. They become Nick Carraway, dazzled by the Jazz Age extravagance and glamour, the Charlestons and bobs and pearls. It's as if luscious prose has to translate to luscious visuals, or, in the case of Baz Luhrmann, a hyperactive toddler who has eaten too many sweets and thrown them up. The *New Yorker* said that *Gatsby* is 'too intricate, too subtle, too tender for the movies' and, while it's perfect in its structure and pacing, I'm not sure I would say it's a subtle novel. There is melodrama and murder, and heavy symbolism of despoilation and corruption abounds, such as the dirt heaps of the desolate 'Valley of Ashes' surrounding New York's wealth.

It's not a tragic love story either. Gatsby isn't chasing a woman; he is chasing money. We learn that 'It excited him, too, that many men had already loved Daisy – it increased her value in his eyes', and that, when they were young, 'He took Daisy one still October night, took her because he had no real right to touch her hand ... He had intended, probably, to take what he could and go – but now he found that he had committed himself to the following of a grail.' When *Gatsby* gets filmed, however, there is too much emphasis on romantic yearning, not enough on ugly grasping, too much on the beautiful, not enough on the damned.

In the words of veteran film critic Philip French, 'F. Scott Fitzgerald did more for Hollywood than it has done for him.' He moved to Tinseltown in the 1930s and worked on several screenplays, including a failed stint on *Gone with the Wind*, and the movies also inspired his unfinished novel *The Last Tycoon* and the short stories about washed-up hack Pat Hobby, who once enjoyed great success in Hollywood during 'the mosaic swimming-pool age'.* In return, Hollywood has gifted Fitzgerald with a series of substandard versions of his greatest novel.

The first was a silent film from 1926 that has since been lost, although we do know that after the Fitzgeralds attended a screening, Zelda wrote to their daughter saying it was 'ROTTEN and awful and terrible and we left.' It didn't get much better with the first surviving version, a 1949 noir thriller that contains some lumpen moralising, including Nick delivering biblical homilies over Gatsby's grave at the start.

Fast-forward to the 1970s and the film rights had reverted to Fitzgerald's daughter, who, according to producer Robert Evans, 'said she never again wanted to see her father's masterpiece as a movie'. But Evans had an incentive to buy them: his then-wife Ali McGraw had loved *The Great Gatsby* since childhood and it was her lasting dream to play Daisy. The deal was done and Truman Capote was brought on board to write the screenplay – 'I know just the way to bring all that purple prose to the screen!' he allegedly said. But in the end Mia Farrow got the part of Daisy (according to Evans, she lobbied for it with a letter containing a pressed daisy), and Francis Ford Coppola got the gig of adapting. He confessed that he was 'terrified' by the task, and it shows in the resulting 1974 film, starring Robert Redford, which is reverential, faithful, beautiful and somnambulant – also,

* Apparently, Fitzgerald approached every screenplay as if it were a novel, with pages of backstories. Billy Wilder described him as 'a great sculptor who is hired to do a plumbing job. He did not know how to connect the pipes so the water could flow.'

for some reason everyone looks disturbingly sweaty in it.* To quote Aaron Sorkin on his first, failed attempts at adaptation, 'I tried to swaddle the book in bubblewrap ... You have to fall out of love with the source material and try to make it your own.'

In Evans's words, 'Fitzgerald ain't easy to lick'. At the other end of the spectrum, we have Baz Luhrmann's deliberately irreverent 2013 *Gatsby* on speed, with Leonardo DiCaprio as the titular hero. I am not a Baz hater: *Strictly Ballroom* is one of my favourite films, although I'm less of a fan of *Moulin Rouge* as I like my musicals to feature stars who can actually sing and dance and pronounce 'Moulin' properly. Like Ken Russell, Luhrmann is enraptured by excess and visual splendour, so his *Gatsby* is party central, swooping, exhausting and deliberately anachronistic, with a Jay-Z and Lana Del Rey soundtrack.† As *Empire* said, he 'cuts straight to the surface of the story. Welcome to the Bazz Age.'

My problem was that, Brexit style, it wanted to have its cake and eat it. 'Isn't this fun, isn't it, isn't it?' scream the frantic party scenes. But the film also wants to remind us that this is a Very Important Work of Literature, and in doing so spells out key passages from the book in typewriter-letters on screen as they are being narrated by Nick. The result is heavy handed and

---

* Mia Farrow's performance is weirdly irritating, and there's a lack of chemistry with Redford, which was blamed on his fixation with watching the Watergate scandal while locked in his trailer – two years later he'd play one of the reporters who broke the story in *All the President's Men*.

† *The Great Gatsby*'s parties look awful, unlike the humdinger of a party at the start of Paolo Sorrentino's masterpiece *The Great Beauty*, which I really want to go to every time I see it.

hollow, the polar opposite of Hitchcock's dictum that 'A lot of writers think they're filling a page with words, but they're filling a screen with images'. Here, they're literally, not figuratively, filling the screen with words. It's kind of embarrassing. The film's saving grace for me was DiCaprio, who can't be bad in anything, although he still plays Gatsby as vulnerable rather than calculating and, well, rapey. For me, the novel is as romantic as its dust heaps and Gatsby is a man stalking a woman. *The Great Gatsby* as a horror thriller? I'd pay to see that.

# 17

# THE UNWATCHABLES: DIVINE DISASTERS

'Movies are so rarely great art that if we cannot appreciate great trash, we have very little reason to be interested in them'

Pauline Kael

Cinema can be a beautiful, awe-inspiring, even transcendental experience. For some filmmakers, it's akin to religion. 'There's a spirituality in films … you want to possess people on film. You want to live through them. You want to possess their spirits,' said Martin Scorsese. Ingmar Bergman described it as 'corresponding with the world around me in a language that is literally spoken from soul to soul'. Something tells me they weren't thinking of Kevin Costner's post-apocalyptic bomb *The Postman*, Madonna's inane train-wreck *Shanghai Surprise* or a host of other Razzie-winning adaptations, though. Or *Cats*.

For those of us who love being hooked to the silver screen (even if the film is a saddening bore), there is an irresistible, rubbernecking joy that comes from terrible films. As Roger Ebert acknowledged, saying, 'After reviewing a truly good movie, the second most fun is viewing a truly bad one.' Perhaps it's even a masochistic pleasure. I have a very high tolerance for shlock, hokum and shark films. My pain threshold for musicals is almost second to none. I will even defend the ill-fated musical of Colin MacInnes's *Absolute Beginners*, and the madly extravagant Lucille Ball vehicle *Mame*, based on Patrick Dennis's highly camp novel, *Auntie Mame*, although I did walk out of one movie musical – The Greatest Shitshow, I think it was called.

There has been plenty of trash scattered throughout this book, but now we come to the big swill bucket of movie adaptations. Some of these can be classed as flops, i.e. they lost money, some as turkeys, i.e. everyone hated them. Some are both, and some are neither. My only rule is that they have to turn a good literary source into a bad film. For this reason I rejected some now camp cult classics – such as the sleaze-fest *Myra Breckinridge*, based on Gore Vidal's satirical novel, which he called the worst film ever made, or the biblical epic *The Silver Chalice*, so bad that Paul Newman took out a trade ad apologising for his performance, or *The Room*, Tommy Wiseau's notorious, logic-free indie catastrophe, based on a 500-page novel he never got published, and now screened complete with plastic cutlery for audiences to throw at it – because none of the sources were masterpieces in the first place.*

Without further ado, let's venture into my rogue's gallery of adaptations gone wrong, a non-magnificent seven. Prepare for

* Vidal's sex-fluid, absurdist novel of a trans woman who wreaks violent revenge on the patriarchy is undergoing a *bit* of a critical reassessment now, however, as it seems to speak so well to our times – although it's still basically insane.

tears, tantrums, acts of God, oversized egos and overinflated budgets. Prepare for what happens when good books (or poems or plays) get transformed into bad art. Sometimes so-bad-it's-good art. Mostly so-bad-it's-bad.

### Worst *Dracula* Adaptation

'How would you like to go around looking like a head waiter for 700 years?' says George Hamilton, he of the eternal spotless suntan, playing Dracula in the vampire spoof *Love at First Bite*.* Ever since the publication of Stoker's novel in 1897 – in fact, just before it too, as the first play, adapted by Stoker, had a reading eight days in advance – our mental image of the bloodthirsty Count has been infected by adaptation. The white tie and swirling cape come from Bela Lugosi on Broadway, a stage role he would then recreate on film in 1931. Dracula's allergy to daylight came from the unauthorised 1922 adaptation *Nosferatu*; the fangs, allegedly, from a 1953 Turkish film called *Dracula in Istanbul*; the debonair, dynamic, lustful Count from Christopher Lee's many Hammer Horror outings.† Dracula has become an immortal, genre-defining archetype, an 'imperishable brand', in the words of Mark Gatiss, with the undead given fresh blood with each new

* Clive James described Hamilton's performance as 'the only Dracula who was ever intentionally funny'. Good one-liners from the film include 'I'm going out to get a bite to drink'.

† As Matthew Sweet says in *Shepperton Babylon*, 'few horror actors can have exerted more influence on the genre'. Lee became increasingly jaded by his role, but kept going because of phone calls from Hammer executives telling him hundreds of staff would be put out of work if he didn't: 'It was a form of blackmail really.'

incarnation – or in some cases floating free of the horror genre entirely.*

There are literally hundreds of *Dracula* adaptations, so it makes sense that, given the law of averages, many of them are very bad indeed (in fact, this entire section could have been made up of awful Counts). There are, naturally, porn versions, including *Dracula Sucks*. Some adaptations embrace the novel's inherent campness, such as the Andy Warhol-produced, giallo--influenced *Blood for Dracula* (starring a very hot Count, Udo Kier, and an equally hot vampire hunter, Joe Dallesandro, whose naked bottom features heavily), *Dracula AD 1972*, which thrusts poor Christopher Lee into a swinging London of hotpants and hipster satanists, and 2004's *Van Helsing*, all unnecessary crashing through windows on ropes, with even ropier CGI wolves, pony tails and overripe accents. Some are just bad, including the woeful *Dracula 3D*, even sadder because it was made by horror maestro Dario Argento; the smug, sour Steven Moffat miniseries; and the abysmal *Dracula 2000*, where a confused-looking Gerard Butler is Dracula but also Judas Iscariot. Or something. (There's even a comedy spinoff featuring the fly-eating minion, *Renfield*, where Nicolas Cage, kitsch king of 'scorched-earth acting', tears his fangs into the scenery as the ultimate bad boss.)

My most divinely disastrous Dracula adaptation, however, is *Bram Stoker's Dracula*, directed by Francis Ford Coppola. I understand that there is much love for this 1992 film, and there's a huge amount to admire in its sumptuous, maximalist

* It's no wonder, as Dracula was born from Stoker's research into oral folklore, and from a dream he had after eating some dressed crab; the perfect ingredients for an immortal fear myth, or as the critic Maurice Richardson put it, an 'incestuous, necrophilous, oral-anal-sadistic all-in-wrestling match'.

aesthetics and magical, old-school special effects, as well as some barnstorming performances by Gary Oldman as an outrageous, razor-licking Count (wearing what looks like a stuffed Playtex bra on his head), and Anthony Hopkins in eyeliner as Van Helsing.* I think this is what makes it worse for me. The ambitions are so grand, but the results are so frustrating; overlong, overreaching and overstuffed.

Its main crime, however, is to turn Dracula into a tragic romantic hero, who (this doesn't appear in the novel) has returned to claim Mina, the reincarnation of his lost wife. This isn't the first Dracula in love – *Nosferatu* staked that claim. But it is the first where we are asked to believe that Mina would be tempted to the dark side by someone who, with his little round sunglasses and long hair, looks like Ozzy Osbourne in a top hat, when she has sweet, sweet Keanu waiting at home. Gary Oldman is at his best playing sweary, rowdy tykes, such as Sid Vicious or Jackson Lamb, or directing the outstanding *Nil by Mouth*. He's just not a romantic lead.† What's worse, by trying to make Dracula someone to 'root for', this film ushered in a host of weedy, soulful *Twilight* vampires who merely twinkle rather than burst into flames. Unforgivable. It's 'a mess, but it's the kind of mess that only a great filmmaker makes', to quote Quentin Tarantino. It's the perfect description of this film, although he was actually talking about the next film on my list.

* The film's stunning effects were created after Coppola famously fired his original team due to their insistence on deploying CGI, hiring his son Roman instead to deliver old-fashioned, practical effects inspired by Méliès and the dawn of cinema.

† Or a hero: his Churchill is my least favourite; the best is John Lithgow in *The Crown*.

**Worst Adaptation of a Mainstream Literary Bestseller**
'The book was insanely popular. But think about it. What were one million readers or even two or three? That would make for a literary phenomenon. But it wouldn't even register a movie's existence.' With these words, writer Julie Salamon gets to the rub of why Brian De Palma's *The Bonfire of the Vanities* became one of the most calamitous adaptations of all time – and why it's so hard to adapt a mainstream literary bestseller in general. These are the sort of acclaimed, prize-winning novels that also happen to sell millions. In publishing terms it's the dream, but to replicate that level of success at the box office, their film incarnations need to be seen by many, many more millions, so the pressure's immediately on to create a prestige project that will also, somehow, appeal to a broad audience.

There are some successes in this field, such as the well-received *The Kite Runner*, *The English Patient* or *Life of Pi*, or long-running series like Netflix's *One Hundred Years of Solitude*. Few of them are likely to make it to the best films of all time lists, though. Often they feel weighed down with expectation, such as the airless *Enduring Love*. Sometimes the film highlights the worst qualities of what was often pretty melodramatic in the first place, such as *Where the Crawdads Sing*. In the case of *Captain Corelli's Mandolin*, the literary sensation of the 1990s, the problem was woeful miscasting – Penélope Cruz as the Greek heroine Pelagia and, our regular in this section, Nicolas Cage, as the titular captain – resulting in a soup of accents that ranged from 'whatsamatta you' Italian to a Scouse Nazi. Frequently, subtleties are squashed: with 2026's inexplicable hit *Hamnet*, a lyrical, light-touch novel became a superficial, heavy-handed piece of Oscar fodder, featuring a 'Re*lax* with Classic FM' soundtrack and overwrought, teary performances that made me think of *Team America*'s 'I'm going to save the entire world by acting!' (Also, *Hamlet* was *not* set in a forest.) The other problem with these sorts of novels is that, invariably, film reviewers have read them (or have at least pretended to), so that if and when the scorn comes, it is unforgiving.

With *The Bonfire of the Vanities*, it was a perfect storm of everything that could conceivably go wrong, and then some. If you haven't read the novel then this is just a pretty poor, tonally strange movie, with the occasional good scene. If you have read the book, it is a travesty. It deserves its place here not just because of that, but because it also yielded Julie Salamon's bestseller, *The Devil's Candy*, documenting the troubled making of the film, which is the most unputdownable book ever written about a Hollywood flop.

It may have been 'the most famous book in the world' in the 1980s, but initially nobody wanted to adapt Tom Wolfe's seething, roaring beast of a blockbuster about greed, inequality and racial tension in New York City. You can see why. Everyone in the novel is awful – venal, lustful, corrupt, like a walking parade of deadly sins – and everyone, Black, WASP, Jewish, is treated with equal contempt by the author, whether they are the 'master of the universe' Wall Street trader Sherman McCoy, who, after taking a wrong turn to the Bronx with his mistress, fatally injures a young Black man called Henry Lamb and sets his own downfall in motion; the celebrity pastor Reverend Bacon, who exploits the tragedy for his own gain; or Peter Fallow, the dissolute tabloid hack who makes a fortune from the story.*

The other problem is that the plot is the least interesting

* The *New York Times* brilliantly summed its message up as 'All men are born trashy. Those few who aren't have trashiness thrust upon them.'

thing about the book. It's memorable for Wolfe's detailed, fetishistic documenting of the grossness of an age, and his trippy, strange language.* A laugh is 'Heh-heggggggggggggggghh hhhhhhhhhhhhh!' At a party: 'Such ecstasy on all sides! Such radiant eyes and fireproof grins! So many boiling teeth! Hack hack hack hack hack hack hack, Inez Bavardage's laugh rose in social triumph. Haw haw haw haw haw haw haw haw haw, the Golden Hillbilly's barnyard bray rose in response.' It's the old Psmith problem again.

The book also, incidentally, contains one of the best descriptions of a hangover I've read:

> Ah! The membranous sac was his head, and the right side of his head was on the pillow, and the yolk was as heavy as mercury, and it rolled like mercury, and it was pressing down on his right temple and his right eye and his right ear. If he tried to get up to answer the telephone, the yolk, the mercury, the poisoned mass, would shift and roll and rupture the sac, and his brains would fall out.

Wolfe himself found the idea of a film unfathomable, although, as he told Salamon over breakfast at the Carlyle Hotel (during which, she noted, he wore a three-piece suit and ate three bowls of cereal with stewed fruit!), 'I did cash the check.' The resulting production has entered Hollywood disaster lore as a kind of primer on how not to adapt a bestseller. The biggest mistake was Warner Bros. execs' insistence on casting well-known stars in

* He deliberately modelled his method of 'highly detailed realism based on reporting' on Dickens – it's no accident both started out as journalists – serialising the work in *Rolling Stone* before reworking it as a novel.

an attempt to make Wolfe's unredeemable characters 'likeable', with Tom Hanks as Sherman McCoy (a move even he described as 'a huge, massive crapshoot'), Uma Thurman passed over as his mistress Maria for Melanie Griffith, who got breast implants during the shoot and ruined the continuity, and, worst of all, Peter Fallow, a dissipated, desiccated husk of a drunken British sleazebag, played by Bruce Willis – luckily he wears glasses so we know he's a writer. The problem is compounded because Willis also narrates the film, which just made me think of his turn as a baby in *Look Who's Talking* (if only).

Production was notoriously hellish – cast and crew were pelted with eggs and lightbulbs from nearby Bronx rooftops; Willis tried to direct the other actors and changed the lighting so that his bald patch wouldn't have to be sprayed continually with black powder; everything went over budget, including $2 million on a swordfighting scene that was never used. Then again, many nightmare shoots have resulted in masterpieces. This just wasn't one of them.

The resulting film strips away everything that makes the book interesting, and leaves us with broad, cartoonish slapstick instead of raging satirical madness (although there's a really great, unbroken tracking shot at the start). It flopped, fatally, reviews called it things like 'Bombfire', and it became a byword for Hollywood excess – and, irony of ironies, vanity. Salamon remained loyally affectionate to all those she had seen at work, and was adamant that no one knew they had a stone-cold turkey on their hands until it was too late. De Palma still stands by it, as 'An interesting movie that I like. It is not Tom Wolfe's *Bonfire of the Vanities*. The problem is that everyone that wrote about the movie, read the book.'

**Worst Adaptation Featuring Talking Animals**

We're really spoilt for choice with the mangy menagerie of awful films on offer here. They say never work with children or animals, but when the animals are talking, the likelihood of a disaster seems even greater – and when the animals pee on your feet too, it's catastrophe time.

Said peeing was just part of the unbelievable catalogue of calamities that befell the cursed 1967 big-budget musical *Doctor Dolittle*, the first in what would become a doomed franchise based on Hugh Lofting's novel about a man who can talk to animals. This legendary flop featured thousands of live animals and, even worse, Rex Harrison, notorious as one of the most horrible men in Hollywood.* The animals peed and shat everywhere, including on Harrison, a goat ate a script and, mind-bendingly, an angry resident, explorer Ranulph Fiennes, tried to blow up a dam that had been constructed on a local trout stream.† The film almost bankrupted Fox and, along with *Cleopatra*, became infamous as the death knell for the bloated studio system, but that didn't stop more dismal Dolittles. Eddie Murphy took on the role in some late 1990s goofy family capers, then Robert Downey Jr. (sporting a baffling Welsh accent Mark Kermode described as 'something from Mars') in *Dolittle*, which was reshot after test audiences hated it but, despite voice actors including Emma Thompson and Ralph Fiennes (a distant

* Harrison was a bully on set and a sociopath off it, loathed by everyone he worked with. When an autograph hunter assaulted him for his rudeness while filming *My Fair Lady*, co-star Stanley Holloway allegedly called the incident 'the fan hitting the shit'.

† For more juicy details on this and other colossal flops, read Tim Robey's excellent *Box Office Poison*.

cousin of the saboteur Ranulph, weirdly), remains charmless and unpleasant – a particular lowlight was Dolittle removing some bagpipes from the anus of a dragon.

This flogging of a dead horse is not the winner of my benighted category, however. Neither is it that flogging of a fat cat, the increasingly inane Garfield franchise, a series of greedy, lazy films based on the comic strip about a greedy, lazy cat.* The winner is not even Andy Serkis's roundly lambasted 2025 animation of George Orwell's *Animal Farm*, which turned this savage, Swiftian satire into a knockabout comedy featuring Seth Rogen as a gangsta pig wearing sunglasses while driving a pink sports car, after he's been tempted into betraying his animal comrades by evil corporate magnates.† Unlike the *Telegraph*, however, I wasn't particularly upset by this film making capitalists the villains – it's one in the eye for all the 'what would Orwell do?' T-shirt-wearing Musk idiots who think that because he critiqued Stalin, the lifelong democratic socialist Orwell was somehow rightwing. It's more that they thought Orwell needed fart jokes. I mean, show trials and purges are just made for them, right?

Yet even this nightmare is not my winner of worst adaptation featuring talking animals. It's *Cats*. Of course it is! Yes, technically, Tom Hooper's 2019 disaster movie is based on a stage musical that's based on a book of poetry, T. S. Eliot's *Old Possum's*

* In two early films he was voiced by Bill Murray sounding jaded, even for him, and later by Chris Pratt, proving that it is possible for somebody to sound even wearier than Bill.

† X went into meltdown: 'Animation servers powered by George Orwell spinning in his grave', said one. 'Thank god someone was finally able to remove the gravity from the story and reimagine it as the slapstick Orwell always intended but could not achieve.'

*Book of Practical Cats*, rather than a novel, but it has more than earned its place in this line-up of freakish fauna. I should start by confessing that I have been a secret fan of Andrew Lloyd Webber's deeply uncool musical, Jellicle Balls and all, ever since I saw it on stage as a youth. I stand by its catchy earworm songs, despite the admittedly odd juxtaposition of 1930s ditties about crocheting with rock opera.* So I was primed, as one of the few people in the world who might enjoy this experience.†

I did not enjoy this experience, despite its astounding cast of Jennifer Hudson, Idris Elba, Dame Judi Dench, Ian McKellen and, okay… James Corden. In fact, I started wondering, around the moment Rebel Wilson in a fat furry cat suit began to eat a troupe of dancing cockroaches, whether somebody had spiked my drink. By the time the credits rolled, I wished they had. I was prepared for weirdness, but this was just *so* weird. It's the cats themselves. When you see the musical on stage, the effect of human beings in cat suits and cat make-up doing incredible acrobatic dancing is pretty exciting – honestly. When you see it on film, with unconvincing 'digital fur technology' that makes everyone look like a genital-less half-breed of cat people, it's wrong and terrifying.‡ Lloyd Webber described it as 'ghastly'

* I didn't even hate the 2004 Joel Schumacher film of Lloyd Webber's *The Phantom of the Opera*, unlike most people.

† I did, however, hate Hooper's miserable *Les Misérables* – who thought it was a good idea to have live singing in a musical, especially when half the cast can't sing? I want magic unrealism from my musicals.

‡ The unfairly rounded-on effects staff worked ninety-hour weeks to get the fur finished, but, under virtual slave labour conditions, still ran out of time so that things like wedding rings and watches could still be seen, leading the production company to send a new, upgraded version of the film to cinemas two weeks *after* it had been released.

and 'off-the-scale all wrong', and bought an emotional support dog because he was so traumatised by the experience.

Please let the memory never live again.

### Worst Erotic Thriller

Ooh, the erotic thriller, that spicy 1980s/'90s genre featuring murder, suspense and softcore sex, often in lifts or upon kitchen surfaces (why do people always have sex like this in movies? Is it easier to film?), and black-and-white posters showing ladies with their mouths open mid-ecstasy. They also, as the critic Ellen E. Jones has noted, often have adjective-noun titles: *Basic Instinct*, *Fatal Attraction*, *Indecent Proposal*, *Jagged Edge* – leading her to speculate that she might create her own addition to the genre called *Intimate Requirements*. These stylised, lurid, male-gazey films, at their height, hit a sweet spot of home video and DVD watching before internet streaming made such pleasures redundant, and before intimacy coordinators, rightly, made everyone calm down a bit (especially as stars like Sharon Stone have now talked about their own unpleasant, possibly coercive, experiences on set). As the podcaster Karina Longworth has noted, these are 'movies that take sex seriously, maybe too seriously'.

Sometimes, however, they are neither erotic nor thrilling. An obvious contender for my hall of infamy would be 1993's *Sliver*, which reunited 'cinema sex goddess of the 90s' (*Premier*) Sharon Stone with *Basic Instinct* screenwriter Joe Eszterhas, but with far less gripping results. Based on one of Ira Levin's many taut, effective chillers to make it to screen (others include *Rosemary's Baby*, *The Boys from Brazil* and *The Stepford Wives*), this creepy, on-trend story about secret surveillance and voyeurism in a high-rise apartment seemed a sure-fire hit, but ended up a colossal flop, with director Phillip Noyce forced to make extensive reshoots in order to get an R rating, and the entire ending – and identity of the film's killer – being changed. The original finale would have seen Stone and her co-star William Baldwin flying a helicopter into a volcano together; we can but dream. Another horror from the same era is 1994's *Disclosure*, based on Michael Crichton's bestseller about the corporate world of hi-tech virtual reality software, where erotic stalwart Michael Douglas is pipped to a promotion and then falsely accused of sexual harassment by 'ballbreaker' Demi Moore. To say it hasn't travelled is an understatement. It's a regressive, reactionary stew of male insecurity about powerful women in the workplace, whose defining ethos seems to be, as one character puts it, 'feminist bullshit has gone too far!' As *Den of Geek* asks, 'has any film of the 90s aged as badly as this one?' Neither of these is my winner, though, as they are based on sources that could be described as workmanlike rather than masterly.*

No, the crown goes to 2022's *Deep Water*, in which erotic thriller *capo di capi* Adrian Lyne (he of *9½ Weeks*, *Flashdance* and *Fatal Attraction*) serves up the worst adaptation of a Patricia Highsmith book ever committed to celluloid. The novel is an icy, cruel story of a married couple locked in a kind of *folie à deux* of mutual loathing and destruction, circling each other like sharks, as the husband Vic tolerates his wife's many infidelities before he is driven to murder. As superfan Gillian Flynn says, it's about 'in-your-face warfare between husband and wife'.

* *Disclosure* could have also won 'Worst Michael Crichton Adaptation', were it not for 1995's *Congo*, a misguided 'lost world' caper featuring diamonds, lasers, Tim Curry with a Romanian accent, and stuntmen in gorilla costumes, including one who orders a martini on a plane using sign language. It won seven Razzies.

'Melinda is dead and so am I', thinks Vic at the novel's close, smiling to himself.

This is definitely not what we get in Lyne's film. Instead we have a slack-jawed, possibly sedated Ben Affleck, a lot of snails (to be fair, these are in the book) and Ana de Armas slinking lithely around with a series of young beaus, until the ending is changed and she just sort of goes along with her husband murdering them. There is, as befits the genre, a lovely kitchen and a steamy bathtub scene – as Christopher Nolan notes, 'nobody shoots bathrooms like Adrian Lyne'.* But, overall, the film is bleary-eyed, tedious and silly, although not in a good way. Is there any reason to watch it? According to NPR, 'If you've ever wanted to see Ben Affleck look on affectionately while snails slither across his open palm, this is the movie for you.'

**Worst Adaptation of a Classic Novel**

Now we're in dangerous territory. There is something about a novel with 'classic' status that invites adaptations which can be too solemnly reverential, such as the already discussed Coppola *Great Gatsby*, or Peter Bogdanovich's *Daisy Miller*, a stately, sumptuous and 'boringly faithful', to quote one critic, rendering of Henry James's novella, which made its director, and its star Cybill Shepherd, box office poison.† They can also be truly

* From the BBC radio documentary *The Adland Five*, charting the fortunes of five British directors who learned their craft in advertising, honed a visually innovative, hugely commercial style, and changed Hollywood.

† This film has its defenders, such as Tarantino, who blames its failure on the fact that Bogdanovich had left his wife for Shepherd – whom he'd cast in the lead role when she said she loved the book – meaning it was seen as a hubristic vanity project from a man blinded by lust.

silly, such as the little-known and extremely cheap pulp curiosity *Cannibal Women in the Avocado Jungle of Death*, which turns Joseph Conrad's *Heart of Darkness* into a spoof caper starring ex-*Playboy* model Shannon Tweed and, bizarrely, Bill Maher, about a tribe of man-eating feminists. Sometimes, they can just be offensive, such as the awful *Benjamin Button*, which turns a sad, slight F. Scott Fitzgerald short story into a two-hour-forty-minutes schmaltz fest of toe-curling whimsy and bad de-ageing effects.

*The Scarlet Letter*, Roland Joffé's infamous 1995 adaptation of Nathaniel Hawthorne's novel, however, somehow manages to be tedious, silly and offensive all at the same time. It was both a critical and commercial bomb. This Razzie-garlanded offence against film takes a novel about self-knowledge, hypocrisy and quiet dignity in a seventeenth-century Puritan colony (the heroine, Hester Prynne, who is unfaithful to her husband and has an illegitimate child, is forced to wear a red letter 'A' for Adultery) and turns it into a softcore banquet of folly and wrongheadedness. It's now become a regular feature in those 'worst adaptation ever made' lists, and with good reason. The line at the start, 'Freely adapted from Nathaniel Hawthorne's novel', has become a joke in itself.

I'm not sure 'adapted' should even be here. The novel does *not* feature sex on a bed of dried beans, Gary Oldman skinny dipping (another film that mistakes this pale and interesting British actor for a sex god), Demi Moore soaping her boobs in a bath while a servant girl watches her through a glory hole and later indulges in onanism with a candle, Robert Duvall dancing around a fire with a deer carcass on his head, or a last-minute reprieve from the gallows. The film includes all of these.* It also has mad editing, even madder performances, yet still somehow wants to pretend we are in ye olde Puritan times, with lines like 'I love thee!' and ''Tis only a bathing tub' making me laugh out loud. My favourite story about this movie disaster is that Leonard Bernstein's score was rejected, leading him to write to the studio thanking them for the decision, because it meant his name was not associated with the film – talk about dodging a bullet.

**Worst H. G. Wells Adaptation**

This is such a surprisingly crowded field that it warranted its own entry. The novels of H. G. Wells, father of modern science fiction, have yielded a rich and varied legacy of cinematic adaptations because their high concepts (invisibility, Martian invaders and time travel to name just a few) are so applicable to each generation's anxiety about technology. Some of them, including *Things to Come*, *The History of Mr Polly*, the 1960 film *The Time Machine*, and, yes, even *Half a Sixpence*, the riotous musical based on *Kipps*, are classics. Many of them, however, are decidedly not.

According to author Alan Gallop, 'Wells loved everything about movies and moviemaking.' I'm not sure he would have loved many of the following, though. There is the sad little 2002 *Time Machine*, starring a sad-looking Guy Pearce, which transplants the story from London to New York, and adds a romantic subplot. I feel bad because it is directed by H. G.'s great-grandson Simon Wells, but it really isn't very good. On

* Obviously my husband's reaction to this was 'Sounds great! When shall we watch it?'

the plus side, it does provide amusing turns from Jeremy Irons in fright make-up, and Philip Bosco (the 'move your bony ass' boss from *Working Girl*).

It is nothing, however, compared to some of the duds that have resulted from *The War of the Worlds*. First off the mark with a zero per cent Rotten Tomatoes score, we have a solid contender in the 2020s abomination starring Ice Cube as a government agent who saves humanity from an alien invasion without leaving his desk. In what has been called one of the worst movies of the decade, and one of the worst movies ever made, Mr Cube, who unfortunately cannot act, watches things on his laptop and reacts to them, and that's it. I also found Steven Spielberg's updated, US-set film of the same book disappointing because, despite some astounding special effects and good lines ('These came from some place else.' 'What do you mean, like, Europe?'), ultimately it all became a boring family drama. I will, however, defend Jeff Wayne's *War of the Worlds* concept album, later a stage show (of course I've seen it) to the last, because of its appropriately steampunk mood, stonking duh duh duuuuh songs, and David Essex.

But there is one H. G. Wells adaptation that I found myself shouting 'Oh god, no, Jesus Christ! No! Christ!' at, like Sergeant Howie in *The Wicker Man*, when I saw it. This is 1996's infamous *The Island of Dr. Moreau* (according to Mark Kermode, 'arguably the stupidest film of that decade'). It's the Ozymandias of adaptations, where we behold the mighty ambitions and budgets and just despair. The third adaptation of Wells's novel of a messianic scientist who violates the laws of nature and creates animal/human half-breeds on a remote tropical island, this is a story of madness and overreaching ambition, both of which can be used to describe the shoot itself – one so bad it was documented in the film *Lost Soul: The Doomed Journey of Richard Stanley's The Island of Dr. Moreau*. For director Richard Stanley, this had been a years-long passion project, for which he'd landed a sizeable budget from New Line Cinemas. But when they reached the Australian rain forest to start filming, everything went wrong. Tropical storms inundated the set, Stanley got thrown off the production (but later managed to sneak back in as an extra), the leading actor begged to be released from the 'complete insanity' to his agent and was replaced by David Thewlis at the last minute, Val Kilmer was a 'prep-school bully' and, to top it all, Marlon Brando caused havoc, refusing to learn his lines and receiving them through an earpiece instead (according to Thewlis he could also pick up local police radio), sporting white kabuki make-up and an actual ice bucket on his head, and having the world's smallest man appear next to him in every scene, wearing the same outfit – this was later parodied with Mini-Me in the Austin Powers films. The result is an offensive, freakish, surreal circus, which can best be summed up by a line from Thewlis that appears in the film: 'This is the most outrageous spectacle I have ever witnessed!'

**Worst Shakespeare Adaptation**

I admit I felt a bit 'do I have to?' when it came to writing about Shakespeare, like a teenager who doesn't want to do their homework (aside from the fact that this book is mostly about novels and short stories). But I think it's worth it, because of what this most adapted of playwrights tells us about adaptation itself. According to Shakespeare scholar Emma Smith, it's the gaps in his work that keep drawing us to him, inviting us to fill them in with our own spins and interpretations. 'Shakespeare's plays are incomplete, woven of what's said and what's unsaid, with holes in between,' she says. 'We don't know what his characters look like, and, apart from the barest of stage directions, we don't know anything else about them outside of their words. Gappiness is Shakespeare's dominant and defining characteristic. And ambiguity is the oxygen of these works, making them alive in unpredictable and changing ways. It's we, and our varied engagement, that makes Shakespeare.'

There's something else too. Because Shakespeare rewrote existing stories and myths, it means there is something impure about his plays that invites more of the same. As Smith notes, his audiences didn't want originality:

> Ideas of originality have a high status in twenty-first-century ideas of art, but that's not the case for the sixteenth century. A humanist education system suspicious of novelty … taught generations of playwrights and poets that translating, reworking and rewriting existing texts was the sign of the artist. For readers and audiences, this intellectual method known as *imitatio* also offered the particular in-crowd pleasure of spotting those sources and appreciating the craft and invention worked on them.

Is it really that different to our culture's much-derided appetite for reimaginings, retreads and regurgitations today, as we settle down to something familiar and spot the references and Easter eggs? It's a consoling idea, although I do wish today's remakes were less 'once more, without feeling'. Why not remake some bad films instead of good ones? I find it interesting that in a game of 'the best of films, the worst of films', so many remakes go from sublime to terrible: the original *The Wicker Man* and its dire offspring, starring, yes, Nicolas Cage; the original *The*

*Haunting*, from Shirley Jackson's novel, and the execrable 1990s version; even, I hate to say it, the original *West Side Story* and Spielberg's update, which seemed to forget that singing and dancing aren't add-ons in musicals; they are the essential language of the art form. Instead, while fixing some of the original's flaws, he added his own, stuffing it with extra backstory. Romeo and Juliet don't go on a date, they're Romeo and Juliet!*

This isn't my worst Shakespeare, however – nor is it Franco Zeffirelli's action-packed 1990 *Hamlet*, where Mel Gibson's Aussie accent poking through is something to behold.† No, it's *Gonks Go Beat*, a happily now-forgotten 1960s musical of *Romeo and Juliet*, which, according to film historian I. Q. Hunter, is a contender for 'the worst British film ever made'. It reminded me of when a friend told me his mother-in-law said he would 'go peculiar' if he retired early. Here, Shakespeare definitely goes peculiar. This jaw-droppingly awful sci-fi caper, set in a future where warring bands are taught to work in harmony by space aliens, stars *Carry On* stalwarts Kenneth Connor and Terry Scott looking extremely shamefaced as they gurn amid wobbly sets and excruciating dialogue. It was clearly marketed at stoned students as 'The *Plan 9 From Outer Space* of British pop movies!', but it's not that good. It's rumoured that the embarrassed director Robert Hartford-Davis ordered

* I was reminded of Steven Pinker's reaction to seeing *Spinal Tap II*, when he quoted a Yiddish expression used with cocky kids who push their luck: '*Eyn mol shayn; tsvey mol a patsch in tuches*' ('once is cute; twice you get a smack in the ass').

† My best Shakespeare adaptations are Peter Greenaway's *Prospero's Books* (*The Tempest*), Kurosawa's *Ran* (*King Lear*) and Gerald Thomas's *Carry On Cleo* (*Antony and Cleopatra*, sort of).

all prints should be destroyed following his death. It might have been an idea.

But equally, it's enjoyable and instructive to have a reminder of what happens when good books go very bad indeed. When hubris, vanity, insanity and generally missing the point collide to transform a great literary source into a cinematic hellscape. When, as Jeff Goldblum says in *Jurassic Park*, those who made them 'were so preoccupied with whether or not they could, they didn't stop to think if they should'.

# PART IV

## And Finally...

# 18

## A BONUS CHRISTMAS SPECIAL

*Rizzo the Rat*: 'Nice story, Mr. Dickens.'
*Gonzo*: 'Oh, thanks. If you like this, you should read the book.'

FROM *THE MUPPET CHRISTMAS CAROL*

If 'storytelling is always the art of repeating stories' (Walter Benjamin), then Christmas is Groundhog Day.* It's the one time of year when most of us want to eat, do and, above all, watch the same thing over and over, whether it's *Love Actually*, *Home Alone* or, in my case, *It's a Wonderful Life*, *The Good Life* Christmas special and ideally a Peter Ustinov Poirot. The comfort and joy come from repetition, especially as I get older and feel I'm not just marking this Christmas, but remembering all those that have gone before. In that strange period when time collapses and emotions are heightened (and not just because we've been drinking Baileys since 11 a.m.), the best Christmas viewing brings laughter, tears or, ideally, 'Laughter through tears, my favourite emotion', as Dolly Parton observes in *Steel Magnolias*.

* It may be set on an endlessly recurring 2 February, but *Groundhog Day*, with its story of supernatural intervention and personal salvation in the snow, still counts as a Christmas movie in my book.

But it all comes from Daddy Christmas himself, Charles Dickens, and what he called 'the ghost of an idea', his 1843 novella *A Christmas Carol*. It's not just the best-known and most frequently adapted of all his works, with over 250 film, TV and stage versions in the last half-century alone – ranging from the Flintstones, Barbie and Bugs Bunny to Matthew McConaughey under a mountain of condoms in *Ghosts of Girlfriends Past*.* It is the DNA of all Christmas movies, even when they are not direct adaptations, and it has influenced the way we see the season as one of fellowship, compassion and goodwill to all ever since – even the fact we eat turkey.† Apparently, in 1870 a London barrow girl was overheard saying, 'Dickens dead? Then will Father Christmas die too?'‡ In fact, according to Christopher Frayling, 'The uplifting story of the miser Ebenezer Scrooge, who sees the error of his ways after being visited by the three spirits of Christmas, has almost taken over from the Nativity as the Christmas story.' If, as the writer John Yorke has put it, stories fill the god-shaped hole in our lives, then the main reason Dickens's miraculous tale of redemption, salvation and second chances has come to define the festive period as a kind of secular gospel is adaptation.

* There was also, bafflingly, a fully mimed version for BBC TV in 1973, and, inevitably, there's been a porn film, *The Passions of Carol*.

† It also cemented the tradition of the Christmas ghost story, perfect for the winter solstice, that liminal time of year when the barrier between this world and the supernatural is said to be at its thinnest, immortalised by M. R. James's Christmas ghost stories and their TV incarnations.

‡ There's now even a film about Dickens called *The Man Who Invented Christmas*, although I suspect the Church might have something to say about that.

Most people know the *Carol* not through reading it, but by a cluster of remembered phrases ('Bah humbug!' 'God bless us, every one!') that have been passed down like a folkloric memory through various screen versions.* As critic John Mullan says, 'it is now like a mythical tale that has always been there'. With the preliterate quality of a fairy tale and the compressed intensity of a short story, both forms especially well suited to adaptation, as we've seen throughout this book, it's no wonder *A Christmas Carol* burst free from its covers as soon as it was published and entered the cultural bloodstream.

As one literary theorist has noted, it actually reversed the usual progress of folk and fairy tales:

> Although the *Carol* began as a written text, it has been passed down orally from one generation to the next ... The *Carol* has inverted the usual folk process. Rather than beginning as an oral story that was later written down, the *Carol* was written to be retold. Dickens was its creator, but it is also the product of its re-creators who have retold, adapted, and revised it over the years ... Its power is creative.†

Dickens wanted to spread the word with this tale – for reasons both compassionate and commercial. He was determined to strike a 'sledge-hammer' blow for social justice after reading a disturbing report on child labour, in what were known as the 'Hungry Forties'. But he was also in debt following the failure

* In an article in *The Atlantic*, Megan Garber called movies 'engines of language', with phrases like 'high-maintenance' popularised in *When Harry Met Sally* and 'gaslighting' coming from the film based on the play *Gaslight*.

† Paul Davis in *The Lives and Times of Ebenezer Scrooge*.

of *Martin Chuzzlewit* and desperately needed a Christmas hit. *A Christmas Carol*, written in a six-week frenzy during which he 'wept, and laughed, and wept again, and excited himself in a most extraordinary manner … and thinking whereof, he walked about the black streets of London, fifteen or twenty miles, many a night', achieved both. Published on 17 December 1843, it had sold out its first print run of 6,000 copies by Christmas Eve.

Its popularity immediately increased through adaptation. Within six months of publication, there were eight different stage productions in London, and Dickens adapted it himself, reconfiguring and fine-tuning the story for his own dramatic public readings. In Dickens's times, Fezziwig's ball and the Cratchit family Christmas proved the most popular scenes with audiences, perhaps because these moments of humble celebration were so precious when holidays were scarce and infant mortality high. Many readers wrote to Dickens to tell him that 'about their homes, how the Carol had come to be read aloud there, and was to be kept upon a little shelf by itself, and was to do them no end of good'.*

When I reread the story, I noticed how it was itching to be performed, especially with its narrator's voice:

> The curtains of his bed were drawn aside, I tell you, by a hand … and Scrooge, starting up into a half-recumbent attitude, found

* The story was immediately acclaimed for its vision of a fairer, less selfish society, apart from in the *Westminster Review*, where one journalist criticised Dickens's ignorance of the laws of supply and demand, asking, 'Who went without turkey and punch in order that Bob Cratchit might get them?' There's always a utilitarian killjoy at the party.

> himself face to face with the unearthly visitor who drew them: as close to it as I am now to you, and I am standing in the spirit at your elbow.

It's no wonder that cinema leaped upon Dickens. Sergei Eisenstein famously noticed that with his visual imagination, detailed close-ups, vivid cityscapes and 'that spontaneous, childlike skill for storytelling, equally typical for Dickens and the American cinema', Dickens was cinematic before cinema existed. Here, Stefan Zweig brilliantly observes the optical quality of his writing:

> If ever a man had the gift of the eye – and not merely of the eye but of the ear, and of the nose – and the faculty of remembering with microscopic accuracy of detail everything ever seen, or heard, or tasted, smelled, or felt, that man was Charles Dickens ... The whole picture arises before us ... he never overlooks anything; his memory and his keenness of perception are like a good camera lens.

These filmic qualities are intensified by the short form of *A Christmas Carol.* 'Now the scene had changed', the narrator tells us, as we move from one visual tableau to another. Nothing is missed, even Scrooge's door knocker, which has 'a dismal light about it, like a bad lobster in a dark cellar'. I've never seen a bad lobster, but I can imagine the luminous glow.

The first, now lost, film version of *A Christmas Carol* was 1901's *Scrooge: or Marley's Ghost*, for which the director, a former stage magician, used trick photography to achieve his spooky effects. As with the best fables, it was a kind of social litmus test, with each generation taking whatever they needed from it. Many people's favourite adaptation is the black-and-white *Scrooge*, starring a wonderful Alastair Sim, which, inspired by John Leech's original illustrations, leans fully into the gothic, funereal aspects of the tale, making Scrooge's conversion to joy ('I'm as merry as a schoolboy! I'm as giddy as a drunken man!') even more cathartic.* This version, like many others, changes the text, adding a new character, the capitalist vulture Mr Jorkin, and a backstory involving the death of Scrooge's mother in childbirth. Many incarnations now, in fact, psychoanalyse Scrooge, as well as changing names, cutting scenes, or adding extra ones like his Christmas Day visit to the Cratchits' house in *The Muppet Christmas Carol*.

Everyone has their own best Scrooge, whether it's Michael Caine and said Muppets, Albert Finney singing 'I Like Life!' in the musical (tagline: 'What the Dickens have they done to Scrooge?') or Bill Murray having the best time playing a cynical TV exec who learns the error of his ways in 1988's *Scrooged*. My favourite is Patrick Stewart, both in the 1999 film and in his one-man stage show, which I was lucky enough to see. In fact, I'd go as far to say it changed my life, not only sending me back to Dickens, but also making me determined not to be a grumpy old git, and instead to squeeze as much joy from life as possible.

It works because Stewart's lean, mean powerhouse of a performance makes the character feel fresh: not a crabbity collection of clichés, but a believable, sympathetic human being

* It's also been noted how powerfully the two child apparitions, Ignorance and Want, who appear with the Ghost of Christmas Yet to Come, would have chimed with postwar audiences after the Beveridge Report had identified the five giants of 'Want, Disease, Ignorance, Squalor and Idleness' to be overcome by sweeping social welfare reform.

who has hardened his heart against the world, creating a prison of his own making. On stage, in a back-to-basics production without costumes or props, I remember that he read the text 'in different voices' (like Sloppy in *Our Mutual Friend*) but somehow managed to step back and make the book shine, holding it up at the end for everyone to see, like a valedictory trophy. In David Jones's stripped-back, faithful, emotional film version, this towering central performance is also complemented brilliantly by Richard E. Grant as Bob Cratchit, Saskia Reeves as Mrs Cratchit and Dominic West as Scrooge's nephew Fred, plus all manner of well-known extras, such as Celia Imrie, who steals the show just by eating a grape. It also adds in some contemporary music-hall songs, and, unlike many versions, shows us the mariners, the miners and the lighthouse keepers celebrating Christmas Day.

I'll grant that there are some now-dodgy effects and child performances, but this is the *Christmas Carol* that has captured my heart, and the one I watch religiously every year. The additions to Dickens's text are judicious and lyrical, such as when Scrooge asks Fred's wife, 'Can you forgive a stupid, selfish old man who doesn't want to be left out in the cold any more?', or my favourite line, which I'd always assumed was in the book until I double-checked and discovered it wasn't: 'Fezziwig always used to say, when happiness shows up, always give it a comfortable seat.' Could there be a better motto for life?

Christopher Frayling counts Frank Capra's 1946 *It's a Wonderful Life* as his 'all-time favourite film version of *A Christmas Carol*'.* This perennial favourite (like so many

* In his excellent BBC radio documentary *The Many Faces of Ebenezer Scrooge*.

Christmas films, it was only a modest success at the time, but grew in popularity with repeat TV viewings) is the story of George Bailey, who contemplates suicide and is given the chance to see what life would be like if he'd never been born in the small town of Bedford Falls. It is the dark inversion of Dickens's tale, with the same supernatural intervention that rebalances a character's compass – although in this case it is the bumbling angel Clarence Oddbody rather than spirits – but here the laws of time and space are suspended to give us a more dystopian vision of a world turned upside down.* There is the same social message of charity and community, in this case delivered by George when he defends the ordinary townspeople, 'This rabble you're talking about, who do most of the working and paying, living and dying', to the avaricious slum landlord and banker Mr Potter (played by Lionel Barrymore, who also became famous for reading *A Christmas Carol* on US radio).† And there is the theme of redemption through family and loved ones, played out in every single Christmas movie – in this case the emotional payoff is financial too, as George is saved from bankruptcy by his friends (unlike Scrooge, who must learn to give).

The genesis of *It's a Wonderful Life* is a kind of Christmas

* Many people point to the origins of havoc at Christmas in Twelfth Night, or the Epiphany, the Feast of Fools, what Jeanette Winterson calls a 'gaudy ragbag of a festival with something borrowed from everywhere – pagans, Romans, Norsemen, Celts, Turks ... its celebratory free spirit, its gift-giving, topsy-turvy misrule, made it anti-authority.'

† A true sign the movie has reached the status of myth is that everyone projects their own political views on to it: Frank Capra was a Republican, but was still hauled before the House of Un-American Activities because they thought he had been unfair to capitalists.

miracle in itself. It's based on the story 'The Greatest Gift' by Philip Van Doren Stern, who, unable to get it published, sent it out in a Christmas card to 200 acquaintances instead – including his agent, who, serendipitously passed it to RKO Pictures. But what's more remarkable is how far the subsequent adaptation went in raising the stakes for our hero George. The film made him not the bored bank clerk of the book, but the owner of a building society, who faces ruin and scandal when his uncle loses a large sum of money. It made him desperate to leave Bedford Falls and travel the world, only to find his hopes scuppered every time. George never gets to do what he wants, and his acceptance of this is both noble and maddening, spilling out into scenes of angry frustration; it's no surprise many critics have noted there's a noir film trying to escape from within the madcap comedy, especially as the mean, hard, guarded world of Pottersville's strip joints and pawn shops feels more real and disturbing every year. George is taken to the absolute abyss of despair in order to make the unbridled joy of his second chance such ecstasy. As he runs around shouting 'Merry Christmas', it's sheer rapture. And it's the old Hollywood adage: get your hero up a tree, throw rocks at him, get him down again. I laugh and cry every time.

It's the same principle with that other seasonal favourite, 1988's *Die Hard*, which is based on Roderick Thorp's novel *Nothing Lasts Forever*, a real-time thriller of one man's battle to save hostages from terrorists in a high-rise tower on Christmas Eve. As well as making nominal changes to the book (the oil company becomes a Japanese firm, the retired New York cop becomes younger with the casting of a cheeky Bruce Willis), the adaptation, again, ups the ante to fever pitch.* In the novel, hero Joe Leland's wife is dead and he's trying to save his daughter. In the film, he's the everyman lone ranger John McClane, whose marriage is on the rocks and whose wife is one of the hostages. The terrorists become thieves here, mostly an excuse for the fun of a heist movie, yet also another reminder that so many of these Christmas films – see also Santa-themed bankrobbing thriller *The Silent Partner*, based on the novel *Think of a Number* – are about money ('It comes in pretty useful down here, Bub,' says George to his angel in *It's a Wonderful Life*). But mostly it's the Bruce show, as our Reagan-era action hero, with his man-of-the-people charm, revels in showing effete Europeans, FBI bureaucrats and media elites who's boss.† As Antonia Quirke has written, 'It was his act that people wanted. Bruce has grace ... An action film is a dance', and what a dancer he is. As Quirke says, actors are 'poets of walking, running, kissing, everything', and I would also add smoking for this film.

At the end of *Die Hard*, John McClane, like George Bailey, has been put through the wringer, pushed to his absolute limits in order to learn the error of his ways.‡ He comes out the other side, bloodied and battered, to save his marriage to Holly, and

* For the textbook example of a screenplay raising the stakes, adding obstacles and generally making everything better, I highly recommend reading about the late Sir Tom Stoppard's inspired script doctoring for *Indiana Jones and the Last Crusade*.

† 'Just another American who's seen too many movies as a child. Another orphan of a bankrupt culture who thinks he's John Wayne', is just one of the lines Alan Rickman's villainous Hans delivers with relish.

‡ In this case, the lesson is that he should grow up and stop being a selfish jerk towards his wife – although I still don't see why she has to express her gratitude by adopting her married surname once more.

to save Christmas. As with all seasonal movies, there is havoc and misrule – whether it's a heist, a haunting, a kid being left alone or Gremlins – followed by healing. As Mark Kermode has noted, Scrooge isn't changed in *A Christmas Carol*; he's mended. By reconnecting with their earlier, better selves, characters learn what, or who, *really* matters.

This idea is at the heart of all Christmas stories, like O. Henry's touching tale of a poverty-stricken couple, 'The Gift of the Magi' (adapted dozens of times), and all Christmas films, like *Meet Me in St. Louis*, *Miracle on 34th Street* and *How the Grinch Stole Christmas*, which are based on stories or books but all, effectively, adapt *A Christmas Carol* in some way. They show us how, through big, cathartic moments of magical transformation, we reconnect with those we love. 'You don't know what you've got till it's gone' may be a trite message, but it's one we seem to need at Christmas. As Bill Murray says in *Scrooged* after his own epiphany:

> It's the one night of the year when we all act a little nicer, we smile a little easier, we cheer a little more, for a couple of hours out of the whole year we are the people that we always hoped we would be. It's a miracle.

Merry Dickensmas, everyone!

# Appendix

## SOME OUTTAKES

'There is nothing more wonderful than a list,' notes Brother Adso in *The Name of the Rose* (see 'Perfect Book, Perfect Film'), as he compiles a record of the abbey's treasures. As the end credits roll on my book, I thought it fitting to include some deleted scenes – the things I couldn't find room for in the final cut – in the form of lists. Some are top tens, some are top fives, some are bottom fives. All are extremely non-scientific. For your viewing pleasure, please enjoy *The Book Was Better: The Director's Cut*.

**Most Oscar-Hungry Adaptations**

Hollywood loves nothing more than giving itself awards, and, with their sweeping epic spectacle (often war-torn), high-octane performances and plucky underdogs, there are certain films that please the Academy more than others. Here are my top ten adaptations that could all be described using the useful compound German word *Oscar-Geilheit*, or 'horny for an Oscar'.

*Atonement* (2007, dir. Joe Wright).
*There Will Be Blood* (2007, dir. Paul Thomas Anderson, based on the book *Oil!* by Upton Sinclair).

*Forrest Gump* (1994, dir. Robert Zemeckis).
*The Last of the Mohicans* (1992, dir. Michael Mann).
*The English Patient* (1996, dir. Anthony Minghella).
*The Hours* (2002, dir. Stephen Daldry).
*Out of Africa* (1985, dir. Sidney Pollack).
*One Flew Over the Cuckoo's Nest* (1975, dir. Miloš Forman).
*Million Dollar Baby* (2004, dir. Clint Eastwood).
*All Quiet on the Western Front* (2022, dir. Edward Berger).

**Films I Didn't Know Were Based on Books Until I Started Writing This One**

Before embarking on *The Book Was Better*, I had no absolutely no idea that *Die Hard* was adapted from a novel – and punched the air when I realised this meant it could go in my Christmas chapter. These are some of my favourite films that I didn't have a clue were adaptations.

*Kind Hearts and Coronets* (1949, based on the 1907 Roy Horniman novel *Israel Rank: The Autobiography of a Criminal*).
*The Towering Inferno* (1974, based on two different novels, *The Tower* by Richard Martin Stern, and *The Glass Inferno* by Thomas N. Scortia and Frank M. Robinson).
*Deliverance* (1972, adapted by James Dickey from his own novel).
*The Lady Vanishes* (1938, based on the novel *The Wheel Spins* by Ethel Lina White. See also: *Spellbound*, *Suspicion*, *Marnie*).
*Rififi* (1955, based on the novel by Auguste Le Breton).

## Adaptations of Books I Haven't Read and Probably Never Will

The Japanese word *tsundoku* means the habit of buying more books than you can read. A lot of films are made from the kind of Great Unread Novels that weigh down many a shelf, which Italo Calvino called 'Books That If You Had More Than One Life You Would Certainly Also Read But Unfortunately Your Days Are Numbered'. This is my guilty top five (I haven't read Proust either, but I like to think I might one day).

*Moby-Dick* by Herman Melville.
*Inherent Vice* by Thomas Pynchon.
*No Country for Old Men* by Cormac McCarthy.
*Love in the Time of Cholera* by Gabriel García Márquez.
*Under the Volcano* by Malcolm Lowry.

## Adaptations Disowned by Their Writers, Actors or Directors

From Harold Pinter trying (and failing) to have his name removed from the credits of *The Handmaid's Tale*, to J. D. Salinger and Donna Tartt getting burned at the movies, there has been much trashing, rejection and conscious uncoupling throughout this book. Here are some other shunned adaptations.

*Greystoke: The Legend of Tarzan, Lord of the Apes* (1984). As seen in 'Silly Book, Silly Film', but making a reappearance because I discovered veteran screenwriter Robert Towne was so unhappy he credited his dog, P. H. Vazak, with the script instead – which, bafflingly, was nominated for an Academy Award.

*London Fields* (2018). The director of this tawdry flop, Mathew Cullen, sued the film's producers for fraud because he hated their cut of it so much.

*The Unbearable Lightness of Being* (1988). Although author Milan Kundera was consulted on the film of his novel, he was so scarred by the experience he allowed no further adaptations of his work.

*Sahara* (2005). One of the worst flops ever made, it also resulted in a lengthy legal battle between disgruntled author Clive Cussler and the film's producer.

The *Percy Jackson* movies (2010 and 2013). Author Rick Riordan refused to see the Disney films of his beloved children's series after reading an initial script, and described them as 'my life's work going through a meat grinder'.

**Adaptations with the Best Soundtracks**

'Without John Williams, bikes don't really fly … There is no Force, dinosaurs do not walk the Earth, we do not wonder, we do not weep, we do not believe,' said Spielberg of his favourite composer, acknowledging the transcendent power of the movie soundtrack. Williams has been honoured in these pages already, as has Jerry Goldsmith for his milestone *Planet of the Apes* score. Here are some others that make brilliant adaptations even better.

*Blade Runner* (1982, score by Vangelis).

*Midnight Cowboy* (1968, score by John Barry – also all his Bond music).

*Psycho* (1960, score by Bernard Herrmann, also *Vertigo*).

*Murder She Said* (1961, Miss Marple theme music by Ron Goodwin).

*The Belles of St. Trinian's* (1954, based on Ronald Searle's comic strip, music by Malcolm Arnold).
*The Third Man* (1949, score by Anton Karas).
*Lift to the Scaffold/Ascenseur pour l'échafaud* (1958, soundtrack by Miles Davis).
*The Graduate* (1967, soundtrack by Simon & Garfunkel).
*A Clockwork Orange* (1971, for its electronic versions of Purcell and Beethoven).
*The Godfather* (1972, score by Nino Rota).

**Most Unusual Musical Adaptations**

It seems you can make a musical from almost any book, whether it's a story of underage criminals (*Oliver!*) or the First Lady of Argentina (*Evita*). Some of the best, and worst (I've seen them: *The Woman in White* and *Love Never Dies*), are based on fiction. Until my editor allows me to write the book of my dreams, *Climb Every Mountain: Life Lessons from Musical Theatre*, these are some of my favourite musicals taken from unexpected, and sometimes unexpectedly grim, literary sources.

*Jesus Christ Superstar* (1973, The New Testament).
*Seven Brides for Seven Brothers* (1954, the ancient legend of the rape of the Sabine women).
*Shockheaded Peter* (1998, Heinrich Hoffmann's terrifying children's book *Struwwelpeter*).
*Gigi* (1958, the Colette novella about a young courtesan).
*A Funny Thing Happened on the Way to the Forum* (1966, Plautus' ancient Roman farces).

**Fantastic Non-Fiction**

Some of the best adaptations aren't of novels, but of autobiographies, biographies, histories and other non-fiction books. Here are my top ten movies 'Based on a True Story', as the film posters like to say.

*The Sound of Music* (1965, Robert Wise, from the memoir *The Story of the Trapp Family Singers*).
*Goodfellas* (1990, Martin Scorsese, from the biography *Wiseguy*).
*BlacKkKlansman* (2018, Spike Lee, from the memoir *Black Klansman*).
*The Elephant Man* (1980, David Lynch, from a memoir and a history).
*10 Rillington Place* (1971, from the true crime book of the same title).
*The French Connection* (1971, William Friedkin, from the non-fiction book of the same title).
*Mean Girls* (2004, Mike Walters, inspired by the self-help book *Queen Bees and Wannabes*).
*Lawrence of Arabia* (1962, David Lean, from Lawrence's autobiography *Seven Pillars of Wisdom*).
*Patton* (1970, Franklin J. Schaffner, from the biography *Patton: Ordeal and Triumph*).
*I'm Still Here* (2024, Walter Salles, from the memoir of the same title).

**Worst Casting Choices**

Whether it's Tom Hanks in *Bonfire of the Vanities*, or Margot Robbie as Cathy (or Elizabeth I), we've seen how miscasting an actor in an adaptation can misfire. These are my top five who reach 'Denise Richardson in hotpants as a nuclear physicist in *The World is Not Enough*' levels of ludicrousness.

Johnny Depp as Sweeney Todd (2007, the Sondheim musical based on the penny dreadful *The String of Pearls*). Because he cannot sing and this is a musical.
Emma Watson as Belle in *Beauty and the Beast* (2017). As above.
Vince Vaughn as Norman Bates in the *Psycho* remake (1998). Because he is simultaneously too creepy and not creepy enough.
William Shatner as Alexi in *The Brothers Karamazov* (1958). Just because.
Tony Curtis as the slave Antoninus in *Spartacus* (1960). Although I enjoy the way he says 'I am a singer of sawngs'.
Which leads nicely to…

**Actors Who Were Wrong for the Role But Surpassed It and Are Now That Person**

In a rare case of an author getting their dream casting, Agatha Christie wrote to a young Joan Hickson after she'd seen her on stage to say she'd be the perfect Miss Marple. Christie's wish was only fulfilled after her death; in her lifetime Marple was mostly played by Margaret Rutherford, who was wrong on paper, yet whose on-screen charisma overrode any need for accuracy. Here are some other miscast actors who made a role their own.

Renée Zellweger as Bridget Jones.
Michael Caine as Harry Palmer in *The Ipcress File* (in

Len Deighton's novels he's a northerner and doesn't even have a name).
Julie Andrews as Mary Poppins.
Omar Sharif as Dr Zhivago.
Matt Damon as Jason Bourne (he was considered too wimpy but ended up redefining the spy thriller).

**Worst Adaptations Starring Nicolas Cage**

Never has such a gifted actor (watch *Leaving Las Vegas*, *Adaptation* or *Raising Arizona* if you don't believe me) spawned such a legacy of cinematic lunacy. Perhaps he can't say no – he took the role in *Left Behind* because his brother asked him to. Or perhaps he's just playing a massive joke on all of us, as he did in his recent meta-film *The Unbearable Weight of Massive Talent*. He has several appearances in this book; here are his worst, gathered and ranked.

*Left Behind* (2014, 0% on Rotten Tomatoes).
*The Wicker Man* (2006, 15%).
*Captain Corelli's Mandolin* (2001, 28%).
*Next* (2007, 28%).
*Renfield* (2023, a surprising 58%!).

**Best Films Based on Poems**

As we've seen, the elliptical intensity of short stories can sometimes result in the most inspired adaptations. And occasionally the poetic muse can spur filmmakers to lyrical heights too, as with:

*O Brother, Where Art Thou?* (2000, from *The Odyssey*).
*The Canterbury Tales* (1972, from Chaucer).

*The Green Knight* (2021, from *Sir Gawain and the Green Knight*).
*Jason and the Argonauts* (1963, from Apollonius of Rhodes' *The Argonautica*).
*Onegin* (1999, from Pushkin).

Or not…

**Worst Films Based on Poems**

*Beowulf* (2007, from the Old English epic).
*Troy* (2004, from *The Iliad*).
*The Raven* (2012, from Edgar Allan Poe's poem).
*Braveheart* (1995, from the fifteenth-century epic *The Wallace* by Blind Harry).
*Jabberwocky* (1977, from Lewis Carroll's nonsense poem).

**Best Three-Star Film Adaptations**

As already discussed with regards to *Ripley's Game*, the reliable, solid satisfaction of a Three-Star Movie, as opposed to its flashy, exhausting Five-Star cousin, should not be underestimated. Here are some more, along with their IMDb scores. When they hover between 6 and 7, that, for me, is the mark of perfection.

*The Three Musketeers* (the 1973 version, 7.1/10, so it just makes the cut).
*Evil Under the Sun* (1982, 7.1/10).
*The Quiet American* (2002, 7/10).
*The End of the Affair* (1999, 7/10).
*Clear and Present Danger* (1994, 6.9/10).
*Stir of Echoes* (1999, 6.9/10).

*Hannibal* (2001, 6.8/10).
*A Most Wanted Man* (2014, 6.7/10).
*The Accidental Tourist* (1988, 6.7/10).
*Cocoon* (1985, 6.7/10).

**Most Lucrative Adaptations**

I was convinced *The Lord of the Rings* was going to be on here! Here are the highest-grossing adaptations of novels, adjusted for inflation because that's more interesting than lots of *Jurassic Park* sequels and live-action Disney remakes. The Marvel Universe is banned.

*Gone with the Wind* (1939, $4.45 billion).
*The Sound of Music* (1965, $3.05 billion).
*The Ten Commandments* (1956, $2.82 billion).
*Dr Zhivago* (1965, $2.68 billion).
*Jurassic Park* (1993, $2.55 billion).

**Best Adaptations Using Voiceovers**

'Any idiot can write a voiceover narration to explain the thoughts of a character,' says screenwriting guru Robert McKee in Spike Jonze's *Adaptation*. Many people say it's the worst way to show the inner life on screen when adapting a novel, but sometimes, as with the following, it can be the best.

*Clueless* (1995, featuring the voice of Alicia Silverstone).
*Barry Lyndon* (1975, Michael Hordern aka Paddington).
*Trainspotting* (1996, Ewan McGregor).
*Fight Club* (1999, Edward Norton).
*All About Eve* (1950, George Sanders aka Shere Khan).

# ‘I’d Like to Thank...’

## ACKNOWLEDGEMENTS

To quote Halle Berry’s famous Oscar acceptance speech, ‘this moment is so much bigger than me’. And until Gwyneth Paltrow plays me in the film adaptation of this book, I would like to stand at my imaginary podium and thank everybody who has made it all possible, from the bottom of my heart, as they say.

First, Cecilia Stein, the maestro, the Spielberg of editors. Chech, you not only made me a writer, but you made me a better one, every step of the way. You showed me the importance of getting the scaffolding right at the start, as per William Goldman, you sharpened my words and you pretty much came up with the idea for this new book. I am humbled and eternally grateful (starts weeping slightly). Thank you also to Hannah Haseloff for her copy magic, Laura Mcfarlane for shepherding the text along, Hayley Warnham for her stunning Saul Bass-inspired cover design, and the entire wider team at Oneworld. Tamsin Shelton, with her wisdom and humour, made the copy-editing process an utter delight once more.

This also goes out to my publishing friends and colleagues, past and present. To Rebecca Lee, my guiding light, who gave me so much inspired advice along the shared journey of that difficult second book. To my copywriting pal Colin Brush, who not only read several early chapters and offered genius suggestions, but, most importantly, reminded me that Cliff Richard had written a *Wuthering Heights* musical. To Sam Binnie for her *Heights* fandom too! To Rob Williams for generously sharing his experiences of screen adaptation, Rowland White for giving me insight into novelisations, Kaliane Bradley for Dickensmas, Ingrid Matts for her unstinting support and kindness during some difficult months, and the whole team at Penguin for being the nicest bunch in the business (weeping fully now). To Madeleine Collinge for her loyal friendship and our shared secret love of *The Da Vinci Code*. Also Jenny Geras for reading my proposal, James Spackman for helping me clarify my earliest thoughts on the book, and Krystyna Plater for talking it through at the beginning. My clever friends from Book-and-Film-Club, Tom Humberstone, Alan Trotter and Andrea Joyce, gave me many ideas. Lee Kenny stopped me getting Bond wrong.

And I wouldn't be here without my family (tears running down face): my mum, Nancy, Derek, and Becca for being the best sister, cheerleader and *Lord of the Rings* enthusiast. I also want to mention three institutions: everyone at the BFI Reuben Library, a sanctuary of calm and knowledge – I still can't quite get over the fact I could just go and read film books there for free. Libraries are incredible! The BBC, which aided my film education with many happy hours of radio documentaries and podcasts from its archives, again, all for free. And the NHS, specifically all the good people at the Breast Clinic at King's College Hospital, who gave me exemplary cancer care in 2024, when I wanted to give up on this book entirely. These small hands keep the wheels of the world turning, as Elrond, Lord of Rivendell says, and they should be cherished forever.

Finally, as the orchestra strikes up and I get wrestled off-stage (man with the stick, I see you!), I would like to dedicate this to my husband Tim, who encouraged me to keep going with the book and then went through the entire thing for me, made it better and spotted a heinous *Dallas* error. My top reader, and top person, really. Every joke was for you, every silly film reference was for you ('It's all for you, Damien!'). Without you there wouldn't be any point to any of it (hysterical now, over-come with emotion, mad with joy). Here's to the many years we have spent at the cinema and in front of the TV together, and many, many more.

# SELECTED BIBLIOGRAPHY

Amis, M., *The War Against Cliché: Essays and Reviews 1971–2000* (London: Vintage, 2001).

Barthes, R., *An Introduction to the Structural Analysis of Narrative* (Baltimore: Johns Hopkins University Press, 1975).

Bazin, A., *What is Cinema?* (Berkeley: University of California Press, 1967).

Bell, J. (ed.), *Gothic: The Dark Heart of Film* (London: BFI, 2013).

Biskind, P., *Easy Riders, Raging Bulls: How the Sex'n'Drugs and Rock'n'Roll Generation Saved Hollywood* (London: Bloomsbury, 1998).

Biskind, P., *The Sky is Falling! How Vampires, Zombies, Androids and Superheroes Made America Great for Extremism* (London: Allen Lane, 2018).

Biskind, P., *Pandora's Box: The Greed, Lust and Lies that Broke Television* (London: Allen Lane, 2023).

Bluestone, G., *Novels into Film: The Metamorphosis of Fiction into Cinema* (Berkeley: University of California Press, 1961).

Bresson, R., *Notes on the Cinematograph* (New York: NYRB Classics, 2016).

Callow, S., *The Night of the Hunter: BFI Film Classics* (London: Bloomsbury, 2000).

Carey, J., *What Good Are the Arts?* (London: Faber & Faber, 2006).

Cohen, R., *How to Write Like Tolstoy: A Journey into the Minds of Our Greatest Writers* (London: Oneworld Publications, 2016).

Ebert, R., *A Horrible Experience of Unbearable Length: More Movies that Suck* (Kansas: Andrews McMeel, 2012).

Eilenberger, W., *The Visionaries: Arendt, Beauvoir, Rand, Weil and the Salvation of Philosophy* (London: Allen Lane, 2023).

Eisenstein, S., *Film Form: Essays in Film Theory* (San Diego: Harcourt, 1949).

Evans, R., *The Kid Stays in the Picture* (London: Faber & Faber, 2003).

Field, S., *Screenplay: The Foundations of Screenwriting* (New York: Bantam, 2005).

Fisher, C., *The Princess Diarist* (London: Black Swan, 2017).

Frayling, C., *The Innocents: BFI Film Classics* (London: Bloomsbury, 2013).

Goldman, W., *Adventures in the Screen Trade: A Personal View of Hollywood* (London: Macdonald & Co. Ltd, 1984).

Goldman, W., *Which Lie Did I Tell?: More Adventures in the Screen Trade* (London: Bloomsbury, 2001).

Greene, G., *Reflections* (London: Vintage, 2014).

Hanson, P. & Herman, P. R., *Tales from the Script: 50 Hollywood Screenwriters Share Their Stories* (New York: HarperCollins, 2010).

Hutcheon, L., *A Theory of Adaptation* (New York: Routledge, 2006).

James, C., *Fame in the 20th Century* (London: Penguin Books, 1993).

Kael, P., *I Lost It at the Movies: Film Writings 1954–1965* (London: Marion Boyars, 1994).

Kermode, M., *The Exorcist: BFI Film Classics* (London: Bloomsbury, 2020).

Kermode, M., *The Good, the Bad and the Multiplex: What's Wrong with Modern Movies?* (London: Arrow, 2012).

Kermode, M., *It's Only a Movie: Real Life Adventures of a Film Obsessive* (London: Arrow Books, 2010).

Klein, M., *The English Novel and the Movies* (New York: Ungar Film Library, 1981).

Lewis, J., *Die Hard: BFI Film Classics* (London: Bloomsbury, 2025).

Lewis, J., *The Godfather: BFI Film Classics* (London: Bloomsbury, 2022).

Lewis, J., *The Godfather: Part II: BFI Film Classics* (London: Bloomsbury, 2022).

Lodge, D., *The Art of Fiction* (London: Vintage, 2011).

Lodge, D., *Consciousness and the Novel* (London: Vintage, 2002).

Luckhurst, R., *The Shining: BFI Film Classics* (London: Bloomsbury, 2013).

Mamet, D., *Bambi vs. Godzilla: On the Nature, Purpose and Practice of the Movie Business* (London: Simon & Schuster, 2007).

Mayo, S. & Kermode, M., *The Movie Doctors* (Edinburgh: Canongate, 2016).

McFarlane, B., *Novel to Film: An Introduction to the Theory of Adaptation* (Oxford: Oxford University Press, 1996).

Mulvey, L., *Death 24x a Second: Stillness and the Moving Image* (London: Reaktion Books Ltd, 2006).

Nabokov, V., *Think, Write, Speak* (London: Penguin Books, 2023).

Newton, M., *It's a Wonderful Life: BFI Film Classics* (London: Bloomsbury, 2023).

Perkins, V. F., *Film as Film* (London: Penguin Books, 1992).

Phillips, J., *You'll Never Eat Lunch in This Town Again* (New York: Random House, 2017).

Polan, D., *In a Lonely Place: BFI Film Classics* (London: Bloomsbury, 1993).

Propp, V., *Morphology of the Folktale* (Austin: University of Texas Press, 1968).

Quirke, A., *Jaws: BFI Film Classics* (London: Bloomsbury, 2025).

Quirke, A., *Madame Depardieu and the Beautiful Strangers* (London: Fourth Estate, 2007).

Robey, T., *Box Office Poison: Hollywood's Story in a Century of Flops* (London: Faber & Faber, 2024).

Salamon, J., *The Devil's Candy: The Anatomy of a Hollywood Fiasco* (Boston: Da Capo Press, 2002).

Sanderson, M., *Don't Look Now: BFI Film Classics* (London: Bloomsbury, 2012).

Seger, L., *The Art of Adaptation: Turning Fact and Fiction into Film* (New York: Henry Holt, 1992).

Snyder, B., *Save the Cat!: The Last Book on Screenwriting You'll Ever Need* (Los Angeles: Michael Wiese, 2005).

Sutherland, J., *How to Read a Novel: A User's Guide* (London: Profile Books Ltd, 2006).

Sweet, M., *Shepperton Babylon: The Lost Worlds of British Cinema* (London: Faber & Faber, 2005).

Thomson, D., *The Big Screen: The Story of the Movies and What They Did to Us* (London: Allen Lane, 2012).

Thomson, D., *'Have You Seen…?'* (London: Allen Lane, 2008).

Thomson, D., *How to Watch a Movie* (London: Profile Books Ltd, 2015).

Thomson, D., *The New Biographical Dictionary of Film: Sixth Edition* (London: Knopf, 2014).

Truffaut, F., *Hitchcock* (London: Faber & Faber, 2017).

Truffaut, F., *What is Cinema? 2nd Edition* (Berkeley, University of California Press, 2004).

Vogler, C., *The Writer's Journey: Mythic Structure for Writers* (Los Angeles: Michael Wiese, 2007).

Warner, M., *From the Beast to the Blonde: Fairy Tales and Their Tellers* (London: Chatto & Windus, 1994).

Warner, M., *Managing Monsters: The Reith Lectures 1994* (London: Vintage, 1994).

White, R., *The Third Man: BFI Film Classics* (London: Bloomsbury, 2003).

Winterson, J., *Christmas Days* (London: Vintage, 2016).

Yorke, J., *Into the Woods: How Stories Work and Why We Tell Them* (London: Penguin Books, 2013).

Yorke, J., *Trip to the Moon: Understanding the True Power of Story* (London: Allen Lane, 2026).

Zipes, J., *The Irresistible Fairy Tale: The Cultural and Social History of a Genre* (Princeton: Princeton University Press, 2013).

# INDEX

Page numbers with the suffix 'n.' refer to notes.

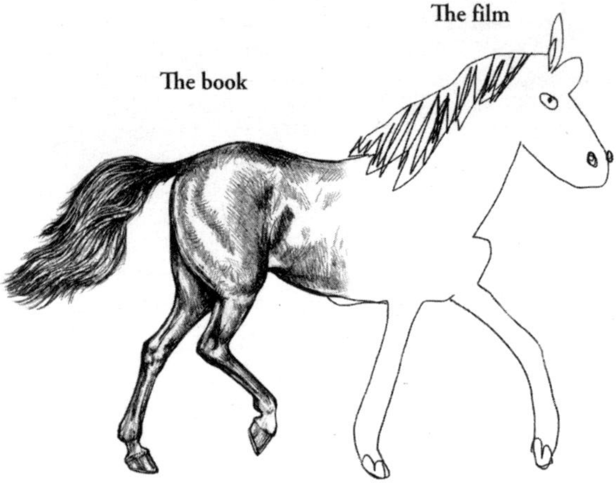


# The End